THE USBORNE
CHILDREN'S
ENCYCLOPEDIA

Researched and written by Felicity Brooks (Our World),
Fiona Chandler (History), Phillip Clarke (Facts and Records),
Anna Claybourne (Science, How Your Body Works), Liz Dalby (Maps of the World),
Ben Denne (How Things Work, Our World, Animals and Plants), Paul Dowswell
(Animals and Plants, Space), Rachel Firth (Science, How Your Body Works),
Laura Howell (Animals and Plants), Sarah Khan (How Your Body Works),
Anna Milbourne (How Things Work), Kirsteen Rogers (How People Live),
Caroline Young (How People Live)

Illustrated by David Hancock

Designed by Francesca Allen, Laura Hammonds, Nelupa Hussein,
Stephanie Jones, Joanne Kirkby, Susie McCaffrey, Keith Newell, Susannah Owen,
Ruth Russell, Karen Tomlins, Candice Whatmore and Helen Wood

Edited by Felicity Brooks, Anna Claybourne,
Anna Milbourne, Kirsteen Rogers, Judy Tatchell
Art Director: Mary Cartwright
Cartography: European Map Graphics Ltd.
Digital manipulation: Roger Bolton, Keith Furnival,
Fiona Johnson, Mike Olley, John Russell, Mike Wheatley
Picture research: Ruth King, Valerie Modd
Internet research: Jacqui Clark and Kenzie Clark
Consultant Cartographic Editor: Craig Asquith
Indexer: Kamini Khanduri

Consultants: Stuart Atkinson (Astronomy, Space), John Davidson (Geography),
Liza Dibble (Farming), Dr. Wendy Dossett (Religions), H.M. Hignett (Ships and Boats),
Professor Michael Hitchcock (How People Live), Sinclair MacLeod (Science),
Dr. David Martill (Dinosaurs), Dr. Anne Millard (History), Eileen O'Brien (Music),
Alison Porter (Technology), Professor Michael Reiss (Science),
Dr. Margaret Rostron, Dr. John Rostron (Biology, Natural History),
Dr. Kristina Routh (Human Biology, Medicine)

Internet links

- Scan the code to watch a video clip about snowflakes.
- For more links, go to
  www.usborne.com/quicklinks

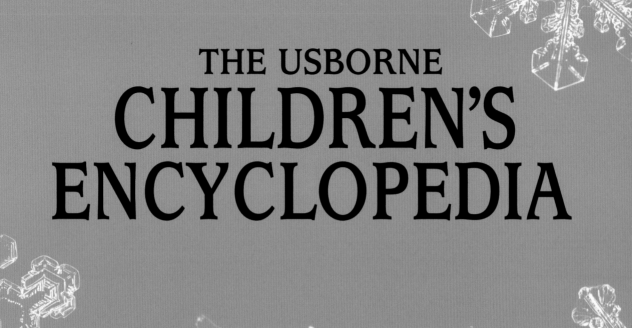

THE USBORNE
CHILDREN'S
ENCYCLOPEDIA

Contents

Internet links

Throughout this book you'll see QR codes, like the one below. These are links that take you straight to websites with video clips or other multimedia content that you can view on a smartphone or tablet.

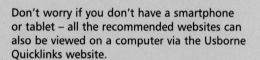

Internet links
- Scan the code for a video of pandas feeding on bamboo.
- For more links, go to **www.usborne.com/quicklinks**

Don't worry if you don't have a smartphone or tablet – all the recommended websites can also be viewed on a computer via the Usborne Quicklinks website.

Usborne Quicklinks

At Usborne Quicklinks you'll find links to click on to visit over 800 recommended websites, plus downloadable pictures from this book, and picture puzzles and quizzes. All the pictures marked with a ★ in this book can be downloaded for home or school use (but not for commercial purposes).

To visit the Quicklinks website go to **www.usborne.com/quicklinks** and enter the letters CE into the search box.

What you can do

Here are some of the things you can do on the recommended websites:

- View Planet Earth from the International Space Station
- See how Egyptian mummies were made
- Watch video clips to explain gravity, friction and other science concepts

Visiting the QR links

To visit the QR links you need a smartphone or tablet with a free app called a "QR reader" that you can download from your device's app store. Just point the device's camera at a QR code and follow your QR reader's instructions to scan the code and visit the recommended website.

Many of the recommended websites include video clips and multimedia, so we recommend you access them via a WiFi connection.

Links to external websites

Usborne internet links go to websites that have been carefully selected by Usborne editors to enhance the information in Usborne books. Usborne Publishing is not responsible or liable for the content or availability of external websites. We regularly review the recommended sites and update our links, so you'll always find a selection of the best sites on the internet at Usborne Quicklinks.

Safety on the internet

Parents – please make sure your children read and follow our three basic rules:

- Always ask an adult's permission before using the internet.
- Never give out personal information, such as your name, address, the name of your school or telephone number.
- If a website asks you to type in your name or email address, check with an adult first.

Help and advice

For more advice on using the internet and scanning QR codes, see the "Help and advice" area at the Usborne Quicklinks website.

You don't have to have a smartphone or tablet to use this book. All the recommended websites are also available at the Usborne Quicklinks website. Just go to **www.usborne.com/quicklinks** and enter the letters CE.

Our world

Our planet

Our planet is called the Earth. It is the only planet where we know that plants, animals and people live. The large areas of land are called continents. Each continent is divided into smaller areas called countries.

This is a house...

in a town...

in a country...

in a continent on planet Earth.

Planet Earth travels around the Sun. It takes one year to go all the way around.

As it travels, the Earth spins around. It takes 24 hours to spin around once.

This is what you'd see if you went up in a spacecraft and looked at the Earth.

Swirling white clouds

Brown or green land

Blue seas and oceans

Internet links

- Scan the code for a view of the Earth from space taken by astronauts on the International Space Station.
- For more links, go to www.usborne.com/quicklinks

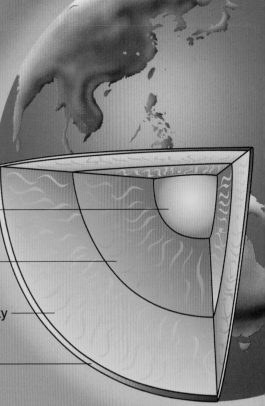

What's inside the Earth?

The Earth is made of rock and metal. If you could cut it open, you would see different layers inside. The picture on the right shows you what's inside the Earth.

In the middle, there's solid metal.

Next there's very hot, soft metal.

Then there's hot, sticky rock which moves.

On the outside, there's solid rock.

The atmosphere

The Earth is protected by an large blanket of gases, called the atmosphere. It stretches from the surface of the Earth over 600km (560 miles) into space. The sky you can see is part of the atmosphere.

The light, hazy blue on this photograph shows part of the Earth's atmosphere.

The atmosphere helps to keep the Earth warm at night.

In the daytime, it helps to protect you from the Sun's heat and light.

Day and night

When it is day for you, it is night for people on the other side of the world. When it is their day, it is your night.

This part of the Earth is in shadow. It's night here.

This part of the Earth is in sunlight. It's day here.

Sunrise

When your side of the Earth turns to face the Sun in the morning, the Sun is said to rise.

The Sun rising over a field

Sunset

When your side of the Earth turns away from the Sun in the evening, the Sun is setting.

The Sun setting over the sea

Turning Earth

Day changes to night, and night to day, because the Earth turns. As it turns, different parts face the Sun.

The part of the Earth with the USA on it is facing the Sun, so it's day in the USA.

A few hours later, the USA has turned away from the Sun, so it's night there now.

The Earth keeps turning all the time.

The Earth travels around the Sun this way.

After 24 hours, the Earth has turned all the way around, so now it's day again in the USA.

Moon in the way

The only time it is dark in the day is when the Moon blocks out the Sun. This is called a total eclipse of the Sun. A total eclipse doesn't happen very often and it only lasts a few minutes.

Internet links

- Scan the code to find out how to make a model of our Solar System.
- For more links, go to www.usborne.com/quicklinks

This picture shows why an eclipse takes place.

The Sun, Moon and the Earth are all in a line.

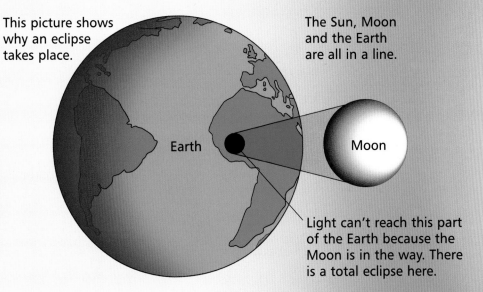

Earth

Moon

Sun

Light can't reach this part of the Earth because the Moon is in the way. There is a total eclipse here.

Make shadows

On a sunny day, you stop some sunlight from reaching the ground. This is what makes your shadow.

Try looking at your shadow on a sunny day. You will see that it always points away from the Sun. As the Sun rises higher in the sky in the morning, your shadow gets shorter. As the Sun sinks lower in the afternoon, your shadow gets longer.

Cloudy days

Even on a cloudy day the Sun is shining on your part of the Earth. You just can't see it because the clouds hide it.

Clouds like these may hide the Sun, but it is always there above them.

The seasons

In most places on Earth, the year is divided into four seasons. They are spring, summer, fall and winter.

Changing seasons

The weather changes from season to season. It is coldest in winter and hottest in summer. Many plants also change with the seasons. You can tell what season it is by looking at some kinds of trees.

In the fall, the leaves on the trees begin to turn red or brown and die.

In the summer, trees like this one are covered in green leaves.

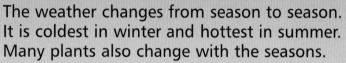

In spring, as it gets warmer, new leaves start to grow on trees.

By winter, all the leaves have died and fallen off.

North and south

The two halves of the Earth are called the northern and southern hemispheres. When countries in the southern hemisphere have their winter, countries in the northern hemisphere have their summer.

The picture on the right shows the Earth's two hemispheres. The imaginary line around the middle is called the equator.

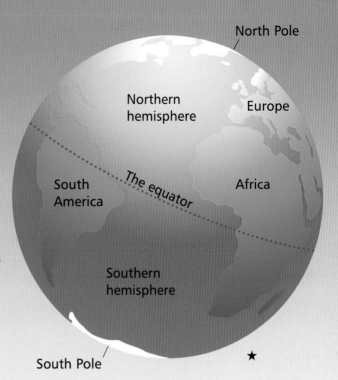

North Pole

Northern hemisphere

Europe

South America

The equator

Africa

Southern hemisphere

South Pole

★

Internet links

- Scan the code to watch a video about the changing seasons.
- For more links, go to **www.usborne.com/quicklinks**

What makes the seasons happen?

The Earth is tilted a little as it goes around the Sun. The hemisphere that is tilted toward the Sun gets more hot sunlight and it is summer there.

The hemisphere tilted away from the Sun has winter. Each year, first one half and then the other is closer to the Sun. This makes the seasons change.

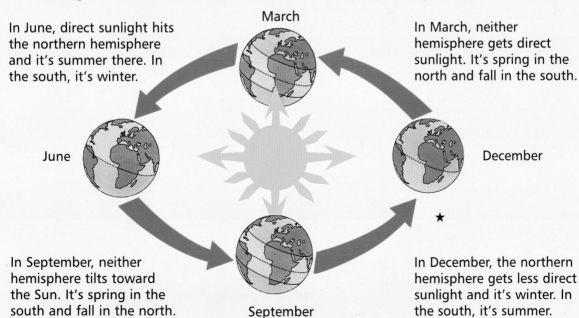

In June, direct sunlight hits the northern hemisphere and it's summer there. In the south, it's winter.

March

In March, neither hemisphere gets direct sunlight. It's spring in the north and fall in the south.

June

December

In September, neither hemisphere tilts toward the Sun. It's spring in the south and fall in the north.

★

September

In December, the northern hemisphere gets less direct sunlight and it's winter. In the south, it's summer.

13

The weather

There are lots of different kinds of weather. It can be rainy, snowy, sunny or windy. The three main things that make the weather happen are the Sun, the air and water.

The Sun gives out heat.

The air moves to make wind.

Water makes rain and snow.

4. The water droplets bump into other droplets and join together to make clouds.

Rainy days

The amount of water in the world is always the same. Rain isn't new water. Follow the numbers to find out where rain comes from.

3. Up in the sky, it's cooler and the water vapor turns back into tiny water droplets.

5. As more water is added, the droplets get bigger and heavier and fall back to the ground as rain.

2. The water turns into water vapor, a gas which we can't see, and rises up into the sky.

6. The rain falls down to the ground where it flows back into seas, lakes and rivers.

1. The Sun heats up the water in seas, lakes, rivers, and snow on mountain tops.

Windy weather

When it's windy, it's because the air is moving around. You can't see the wind, but you can see it blowing leaves around and feel it on your face.

A gentle wind is called a breeze. It can help dry wet clothes.

Gales are much stronger winds. They can blow tiles off roofs.

Hurricanes are very strong winds that can do a lot of damage.

Rainbows

Sometimes it rains even though the Sun is shining. Raindrops split sunlight into different colors. When this happens you might see a rainbow. From the ground, it usually looks like an arch, but from an aircraft, it may be a circle.

Icy snowflakes

Snowflakes are made when it gets so cold that the water in a cloud freezes and turns into ice. Snowflakes all have six sides or points, but they form millions of different patterns.

Make a rainbow

You can make your own rainbow even when it's not raining, as long as the Sun is shining. You will need:

a plastic tray or bowl; a piece of paper; a mirror.

1. Put the tray of water in a sunny place, such as on a windowsill, or outside.

2. Stand the mirror in the tray so the Sun can shine through the water onto the mirror.

3. Hold the paper above the tray. Tilt the mirror until you see a rainbow on the paper.

Every snowflake has a different shape.

Internet links

- Scan the code to watch a video clip about clouds.
- For more links, visit the Quicklinks Website

Storms and floods

In a big storm, the wind blows very hard. There's usually lots of rain or snow. There may be thunder and lightning too.

Types of storms

The pictures below show some of the things that can happen during different types of storms.

Lightning is a big spark of electricity in the sky. Thunder is the noise that the spark makes.

A tornado is a spinning funnel of wind. It whirls along sucking up anything in its path.

A hurricane is a huge storm with lots of wind and rain. It can destroy towns and forests.

The swirling clouds on this photograph of the Earth are a hurricane – a huge storm with lots of wind and rain.

Storms at sea

At sea, violent storms and huge waves can appear suddenly and cause terrible damage. Tornadoes, called waterspouts, sometimes pull sea water up into a spinning column. This sucks up anything in its path as it moves across the sea.

Giant sparks of electricity zigzag through the air during a lightning storm in Arizona, USA.

Floods

If a lot of rain falls in a short time, or if it rains for a long time, rivers get too full and spill onto the land. This causes floods, which cover land that is usually dry.

A flash flood is a sudden rush of water. It happens when a lot of rain falls in a short time.

Some floods happen when snow and ice melt. The soil is still frozen so water can't soak into it.

Huge waves can cause floods. They are made by storms, undersea volcanoes or earthquakes.

Monsoon floods

A monsoon is a wind that blows one way all summer and the other way all winter. In Asia, the monsoon in summer brings very heavy rain from the oceans.

Each year, homes and villages in southeast Asia are flooded by heavy monsoon rains. This photograph was taken in Vietnam.

Internet links

- Scan the code to watch a video of hurricanes and how they form.
- For more links, go to www.usborne.com/quicklinks

Rocks and fossils

There are lots of kinds of rocks.
Some are made by heat inside the
Earth. Others are made from sand, mud
and pieces of dead plants and animals.

This is
a fossil of a
sea animal called
an ammonite.

Rocky layers

Sand, mud and pieces of
plants and animals that
sink and settle at the
bottom of the sea
are known as
sediment.

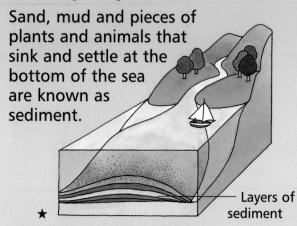

★   Layers of
sediment

Layers of sediment build up slowly.
Over millions of years, the bottom
layers get squeezed and stick together
to become sedimentary rocks.

Fiery rocks

Sometimes, hot,
sticky rock from
inside the Earth
breaks through
the surface.

Volcano

★   Hot,
sticky rock

Hot, sticky rock pours out of a
volcano. When it cools, it becomes
hard. This kind of rock is known as
igneous rock. Igneous means "fiery".

The Grand Canyon in Arizona,
USA, is formed from layers
of sedimentary rock.

This is a fossil of a sea animal called a trilobite.

This is the fossil of a sea creature called a sand dollar.

Fossils

Fossils are the stony remains of animals that lived millions of years ago. Most fossils are found in sedimentary rock.

Internet links

- Scan the code to see lots of different fossils.
- For more links, go to www.usborne.com/quicklinks

When an animal dies, its soft parts rot away leaving its bones. If they sink into mud, they get covered in sediment.

Over millions of years, the sediment layers slowly harden into rock. This keeps the shape of the animal's bones in it.

Millions of years later, people sometimes find fossil bones or shells inside rocks. They have to dig them up carefully.

The Colorado River made the Grand Canyon. It started to wear the rock away millions of years ago.

Earthquakes

An earthquake happens when huge rocks deep under the ground slip and push against each other. This makes the ground above shake.

The red dots on this map show where earthquakes are most likely to happen.

Start of an earthquake

The place underground where an earthquake starts is called the focus. On the surface, the place right above the focus is the epicenter. The effects of an earthquake are strongest here.

Internet links

- Scan the code to watch a video clip about tsunamis.
- For more links, go to **www.usborne.com/quicklinks**

This house fell down in a big earthquake in California, USA, in 1994.

Earthquake effects

Most earthquakes are too weak to be felt by people, but some can cause great damage. The pictures below show some of the effects of an earthquake.

In a weak earthquake, hanging things, like birdcages, swing. Windows and dishes may start to rattle.

A stronger earthquake makes walls crack and pictures fall. Frightened people run outdoors.

In a very strong earthquake, buildings and trees fall down.

Staying safe

In countries where there are a lot of earthquakes, people are taught ways to stay safe. Children have earthquake-safety lessons at school.

Indoors, it is safest to shelter under a table. ★

Outdoors, you are safest in a big open space. ★

Earthquakes at sea

An earthquake that happens under the sea shakes the seabed. This sometimes creates huge waves, called tsunami (say "soonaamee").

In the deep ocean, tsunami are not dangerous and may pass under ships without anybody noticing. They only become enormous if they reach shallow water. Then they break and crash onto the land.

As the seabed moves, the sea above forms long, low waves.

If tsunami reach the coast, they are squeezed up into huge waves.

Earthquakes can cause huge waves, like this one. The biggest wave ever recorded was 574 yards high, in Alaska in 1958.

Volcanoes

A volcano erupts when hot, sticky rock from inside the Earth bursts through the surface. The hot rock, called lava, pours down the sides of the volcano and over the land.

This photograph shows a fountain of hot, sticky rock shooting out of a volcano.

Volcanic eruption

When a volcano erupts, lava comes out of a vent (opening) in the volcano's top or side. "Bombs" of rock may shoot up into the sky, and thick clouds of ash and gas may billow out. Sometimes a vent is in a hollow called a crater.

Lava is so hot it destroys everything it touches. The heat of the lava has set this wooden house on fire.

Volcano shapes

The lava cools and hardens into rock. Layers of lava and ash build up each time the volcano erupts, giving the volcano its shape. Some volcanoes are tall cones with steep sides and some are fairly flat with gentle slopes.

Many volcanoes are tall and steep. Their thick, sticky lava does not flow far before it hardens.

Some volcanoes are flatter. Their lava is runny. It spreads out quickly before it hardens.

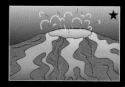

Sea volcanoes

There are lots of volcanoes under the sea. When one gets tall enough to appear above the waves, it makes an island.

This photograph shows clouds of steam and ash billowing from Surtsey, a volcanic island near Iceland.

A red-hot river of liquid rock is flowing down the side of this volcano.

Lava often moves quite slowly, so people usually have time to escape.

Alive, asleep or dead?

A volcano may be active (alive), dormant (asleep) or extinct (dead).

 ★

A volcano that erupts quite often is called an active volcano.

 ★

A dormant volcano hasn't erupted for a long time, but may erupt again in the future.

 ★

An extinct volcano hasn't erupted for at least a million years. Some towns are built on extinct volcanoes.

Internet links

- Scan the code to find out about volcanoes and watch them erupt.
- For more links, go to **www.usborne.com/quicklinks**

Following a river

A river starts high up in hills or mountains. The water comes from rain or melted snow. It flows downhill until it reaches the sea. Follow this river to see how it changes.

1. The start of a river is called its source. This may be where lots of streams join together.

2. The water wears the rock away to make a valley shaped like a V.

3. Other smaller rivers called tributaries may join the river and make it bigger.

The sides of the river are called riverbanks.

People sometimes put big, flat stepping stones in a river. You can step on them to cross it.

These fishermen are trying to catch fish that live in the river.

4. Here the river flows fast over rocks and stones.

This is a waterfall. The water flows very fast here.

Waterfalls

A waterfall forms where a river flows from hard rock to soft rock. The water wears away the soft rock faster than the hard rock. This makes a big step.

This photograph shows water rushing over the Kanchan Waterfall in Cambodia.

9. The place where a river joins the sea is called the mouth of the river.

Lots of birds feed on the little animals that live in the sand.

Bank of sand

7. The river carries lots of sand and mud to the sea.

8. The river drops most of its sand and mud when it reaches the sea.

6. The river is deeper and wider on the outer edge of the bend.

5. Here the river starts to flow in big loops called meanders.

Internet links

- Scan the code for facts about the world's longest rivers.
- For more links, go to **www.usborne.com/quicklinks**

The arches on this stone bridge make it strong.

Mountains

Mountains form over millions of years. Vast pieces of rock on the Earth's surface push against each other and force part of the land up into mountains.

Parts of a mountain

Some mountains have snow on their peaks (tops) all year around. The level where the snow ends is called the snowline.

Trees often grow on a mountain's lower slopes, but it's too cold for them to grow above a certain level. This is known as the treeline.

A group of mountains is known as a range. These mountains are part of a range called the Rocky Mountains in Canada.

A gap between two peaks in a range is called a pass. ★

Peak

Treeline   Snowline

Pass

This picture shows the parts of a mountain.

Glaciers

On the coldest parts of some mountains, snow builds up and turns into ice. Solid rivers of ice, called glaciers, move very slowly downhill.

Internet links
- Scan the code to watch climbers scale the world's highest mountain.
- For more links, go to www.usborne.com/quicklinks

Glaciers like this one carry stones and rocks downhill. As it warms up farther down the mountain, the glacier melts, forming streams.

Mountain life

Some plants and animals can live on mountains. They need to be able to survive in very cold temperatures and strong winds.

Mountain flowers such as purple saxifrage grow in short, round clumps.

Conifer trees have tough, narrow needles instead of broad leaves.

Golden eagles build their large nests on mountain rocks and ledges.

Mountain hares have thick fur which turns white in winter.

In the desert

Deserts are the driest places in the world. Sometimes it doesn't rain for many years. Most deserts are very hot in the day, but cool at night.

Internet links

- Scan the code to watch fennec foxes and see their huge ears.
- For more links, go to www.usborne.com/quicklinks

Sahara Desert

AFRICA

Deserts cover over a quarter of our planet. The biggest is the Sahara Desert in North Africa.

Desert homes have flat roofs, and small windows to keep out the sun.

Palm trees

An oasis is a place where there is water so plants can grow.

Camels can last a week without water.

Euphorbia plant

Antelopes

Most deserts are rocky and bare. Only parts of them are covered in sand.

Sandgrouse

Jerboas hop along like miniature kangaroos.

28

Desert plants

Many desert plants have long roots, and stems which can soak up water. Some, like the barrel cactus, can store water inside.

Before rain

After rain

A barrel cactus swells with water when it rains.

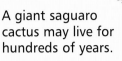

A giant saguaro cactus may live for hundreds of years.

When the wind blows, the sand piles up into hills called sand dunes.

Lanner falcon

Desert people live in groups and move from place to place. They keep sheep, goats and camels.

Fennec foxes have huge ears which help them to lose body heat.

Saw scaled adders slither along with an S-shaped wiggle.

Grasslands

Plains, or grasslands, are big areas of land covered in grass. Bushes and some trees may grow there too. The picture below shows part of a grassland in Africa.

Grasslands, shown in orange on the map, cover about a quarter of the Earth's land.

Baobab trees can store water in their trunks.

Ostriches

Rhinos

Elephants

Thousands of insects called termites make these big mounds.

Baboons live in large groups called troops.

Lions live in groups called prides.

Weaver birds make complicated nests.

Acacia tree

Wildebeest

Hyenas

Tourists come in trucks and buses to see the animals.

30

Tourists in a
hot air balloon

Vultures

Internet links
- Scan the code to watch a cheetah chasing its prey.
- For more links, go to **www.usborne.com/quicklinks**

The dry grass catches fire easily. It grows again when it rains.

Giraffes

Lots of animals come to a waterhole to drink and stay cool.

Antelopes

Warthogs

Zebras

Cheetahs

Prairies and steppes

There are many names for grasslands around the world. Grasslands in Russia are known as steppes.

In North America, grasslands are called prairies. Most prairies are now used as farmland. Wheat grows well there.

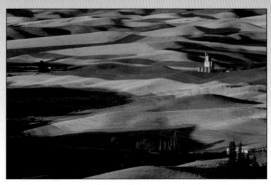

Huge fields of wheat stretch across the grasslands of North America.

In the rainforest

Thick, green rainforests grow in hot, wet places near the equator. It is warm all year there and it rains nearly every day. Rainforests are home to thousands of different plants and animals.

Internet links
- Scan the code for a video about the Amazon rainforest.
- For more links, go to **www.usborne.com/quicklinks**

SOUTH AMERICA

Amazon River

The biggest rainforest is the Amazon Rainforest in South America. The Amazon River runs through it.

Rainforest trees grow very tall.

Spider monkeys

Morpho butterfly

Lichen

Arrow-poison frog

Jaguar

Hummingbird

Orchids

Plants on trees

Many rainforest plants grow on the branches of trees. This is because there is more light up there than on the ground.

Ferns

Scarlet macaws

Toucans

Bromeliad

Howler monkeys

Lianas are plants with long stems like ropes.

Sloths move very slowly.

Capybaras look like large guinea pigs.

Caiman

These big buttress roots hold the tall trees upright.

Giant armadillo

Scarlet ibis

Anacondas are huge snakes.

Matamata turtle

Giant water lily leaves

Seas and oceans

More than two-thirds of the Earth is covered with salty water. This makes the planet look blue from space. The water is divided into five large areas called oceans. In some places these are divided into smaller areas called seas.

Watery world

It is like a different world under the oceans. There are deep valleys, huge mountains, forests of seaweed and many amazing sea animals.

Internet links
• Scan the code for fascinating facts about oceans and ocean wildlife.
• For more links, go to www.usborne.com/quicklinks

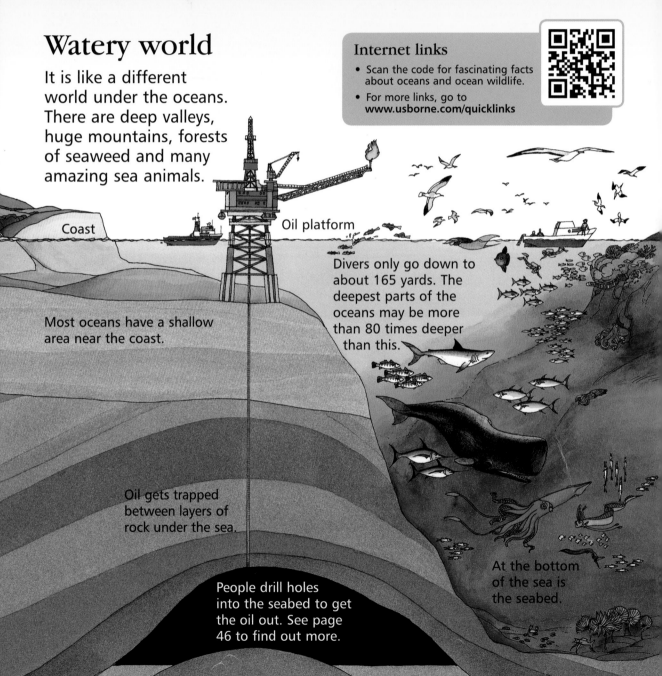

Coast

Oil platform

Most oceans have a shallow area near the coast.

Divers only go down to about 165 yards. The deepest parts of the oceans may be more than 80 times deeper than this.

Oil gets trapped between layers of rock under the sea.

People drill holes into the seabed to get the oil out. See page 46 to find out more.

At the bottom of the sea is the seabed.

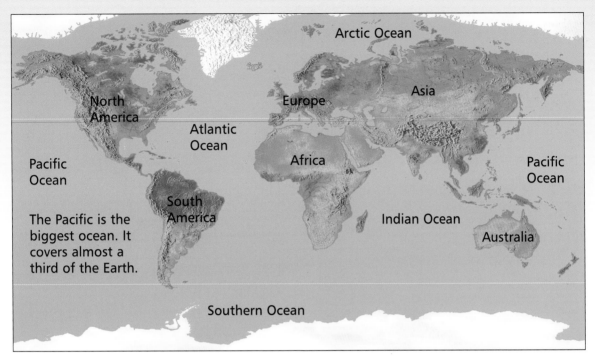

This map shows the five different oceans. Remember that the world
is round, so the two parts of the Pacific Ocean join up.

Some islands are the tops of enormous undersea mountains.

Undersea volcanoes throw out boiling melted rock called lava.

Darkest depths

The deepest place in any ocean is the Mariana Trench in the Pacific. If you dropped a 2lb rock into the water there, it would take over an hour to reach the seabed.

The 88-floor Petronas Towers in Malaysia are among the world's tallest buildings. Even 28 of them stood one on top of the other in the Mariana Trench wouldn't quite reach the water's surface.

The bottoms of deep trenches are completely dark, but some animals live down there.

The Pacific is the biggest ocean. It covers almost a third of the Earth.

37

Waves

Waves are made far out at sea by the wind. They sometimes travel enormous distances across the oceans before finally crashing onto the seashore.

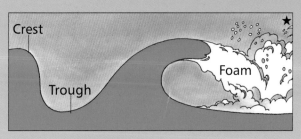

This picture shows what the different parts of a wave are called.

Crest

Trough

Foam

Making waves

Wind blowing across the sea makes ripples on the water. If the wind continues to blow, the ripples will get bigger and bigger, until they turn into waves.

When the wind blows across the tops of waves it creates foam on them and makes them grow.

Breaking waves

The shape of a wave is affected by the depth of the sea. This makes waves change shape as they get closer to the coast.

Internet links
- Scan the code to see amazing photos of waves.
- For more links, go to www.usborne.com/quicklinks

Water drags on seabed.

As a wave gets closer to land, the water gets shallower. The bottom part of the wave starts to drag on the seabed and slows down.

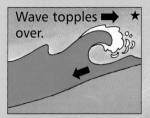

Wave topples over.

The top of the wave now moves faster than the bottom. This makes the top of the wave fall forward and topple over. This is called breaking.

Underwater energy

Waves are a kind of energy, moving through the water. Although the wave moves through the water, the water actually stays in the same place.

If you watch a wave, it looks as if the water moves along, but it doesn't.

When a wave passes under something such as a seagull, it just lifts it up.

When the wave has passed, the seagull is still in the same place as it was before.

Monster waves

The size of a wave depends on how strongly the wind is blowing and the distance it has covered. During storms at sea, strong winds create huge, powerful waves, which are big enough to sink a ship.

In some places, waves can be over 13 yards high. That's higher than a two-floor house.

Currents

Currents are like big rivers which flow through the oceans. Different currents flow at different speeds. Some only move seven miles a day. Others move up to 100 miles a day.

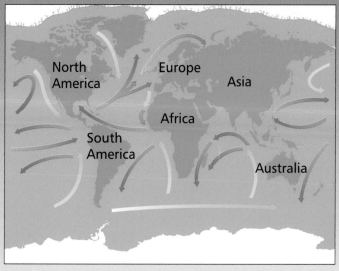

North America

Europe

Asia

Africa

South America

Australia

The map above shows the world's main currents.

 Warm current Cold current

Carried by currents

Plant seeds are sometimes carried a very long way by a current. The new plant can grow a long distance away from its parent.

Internet links
- Scan the code to see a rocky shore when the tide goes out.
- For more links, go to **www.usborne.com/quicklinks**

Plant seeds, such as this coconut, fall into the sea. The current carries them away.

The seed sometimes travels for a long distance before reaching land.

Waves carry the seed onto another shore, where it may put down roots and grow.

Tides

The height of the sea is called sea level. The sea level in most places is constantly changing through the day as the sea moves up and down the beach. This movement is called the tide.

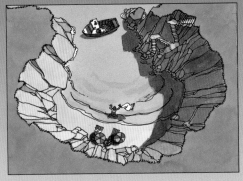

Tides sometimes come in very fast and trap people on beaches.

Tidelines

When the water reaches its highest point on a beach, it leaves behind a line of things from the sea. Then it starts to move back down the beach again. This line is called a tideline.

Seagulls search the tideline, eating pieces of food they find.

There is often lots of seaweed left behind when the tide goes out.

The bones of cuttlefish, called cuttlebones, are often washed up on beaches by the tide.

This is a dogfish egg case. It is called a mermaid's purse.

Coasts

Coasts are the places where the land meets the sea. Coasts are always changing shape as waves and the wind wear them away.

Waves throw pebbles and rocks against the coast. Over time, this wears it away.

Bigger stones are at the back of the beach.

Small stones and sand are near the sea.

Making beaches

Beaches form on low, flat parts of the coast. Waves grind down big rocks and cliffs into smaller stones and pebbles, and finally into sand. Sand often also contains tiny pieces of broken seashells.

Internet links

- Scan the code to fly along a rocky coast.
- For more links, go to www.usborne.com/quicklinks

Changing coasts

Some parts of a coast are made of harder rock than others. These parts are worn away more slowly by the sea, and form a headland.

Headland

When the top of an arch collapses, a stack or stump is left.

Waves wear away softer rock in the cliffs to make caves.

An arch forms when waves wear away a hole through a headland.

Sorting the stones

The smallest stones on a beach are always the ones nearest to the sea. This is because of breaking waves. As waves crash onto a beach, they slowly sort the stones into different sizes. Here is how it happens:

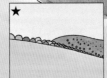

As waves break, they throw pebbles and stones onto the beach.

As the water flows back to sea, it carries little pebbles back with it.

The bigger stones and pebbles are left farther up the beach.

Icy world

The places near the top and bottom of the Earth are called polar regions. They are very cold. Huge areas of land and sea are covered in ice and snow.

The area around the North Pole is called the Arctic.

The area around the South Pole is called the Antarctic.

Polar ice

The ice in the polar regions forms flat sheets and glaciers, and covers high mountains. In the summer, some of the ice melts, but in the winter it freezes solid again.

Many penguins live in the Antarctic. They have a thick layer of feathers and fat to keep out the cold.

What is an iceberg?

Icebergs are huge chunks of ice floating in the water. The small top part, or tip, floats above the water. The rest is hidden below. The pictures on the right show how an iceberg forms.

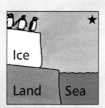

A sheet of ice moves over the land to the sea.

At the sea, the ice moves out over the water.

A piece of ice breaks off. This is an iceberg.

Life near the poles

Not many people live in the Arctic, compared with most other areas of the world. No one lives in the Antarctic all the time, but scientists go there to study its animals, weather and land. Tourists go to both places to climb, ski, and see the wildlife.

Internet links

- Scan the code to see penguins and seals that visit the Antarctic.
- For more links, go to **www.usborne.com/quicklinks**

Surviving the cold

Animals that live in the polar regions have to survive in very cold weather. They must keep warm and find food in icy conditions.

Polar bears make long journeys over the Arctic snow and ice in search of seals, birds, fish and plants to eat.

★

Antarctic icefish have special liquid in their blood to stop it from freezing.

★

Walruses live in the Arctic. A layer of fatty blubber under their skins keeps them warm.

★

Weddell seals hunt for food under the Antarctic ice. They make breathing holes in the ice.

★

Caves and caverns

A cave or cavern is like an underground room with walls made of rock. Some caves are just below the surface. Others are very deep underground.

Caves like this one form slowly over many thousands of years.

How caves are made

Each time it rains, the rainwater seeps through cracks in the rock.

Over a long, long time, the water dissolves the rock and wears it away.

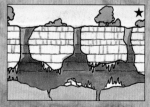

When the level of the water drops, empty caves and passages are left.

This man is one of a group of French cavers who climbed down into this cave in Hunan, China, to explore it.

Internet links

- Scan the code to watch a video of cavers exploring a cave.
- For more links, go to www.usborne.com/quicklinks

Rocky shapes

Some caves are full of strange, rocky shapes. These are made by water which has trickled through the rock and dissolved some of it. When the water drips, it leaves behind some of the dissolved rock. This builds up very slowly to make the rocky shapes.

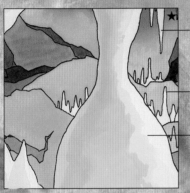

Stalactites hang from the roof.

Stalagmites form on the floor.

Sometimes stalactites join up with stalagmites.

Cavers

Cavers are people who explore caves for fun, or to find out more about them. Cavers often squeeze through narrow passages or wade through deep water to reach a cave. They have special clothes and equipment to keep them safe and help them explore the caves.

Helmet with lamp

Thick overalls

Strong rope

Waterproof boots

Bears, bats and bison

Brown bear

Brown bears and black bears sleep inside caves through the winter.

Horseshoe bat

Many kinds of bats spend the winter in caves. They fly out in the spring.

Cave painting of a bison

A long time ago, people lived in caves. They made pictures on the walls. These pictures help to tell us what life was like then.

45

Useful Earth

We depend on the Earth to survive. It gives us food, water, air and all we need for building and making things. It also gives us the fuel we need for cooking, heating and making machines and engines go.

Sand is used to make glass.

We eat many kinds of plants. Some are made into material, such as cotton, for clothes. Others are made into medicines.

Coal and oil

Coal is made from rotted trees and plants from millions of years ago. Oil began as tiny, dead sea animals. Coal and oil are taken from under the ground and used as fuels, but they are also used to make lots of other things.

Coal can be used to make paint, plastic, perfume, soap and the "lead" in pencils.

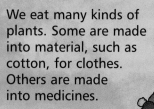

★

Oil and natural gas come from under the ground or under the seabed. People drill for them from rigs.

★ Oil can be used to make dishwashing liquid, plastic, gasoline, and dye to color material.

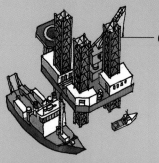

Oil rig

46

Wood from trees can be made into many things, such as furniture and paper.

Animals give us leather and wool as well as milk, meat and eggs.

Metal, coal, stone, clay and other useful things are dug out of the ground in places called quarries or mines.

Fishing boats catch fish from the sea.

Non-stop power

Oil, gas and coal may one day run out. There are many other ways of making power. They use things that will not run out, such as wind, water and sunshine.

Internet links

- Scan the code for a video about how wind turbines make electricity.
- For more links, go to www.usborne.com/quicklinks

These are wind turbines. The turning blades drive machines to make electricity.

Solar panels can soak up heat from the Sun and use it to make water hot.

Like the wind, flowing water can also drive turbines to make electricity.

World in danger

There are many things that we do to our world which put animals, plants and people in danger.

Smoke and fumes from factories and cars pollute the air.

Rainforest damage

Every year, huge areas of rainforests are cut down or burned. This is done for the wood, and to make space for farms. It destroys the homes of the animals that live there.

These rainforest trees are being burned to make space for farming.

Pollution

Litter, smoke from factories and cars, and oil spilled from ships at sea are all kinds of pollution. Pollution harms animals and people and the places where they live.

★ Litter looks horrible and can be dangerous for wildlife.

★ Chemicals from factories and farms can get into the water and soil.

★ Oil which spills from ships can harm sea animals.

Internet links

- Scan the code to find out about endangered wildlife, including leopards and rhinos.
- For more links, go to **www.usborne.com/quicklinks**

Animals in danger

Some animals are endangered – there are only a few of them left and they could easily die out. This is because we have hunted them or destroyed the places where they live.

Rhinos are killed for their horns. This one has had its horns cut off so hunters will leave it alone.

★

★

Golden lion tamarins became endangered when rainforests were cut down.

Some types of leopards are endangered because people hunt them for their skins.

Fishing dangers

When fishermen catch too many fish of the same kind, the number of fish starts to go down. This is called overfishing. If this doesn't stop soon, some kinds of fish will die out completely. Fishing can also endanger ocean life in other ways.

Purse seine nets are like big bags. They are used to catch tuna fish, but dolphins often get caught in the nets by mistake.

Trawl nets drag along the seabed to catch fish. They also pull up plants, and so destroy the homes of many sea creatures.

Getting warmer

Temperatures around the world are slowly rising. This is called global warming. There may be several reasons for it. Scientists think that it may be caused by certain gases, known as greenhouse gases, in the Earth's atmosphere.

Greenhouse gases

Greenhouse gases trap heat around the Earth, making it warm enough for life to exist. But some things that people do make more greenhouse gases. These trap more heat, so the Earth gets warmer.

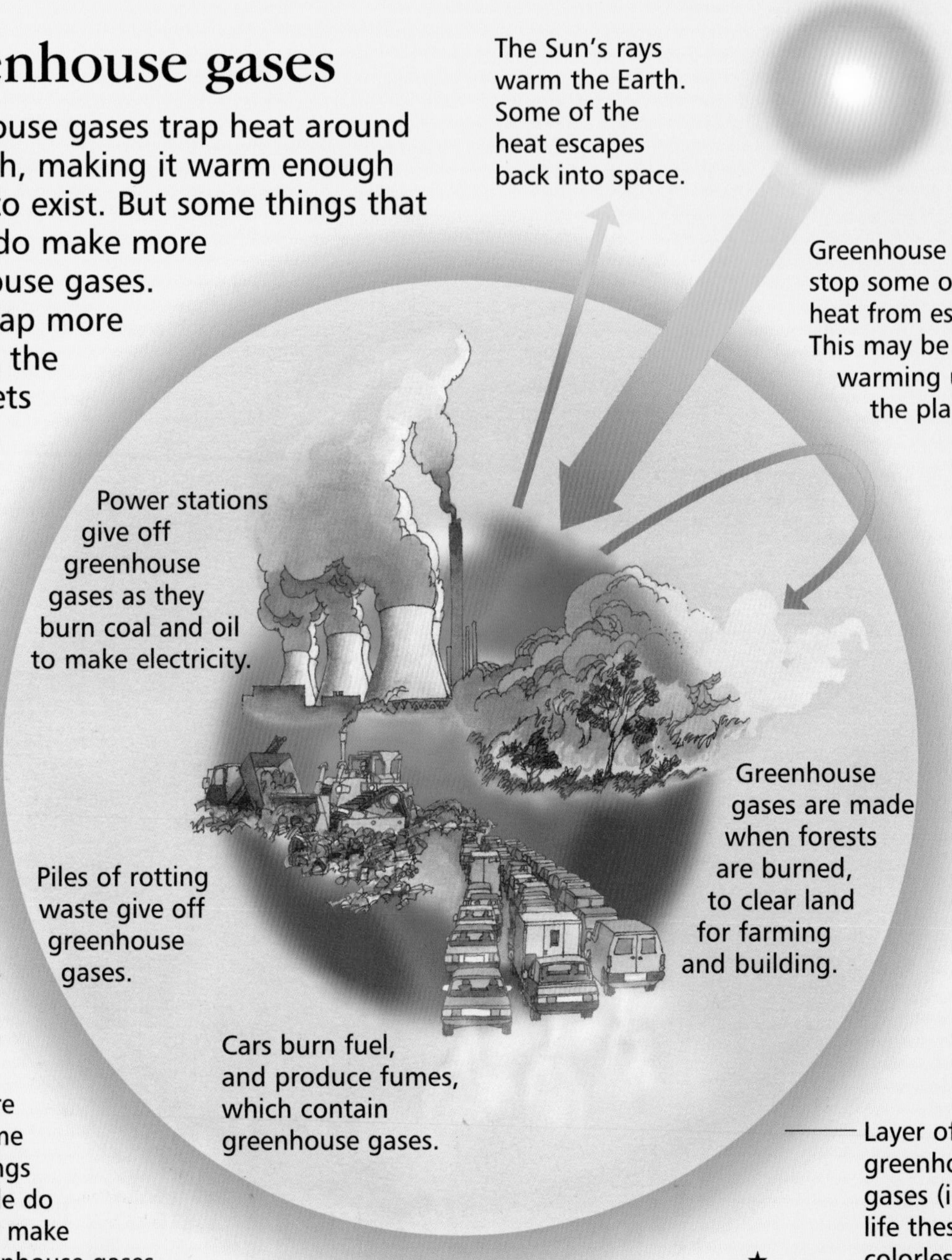

The Sun's rays warm the Earth. Some of the heat escapes back into space.

Greenhouse gases stop some of the heat from escaping. This may be warming up the planet.

Power stations give off greenhouse gases as they burn coal and oil to make electricity.

Greenhouse gases are made when forests are burned, to clear land for farming and building.

Piles of rotting waste give off greenhouse gases.

Cars burn fuel, and produce fumes, which contain greenhouse gases.

This picture shows some of the things that people do which can make more greenhouse gases.

Layer of greenhouse gases (in real life these are colorless).

★

Melting ice

As the atmosphere warms up, the ice in the Arctic and the Antarctic slowly starts to melt. The water goes back into the oceans, making the sea level rise.

The air gets warmer.

Ice melts into the sea.

The sea level rises.

Rising seas

If all the ice in the world melted, it would cause a worldwide disaster. The sea level everywhere would rise by more than 66 yards.

We can help to stop this by finding ways to make energy without burning fuels such as coal and oil (see page 47).

Internet links
- Scan the code to watch a short video about climate change.
- For more links, go to www.usborne.com/quicklinks

This picture shows what would happen to a town by the sea if the sea level rose by 66 yards.

Many islands in the sea would be flooded if all the ice in the world melted.

As ice melts at the poles, huge chunks of it fall into the sea.

Helping our planet

Everyone can do things to help our planet. Governments can make laws, for example, that control pollution and the way that areas of open land are used. There are many ways in which you can help, too.

Look out for this recycling symbol on cans, bottles or boxes.

How can you help?

Internet links

- Scan the code for simple ways to help stop global warming.
- For more links, go to **www.usborne.com/quicklinks**

 Take used cans, bottles and paper to a recycling center. The metal, glass, plastic and paper can be made into new things.

 Save electricity by using low-energy light bulbs and switching off the light when you go out of a room.

 Walk or cycle short distances, and go on longer journeys by bus or train. This helps to reduce pollution from cars.

 Put up a bird table in your yard, and plant shrubs that give birds and other creatures food and shelter.

Some African governments are helping endangered animals, such as chimpanzees, by setting aside land where they can live safe from hunters.

Animals and plants

Living things

There are millions of living things on planet Earth. These include plants, animals and people. All living things share certain features.

Living things need a gas called oxygen. A fish gets oxygen from the water it takes in through its mouth.

Air and food

To stay alive, most living things need a gas called oxygen. They also need food. Plants make their own food using energy from the Sun. Animals get energy by eating plants or other animals.

A buttercup plant uses energy from sunlight to grow.

The snail gets its energy from eating the buttercup.

A thrush eats the snail, and gains its energy.

New life and growth

Living things can make new living things. These live on after their parents have died. Animals make babies, and plants produce new plants. As they get older, most living things grow and change.

These baby penguins look like small versions of their parents.

Some animals give birth to live babies. Penguins, like other birds, lay eggs with the babies inside.

Internet links
- Scan the code to see a Venus flytrap catch an insect.
- For more links, go to www.usborne.com/quicklinks

Moving

All living things can move. Most animals can move from one place to another. Plants can only move parts of themselves, and they usually move too slowly for you to see.

Some animals, such as this cheetah, can move at very high speeds.

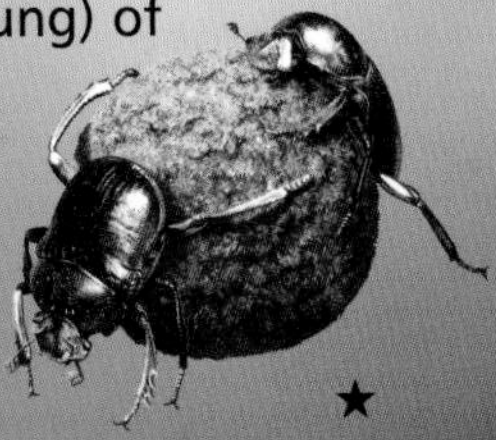

Sensitivity

Living things are sensitive to changes in the world around them, such as changes of light or heat. Animals usually react to these changes more quickly than plants.

A sunflower slowly turns so the flower always faces the Sun.

Waste

Plants and animals produce stuff inside them that they don't need. They all have ways of getting rid of the waste.

Dung beetles eat the solid waste (dung) of other animals.

Fly

Venus flytrap

When a fly touches sensitive hairs on the leaves of a Venus flytrap, the leaves snap shut and trap the fly.

55

Cells

All living things are made up of tiny units called cells. Most cells are much too small to see. Scientists have to look at them through microscopes.

Internet links

- Scan the code to watch a video clip about cells in your body.
- For more links, go to www.usborne.com/quicklinks

What is a cell?

A cell is a tiny structure with its own protective skin. Inside, a cell has even smaller parts called organelles. In many living things, such as humans, millions of cells stick together to make up body tissues such as skin, muscle and bone.

This picture shows human fat seen through a microscope. The pink blobs are cells.

Plant or animal?

Animal cells have a skin called a cell membrane. Inside, the parts of the cell float in a watery gel. Plant cells have a cell membrane and a tough cell wall that gives them a fixed shape.

Both plant and animal cells have a nucleus, which controls the cell

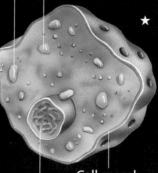

Organelles (cell parts)

Nucleus   Cell membrane (skin)

This picture shows an animal cell, cut in half so you can see inside it

Nucleus   Tough cell wall

Cell membrane   Organelles

This picture shows a plant cell, cut in half so you can see inside it

Single-celled creatures

Some very small living things have only one cell. There are single-celled animals called amoebas, and single-celled plants called algae.

Bacteria also have only one cell each. They are not plants or animals, but belong in a group of their own.

Bacteria are all around us. Most are harmless, but some, like these salmonella bacteria, can make you sick.

Bacteria are extremely tiny. This photograph was taken using a very powerful microscope.

Looking at cells

Microscopes make things look bigger. When microscopes were invented, over 300 years ago, scientists could begin to look very closely at living things, and cells were discovered.

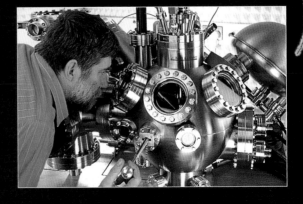

Today, powerful electron microscopes like this one help scientists to look deep inside cells.

57

Animal world

There are millions of different animals, from tiny bugs to huge whales. Here are some of the different types of animals you can find out about in this book.

This Arctic tern's shape helps it to fly.

Mammals

Mammals feed their babies milk. Almost all have hair or fur, and most are lively and curious. From polar bears to camels, mammals can be found all over the world.

Like all baby mammals, this lion cub is taken care of by its mother.

Birds

Birds are the only animals that have feathers. They all have wings, but not all of them can fly. Some are powerful runners or swimmers. All birds lay eggs, and take care of their babies.

Reptiles

Reptiles have dry, scaly skin and almost all lay eggs. You can find reptiles in most countries, especially in the warmer parts of the world.

This reptile is a type of African lizard called an agama. It has tough, dry skin, and spikes along its back.

Amphibians

Amphibians are animals with soft, damp skin. They can breathe on land or in water. An amphibian needs to keep its body moist to stay alive, even if it lives on land.

Frogs are amphibians. They are excellent swimmers and can breathe underwater.

Creepy-crawlies

The world is teeming with creepy-crawlies such as insects, spiders, centipedes and snails. The most common creepy-crawlies are insects. They all have six legs, and most have wings. There are nearly two million different types of insects.

Like most insects, this wasp can fly.

Water life

Many different animals live in water – from fish to mammals such as dolphins and seals, and creatures such as jellyfish and lobsters. Some animals are even able to live in the deepest ocean.

Sea anemones and fish are just two of the many types of animals that live in water.

Internet links
- Scan the code to see some amazing animals.
- For more links, go to **www.usborne.com/quicklinks**

59

Mammals

The animals on these two pages look different, but they are all mammals. There are more than four thousand different kinds of mammals, including you – humans are mammals, too.

Chimpanzees live in the forests of Africa.

Keeping warm

A mammal's body makes its own warmth and it can keep its temperature the same whether the day is hot or cold. This is called being warm-blooded.

The fur on this chimp helps to keep its body warm when the weather is cold.

Food for baby

All mammal mothers feed their babies milk. They make the milk in glands, called mammary glands, on their chests or bellies. Milk is a rich food but it is easy for a baby to swallow.

This baby deer is sucking milk from nipples on its mother's belly.

Flying mammal

Bats are the only mammals that can fly. Their wings are made of flaps of skin, which stretch over the bones of their arms and fingers.

Here you can see how a bat uses its arm as a wing. Long fingers support the wing skin.

★

Fruit bat

Internet links

- Scan the code for a video clip about baby chimpanzees.
- For more links, go to www.usborne.com/quicklinks

Swimmers

Some mammals, such as whales, live in the sea. Like all mammals, they breathe air, so they come to the surface regularly.

Humpback whale

Whales are the biggest animals in the world.

Egg layers

A few mammals lay eggs, rather than give birth. One is the duck-billed platypus. It lays its eggs in a nest in a riverbank burrow.

★

Duck-billed platypus

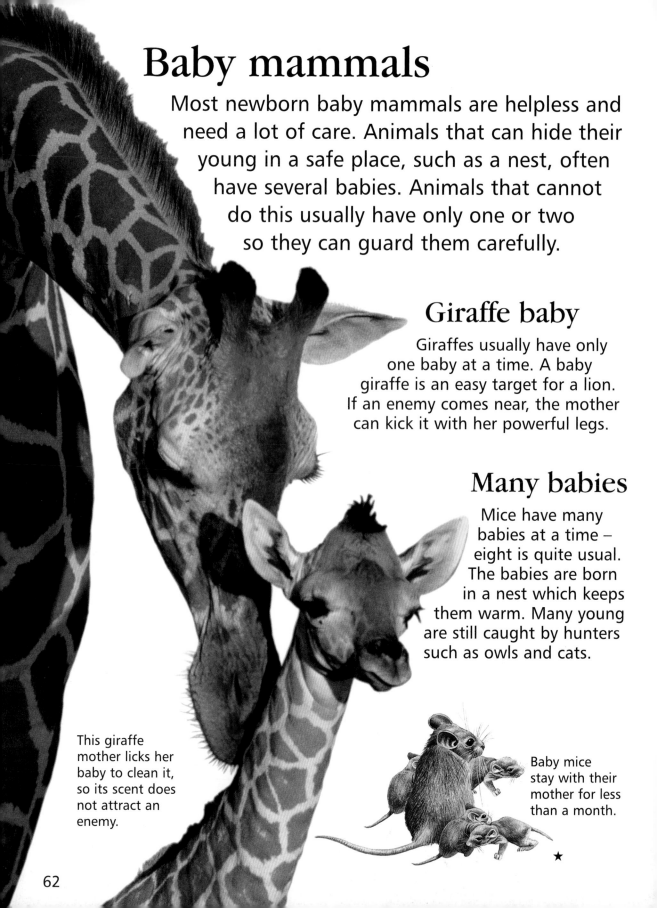

Baby mammals

Most newborn baby mammals are helpless and need a lot of care. Animals that can hide their young in a safe place, such as a nest, often have several babies. Animals that cannot do this usually have only one or two so they can guard them carefully.

Giraffe baby

Giraffes usually have only one baby at a time. A baby giraffe is an easy target for a lion. If an enemy comes near, the mother can kick it with her powerful legs.

Many babies

Mice have many babies at a time – eight is quite usual. The babies are born in a nest which keeps them warm. Many young are still caught by hunters such as owls and cats.

This giraffe mother licks her baby to clean it, so its scent does not attract an enemy.

Baby mice stay with their mother for less than a month.

★

Learning to hunt

Polar bear cubs spend two to three years with their mother, learning how to survive. The mother teaches them how to hunt. They leave her when they are old enough to hunt alone.

★

Baby polar bears stay close to their mother.

Pouch home

Marsupial mammals, like kangaroos, carry their babies in a built-in pouch. The baby feeds on milk from a nipple in the pouch. It also goes into the pouch if it is frightened or tired.

★

A baby kangaroo can travel this way until it is a year old.

Internet links
- Scan the code to watch baby elephants play.
- For more links, go to **www.usborne.com/quicklinks**

Long childhood

Elephants take care of their babies for longer than any other animals except humans. A young elephant stays with its mother for up to ten years.

This baby elephant is learning to use its trunk to drink and bathe.

Bird life

Birds are the only animals that have feathers. Not all birds fly, but those that can't are usually superb swimmers or runners.

Fit for flying

Many birds are excellent fliers. Most of their bones are hollow, so they are light. Strong chest muscles power birds' wings. The sleek shape of their bodies helps them move quickly through the air.

A goose coming in to land lowers its feet, and spreads out its wings to slow down.

Body shapes

Birds have different body shapes. A goose's sturdy, muscular body is ideal for making long flights to warmer countries in winter. A kingfisher's arrow-like body lets it dart in and out of the water as it hunts.

A kingfisher uses its long, sharp beak to spear fish.

★

Internet links

- Scan the code to watch snow geese in flight.
- For more links, go to www.usborne.com/quicklinks

Types of feathers

Birds have three different kinds of feathers. Fluffy feathers, called down, keep them warm. Short, sturdy body feathers keep them dry. Long flight feathers help them take off, fly and land.

You can see this eagle's flight feathers on its wings.

Long flights

Birds are the greatest travelers in the animal world. Half of all types fly long distances to places where there is lots of food or where they can have babies. This is called migration.

★

In winter, these geese fly from Canada to Mexico in search of food.

This baby bird has a down coat to keep it warm in its cliff top nest.

Feather growth

Baby birds are covered in down feathers. They grow body and flight feathers when they are older. All feathers get dirty and untidy. Birds clean and smooth them down with their beaks to keep them working properly.

This heron is cleaning its feathers.

★

Bodies and beaks

The shape of a bird's body and beak help it to find and eat the kind of food it likes. You can see here that there are huge differences in body and beak shapes.

Sea life

Puffins live by the sea and hunt fish. Their stubby, muscular bodies and short wings help them swim well underwater. They can fly, but they are much clumsier in the air than in the sea.

Wings and claws

This bald eagle's huge wings let it glide effortlessly over water as it searches for fish. Its sharp claws hold fish tightly as it returns to its nest to feed.

★

This bald eagle has sharp claws for grasping fish.

This is a puffin. Its webbed feet help it paddle in the sea.

Beak shapes

Birds use their beaks as tools to help them find food. This toucan's long beak lets it reach for fruit among dense forest branches.

The toucan's jagged beak helps it to grip fruit firmly.

Diggers

Like many river and seashore birds, the scarlet ibis has a long, thin beak. It uses it to poke around for small shrimp and worms at the muddy edges of rivers.

Scarlet ibis

Spears and nets

Many birds eat other animals. Some are fierce hunters that can kill animals as big as a monkey. Here are three flesh-eating birds that use their beaks in different ways.

★ A heron uses its dagger-like beak to spear fish.

★ A vulture's hooked beak lets it tear meat from a dead animal.

★ A pelican uses its sack-shaped beak like a fishing net.

Internet links

- Scan the code to see an eagle catch fish with its claws.
- For more links, go to www.usborne.com/quicklinks

Nests and chicks

Once she has laid her eggs, a female bird needs to sit on them to keep them warm. If the eggs get too cold, the babies inside will die.

A safe spot

Most birds build nests to protect the mother and her eggs from enemies. Nests also make a safe place for the babies when they hatch.

Internet links
- Scan the code to watch a hummingbird mother and her chicks in a nest.
- For more links, go to **www.usborne.com/quicklinks**

Types of nests

Each type of bird has its own way of building a nest. Many are cup-shaped, and made of mud, hair, feathers and twigs.

A swallow's nest is made of mud and stuck to a wall.

A tailor bird sews big leaves together with plant parts.

A long-tailed tit makes a nest of moss, lichen and cobwebs.

This Eurasian tit's nest is made of twigs and reeds.

Breaking out

Birds sit on their eggs for two weeks or more. (Bigger birds sit for longer.) When the baby is ready to hatch, it chips its way out of the egg. Most bird babies need a lot of looking after.

★

This baby moorhen is chipping its way out of its egg.

A hoopoe feeding a hungry chick

Hungry babies

Baby birds are always hungry, and need a constant supply of food. An adult hoopoe, for example, must make hundreds of journeys to and from its nest every day. It brings insects and grubs for its chicks.

Protecting the family

Swans build large waterside nests from plant stalks. Their babies (called cygnets) stay with them for around four months. The parents protect their young and take them to feeding places. When the cygnets leave, they live alone until they find a mate.

This mother swan and her cygnets are gathered around their nest.

Reptile life

What makes a reptile a reptile? It has scaly skin, it lays eggs and it is "cold-blooded". This means its body does not make heat and is as warm or as cold as the air around it. Lizards, snakes, turtles and crocodiles are all reptiles.

This snake is a green tree python. It hunts birds.

Snakes

All snakes are meat-eaters. Some eat insects and worms. Some can eat animals as big as a crocodile. You can find snakes all over the world, except in Antarctica.

Lizards

Most lizards are small, nimble creatures, although a few can grow to be as much as 10ft long. Like snakes, they can be found almost everywhere on Earth.

Internet links

- Scan the code to see baby turtles leave their nest and scurry to the sea.
- For more links, go to **www.usborne.com/quicklinks**

Crocodiles

Crocodiles, and their close relatives, alligators, are fierce hunters. They can be found on riverbanks in hot countries. In the right conditions, crocodiles can live for over 100 years.

Nile crocodile

This leaf-tailed gecko lives in the forests of Madagascar.

Its flat, leaf-shaped tail helps it to camouflage among the plants and trees.

Hawksbill turtle ★

Turtles

Turtles spend their lives in warm, shallow seas, and only ever come onto land to lay eggs. Some swim very long distances to find a place to have babies.

This iguana's leathery skin helps prevent it from drying up.

Tortoises

Tortoises are similar to turtles, but they live on land instead of water.

Tortoises are well protected by their hard outer shells.

★

Hot and cold

As reptiles are cold-blooded, heat and cold affect them more than warm-blooded animals. If they are too cold, they become sluggish. If they are too hot, they dry up and die. A reptile spends a lot of the day trying to stay at the right temperature.

Morning. Sits in sun to warm up after cool night.

Noon. Hides in shade at hottest time of day.

Afternoon. Moves in and out of sun, to keep warm or cool.

Amphibians

Amphibians look a little like reptiles, but with soft, moist skin. They lay squishy eggs in water, where their young hatch and grow. Adults can live on land and in water. Frogs and toads are amphibians.

Slimy skin

Many amphibians have shiny, slimy skin. They need to keep their skin moist, even when they are on land. If their skin becomes too dry, they may die.

This tree frog lives in rainforest trees. Moisture in the air helps to keep its skin damp.

Getting air

Amphibians are clever breathers. They can take in air through their skin on land and underwater. Some have gills, like fish (see page 81). On land, many amphibians breathe through their mouths.

The frilly growths on this axolotl's head are gills. It uses them to breathe underwater.

Swimming

An amphibian's body has special features that let it walk or swim. Frogs, for instance, have webbed toes. They use these like flippers to push themselves through the water.

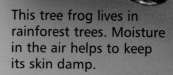

★

Webbed toes

Frogs and toads

Frogs have long, strong back legs. They use them to leap around on land, and swim in water. Many frogs have beautiful, bright skin. Toads have drier, warty skin.

★ Toads have shorter back legs than frogs. They waddle rather than hop.

Toad

★

Frog

Salamanders

A salamander has a long tail like a lizard. Most salamanders have foul-tasting skin which is brightly patterned. This warns their enemies not to try eating them because they will taste horrible.

The pattern on this salamander warns its enemies that it tastes bad.

Babies

Many frogs and toads lay lots of eggs at once. When they hatch, the babies live in water. They don't look like their parents at all. When they grow up, they move onto land.

These squishy blobs are frogs' eggs, called spawn. The babies, called tadpoles, hatch out of them.

After a few weeks the tadpoles start to grow legs. The back legs grow first, then the front legs.

Eventually, the tail shrinks away and the tadpole grows lungs. It can now breathe on land.

It takes about 16 weeks for a tadpole to become a frog. It still has a lot of growing to do.

Creepy-crawlies

The world is full of tiny creatures. Over four-fifths of all known types of animals are creepy-crawlies. Here you can see some of the different kinds found within this miniature world.

Types of insects

Although they look different, a bee and a dragonfly are both insects. They behave very differently though. For example, many bees live together in big groups, but dragonflies live alone.

The dragonfly (left) and bee (below) look very different, but they are both insects.

Southern hawker dragonfly

Head

Thorax

Abdomen

Insect parts

All adult insects have six legs and three parts to their bodies – a head, a thorax, and an abdomen. Most insects have wings at some stage of their lives.

White-tailed bumblebee

Spiders

Spiders are not insects. They are a type of animal known as an arachnid. Spiders have eight legs and two parts to their body. They never have wings. Many spiders spin webs to catch their food.

The golden orb weaver is one of Australia's biggest spiders. Females can be 2in long.

Lots of legs

Millipedes and centipedes have the most legs of any animal. Centipedes have up to 100 legs, while some millipedes have up to 700. Their bodies are divided into a series of segments. Like many creepy-crawlies, they have feelers called antennae on their heads.

★

Two rainforest millipedes

★

Internet links

• Scan the code to watch a video clip of a stag beetle.
• For more links, go to www.usborne.com/quicklinks

Slimy snails

Snails have a hard shell they can curl up in. This protects their bodies from enemies. Land snails, such as the one on the right, lurk in damp places, such as under leaves and stones. Some snails can live underwater.

This is a kind of snail called a grove snail. Like all snails, it slides along on its slimy belly.

A snail can pull its whole body into its shell if it is in danger.

Butterflies

Butterflies are among the most colorful types of insects. Most live for only a few weeks. They find a mate, lay eggs, then die.

Butterfly wings

Butterfly wings are covered in tiny colored, shiny scales. The shiny scales reflect light, which is why butterflies shimmer when they fly.

Butterflies visit plants to drink a liquid, called nectar, from flowers.

This butterfly is called a common blue. It has spread its wings to soak up the Sun's heat.

Open and shut

When a butterfly holds its wings open, it is gathering warmth from the Sun. This helps give it the energy to fly. When its wings are closed, it is resting. It faces the Sun, so its shadow is small and enemies are less likely to spot it.

Butterfly with wings open

Butterfly with wings closed

Internet links
- Scan the code to watch butterflies feeding on a plant.
- For more links, go to www.usborne.com/quicklinks

Wing patterns

A butterfly's beautiful, patterned wings help other butterflies spot their own kind. Their wing patterns help butterflies in other ways, too.

A comma's ragged wings disguise it as a dead leaf when it is on the ground.

The circles on a peacock butterfly's wings look like eyes. This frightens enemies. ★

★

The African monarch is poisonous. Birds learn not to eat it.

★ An Arctic ringlet's dark wings help it soak up heat.

This mocker swallowtail is not poisonous, but birds think it is an African monarch and do not eat it. ★

The patterns on this tortoiseshell's wings help it attract a mate.

Making butterflies

A female butterfly lays her eggs on a plant. When an egg hatches, a caterpillar comes out and feeds on the plant. When the caterpillar is fully grown, it turns into a pupa, and then into a butterfly.

A caterpillar ready to turn into a pupa

The pupa forms inside the body. It splits the skin.

The pupa hardens. Inside, it is changing.

After two weeks a butterfly comes out.

The butterfly's body hardens and it flies off.

Seashore life

There are lots of things to spot on the seashore. Every day when the tide goes out, it leaves pools of water trapped among the rocks. Plants and animals make their homes in these pools.

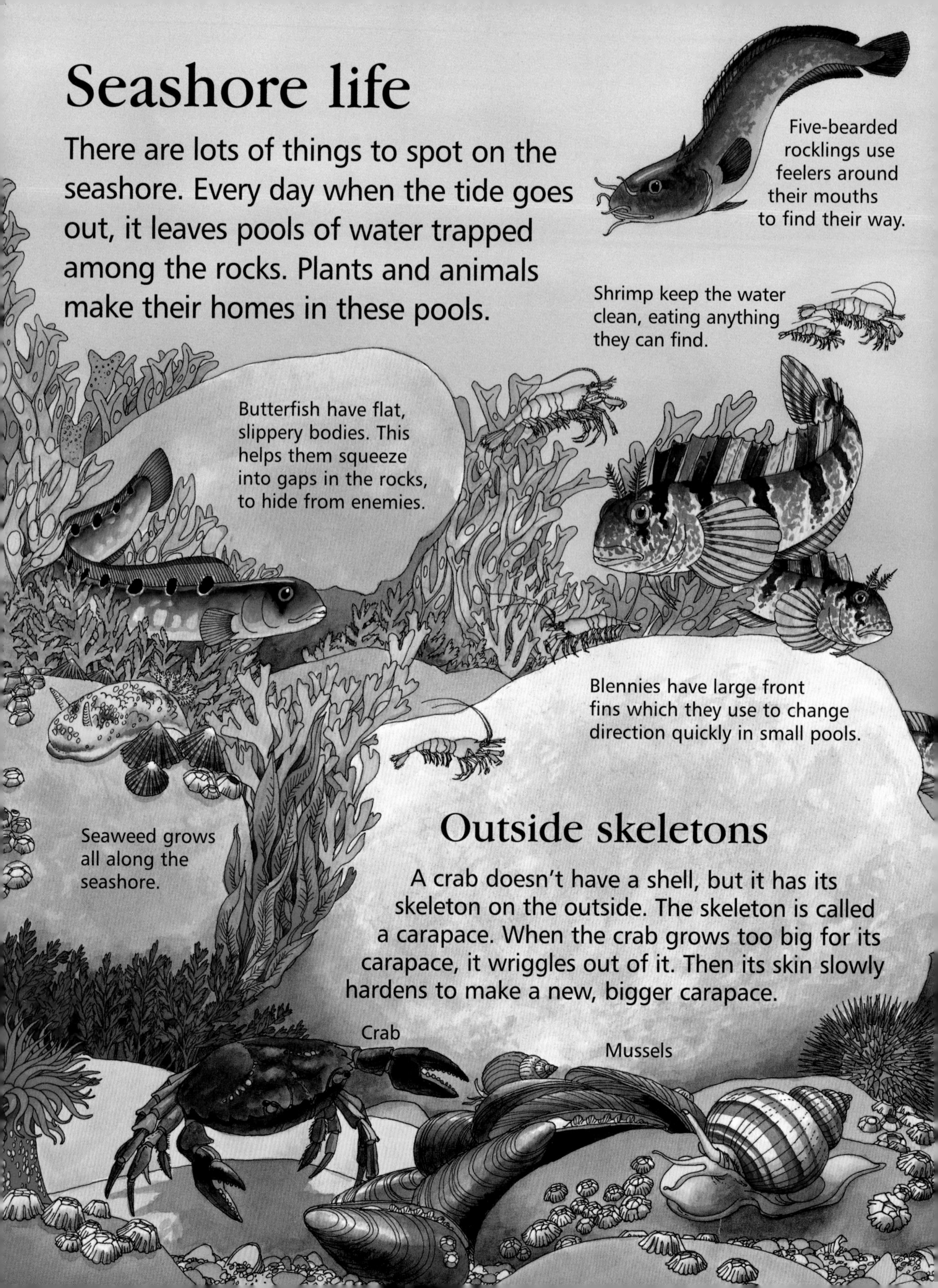

Five-bearded rocklings use feelers around their mouths to find their way.

Shrimp keep the water clean, eating anything they can find.

Butterfish have flat, slippery bodies. This helps them squeeze into gaps in the rocks, to hide from enemies.

Blennies have large front fins which they use to change direction quickly in small pools.

Seaweed grows all along the seashore.

Outside skeletons

A crab doesn't have a shell, but it has its skeleton on the outside. The skeleton is called a carapace. When the crab grows too big for its carapace, it wriggles out of it. Then its skin slowly hardens to make a new, bigger carapace.

Crab

Mussels

Upside down

Barnacles cover the rocks along the seashore. They feed by sticking their legs out of the tops of their shells.

Tiny barnacles cling to the rocks in big groups. Their tough shells protect them from danger.

Barnacles open the tops of their shells to feed. Their legs stick out to pick up bits of food in the water.

Special air bubbles keep this seaweed floating near the surface of the water, where there is light.

Sea scorpions are fierce hunters. Their huge mouths can open very wide.

Internet links

- Scan the code to spot seashore life in a tide pool.
- For more links, go to www.usborne.com/quicklinks

Starfish have five arms. If they lose an arm, another one grows in its place.

Hermit crab

Sea urchins have sharp spines on their shells to protect them.

Sea lemons scrape food off the rocks with their tongues.

Strawberry anemones

Limpets

Barnacles

Dog whelk

Underwater life

The oceans are full of living things. Some sea creatures are gentle and friendly, but others are fierce hunters.

Internet links

- Scan the code to see unusual-looking creatures that live in the oceans.
- For more links, go to www.usborne.com/quicklinks

Most types of sharks are deadly hunters. They have sharp teeth for eating other animals.

Dolphins are one of the most intelligent and playful kinds of sea animal.

Coral reefs are beautiful underwater structures. They are home to many different sea animals.

Sea slugs collect other animals' poison and use it themselves against their enemies.

What are fish?

Fish are a group of animals that live in water. There are thousands of different kinds. They come in different shapes and sizes, but they all have gills and fins. Gills allow them to breathe underwater, and fins help them to move around.

Caudal fin

Most fish have flat tails, which they move from side to side to swim. Their strong tail muscles make swimming easy.

Fish use these top fins, called dorsal fins, to help keep their balance.

This flap, called the operculum, covers the fish's gills.

Pelvic fins help fish to change direction quickly.

Fish use these fins, called pectoral fins, for turning.

Slimy skin helps fish to move easily through water.

This line, called the lateral line, helps fish to sense movement in the water.

Breathing

Fish breathe by taking oxygen out of the water. Here's how they do it.

Gills under here

As a fish moves forward, it takes in water through its mouth. The water passes over its gills.

The fish's gills take oxygen from the water. The water then passes out under the fish's operculum.

Fish scales

Most fish are protected by a covering of tiny plates, called scales. These scales are waterproof, and help to protect the fish from pests and hunters.

Fish scales overlap each other, to make a protective cover.

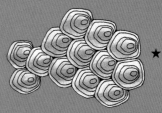

The rings on a fish's scales show how old the fish is. Some fish can live for up to 80 years.

Coral reefs

Corals live in warm, shallow seas.
Although they look like plants,
corals are really made of
thousands of small animals.
Large areas of coral are
called coral reefs.

Internet links

- Scan the code to watch clownfish
  in a sea anemone on a coral reef.
- For more links, go to
  www.usborne.com/quicklinks

Angelfish live among corals. Their bright markings
help them blend in with their background.

Coral animals

Coral animals, called polyps, are
protected by hard skeletons. When
they die, the skeletons remain and
new polyps grow on top of them.
Over time, a coral reef slowly forms.

A coral polyp,
cut in half

Poisonous tentacles
for catching food

Mouth

Stomach

Stony base

There are four fish and an
eel hiding in this coral reef.
Can you spot them all?

★

Sponge

Sea fan

Sea urchin

Brittle star

Brain coral

Reef life

Coral reefs are full of nooks and crannies where animals can hide and make their homes. This means there are always lots of living things around them.

A coral meal

The animals in coral are well protected by their shells, but some fish, such as parrotfish, are able to eat them.

A parrotfish's teeth are all joined together to form a hard beak.

The parrotfish breaks off a chunk of coral, then uses its beak to crunch it up.

Giant clam

Feather star

Sea anemone

Sharks

Sharks are fish which live in oceans all over the world. There are more than 300 different kinds. Most are fierce hunters, with sharp teeth for catching and killing other animals.

Internet links

- Scan the code to watch a video clip of hammerhead sharks.
- For more links, go to **www.usborne.com/quicklinks**

Whale sharks are not a danger to people. Divers can swim with them safely.

Great white shark

People killers?

Great white sharks like to surprise their prey from below and kill it with only one bite, to save energy. They sometimes attack swimmers, but scientists believe they do this by mistake, thinking that humans are other sea animals.

Great white sharks kill their prey by biting it. They can open their mouths very wide.

As their mouths open, their teeth point forward, helping them to take a bigger bite.

Whale sharks are the world's biggest fish. They can grow up to 40ft long.

Hammerhead sharks have eyes on each end of a long, flat head. This helps them to see all around as they swim.

Sharks swim by moving their tails from side to side.

Fin shapes

Sharks, like dolphins and whales, sometimes swim near the surface of the sea with their dorsal (back) fins sticking out of the water. Dorsal fins of different animals look different, as you can see below.

A common dolphin has a small, gently curved fin.

A great white shark's fin is sharp and triangular.

The fin of a killer whale can be as tall as a person.

Hundreds of teeth

Most sharks have at least three rows of teeth. As they lose the ones in front, teeth from the rows behind move forward to replace them.

A sand tiger shark's teeth point back so that fish it catches can't wiggle free.

Whales

Whales are the biggest animals in the world. They look like fish, but whales are actually mammals (read more about mammals on pages 60-61). Unlike most mammals though, whales do not have hair on their bodies.

This sperm whale is as heavy as six elephants. The heaviest animals on Earth are blue whales, which can weigh as much as 20 elephants.

Spout shapes

Mammals can't breathe underwater, so whales come to the ocean's surface to breathe. They breathe through holes called blowholes on top of their heads. When they breathe out, they shoot out sprays of water. This is called spouting.

Different whales spout in different ways. By looking at the shape of a whale's spout, you can tell what kind of whale it is.

Humpback whale

Blue whale

Right whale

Sperm whale

Minke whale

Sperm whales are the deepest diving whales, and can hold their breath for over an hour. They dive deep to catch giant squid to eat.

Internet links

- Scan the code to listen to a humpback whale.
- For more links, go to www.usborne.com/quicklinks

Energetic whales

Even though they are huge, whales can be very energetic. Big whales, such as humpback whales, often throw themselves right out of the water. This is called breaching. Nobody knows exactly why they do it.

★

The whale on the right is breaching. It may be trying to knock the barnacles off its skin.

Whales often throw their tails in the air when they dive. This is called fluking, and helps them dive deep.

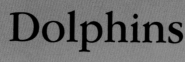

Dolphins

Dolphins are mammals that live in oceans all over the world. They often live in big groups. They are some of the most intelligent animals in the sea.

A group of dolphins is called a school. Some schools contain over a hundred dolphins.

Internet links

• Scan the code to watch a video clip of a bottlenose dolphin.

• For more links, go to **www.usborne.com/quicklinks**

Learning to breathe

Dolphins breathe air, so when a baby dolphin is born, its mother must quickly push it to the surface of the sea and teach it to breathe, or else it will drown. Sometimes, another dolphin helps her do this.

This dolphin has just had a baby. Now the baby must learn how to breathe.

The mother swims under her baby, and gently pushes it up.

The baby takes its first breath of air. Now it will know what to do.

Dolphins can swim at speeds of up to 25mph.

Fun and games

Dolphins are fast swimmers and amazing acrobats. Their speed helps them catch fish, but they also love to play and perform tricks. They can jump right out of the sea.

Spinner dolphins can jump up to 10ft out of the water, and spin around as many as seven times in the air.

These bottlenose dolphins are taking a look around. This is called spy hopping.

Using echoes

Dolphins find their way in the sea by making sounds which send back echoes. They can then tell what's around them by listening to the echoes. This is called sonar. Dolphins also use sonar to catch fish.

A dolphin makes a clicking sound which travels through the water.

When the sound hits some fish, it bounces back as an echo.

The dolphin can tell where the fish are by listening to the returning echo.

Deep sea

The deep sea is a very dark, cold place where some of the strangest creatures in the world live. There are no plants in the deep sea, so all the fish are hunters.

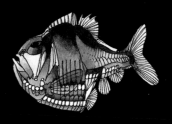

Hatchetfish have eyes on top of their heads so they can see fish which swim above them.

Internet links

- Scan the code to watch a gulper eel swallow a fish.
- For more links, go to www.usborne.com/quicklinks

Gulper eels have enormous mouths. They can eat animals which are much larger than themselves.

Vampire squid

Vampire squid live as deep as 3,000ft. Their big eyes help them see in the murky depths.

Vampire squid have a clever way of escaping from enemies. They can turn themselves inside out. The undersides of their tentacles are covered in sharp spikes, to stop other animals from eating them.

Vampire squid escape from enemies by putting their tentacles over their heads.

Their tentacles cover their bodies, making a spiky shield which protects them.

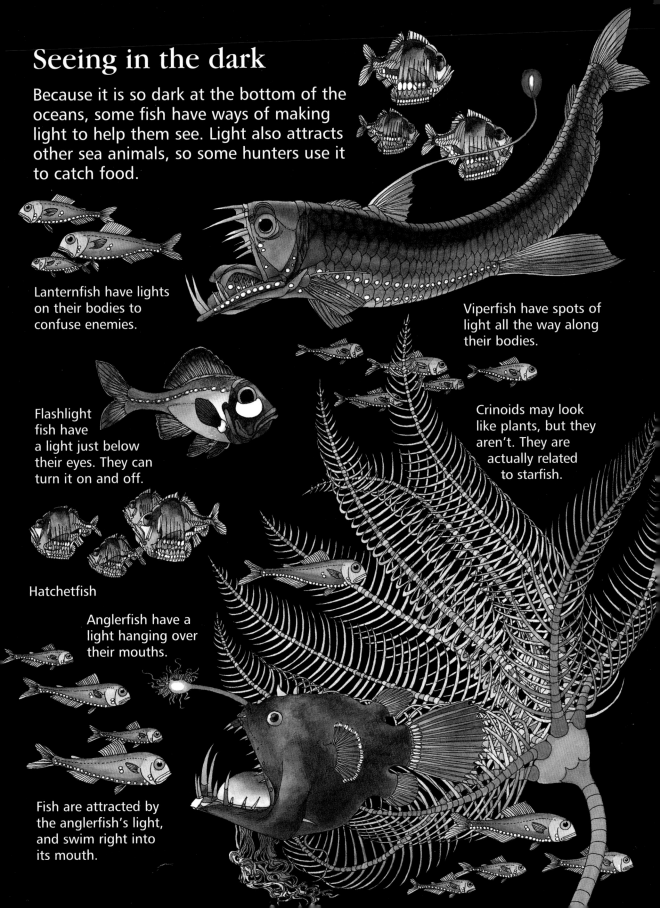

Seeing in the dark

Because it is so dark at the bottom of the oceans, some fish have ways of making light to help them see. Light also attracts other sea animals, so some hunters use it to catch food.

Lanternfish have lights on their bodies to confuse enemies.

Viperfish have spots of light all the way along their bodies.

Flashlight fish have a light just below their eyes. They can turn it on and off.

Crinoids may look like plants, but they aren't. They are actually related to starfish.

Hatchetfish

Anglerfish have a light hanging over their mouths.

Fish are attracted by the anglerfish's light, and swim right into its mouth.

Plant world

Plants are different from animals in several ways. They can't move from place to place, and most can only react slowly to changes around them. Unlike animals, plants make their own food.

Plant groups

There are over 280 thousand different kinds of plants. They can be looked at in groups which are similar in some ways.

Ferns have stems, leaves and roots but no flowers.

★ Conifers have needle-shaped leaves and their seeds are made in cones.

Algae are simple plants with no stems, roots or leaves. ★

★ Flowering plants have roots, leaves and a stem. Their seeds develop from a flower.

★ Mosses have thin leaves but no actual roots. They grow near the ground in damp places.

Making food

Green plants use the Sun's energy to make food in their leaves. They turn water and minerals from the soil, and carbon dioxide gas from the air, into sugar. Sugar is food for plants. This process, called photosynthesis (say "foe-toe-sin-thuh-sis"), also makes oxygen.

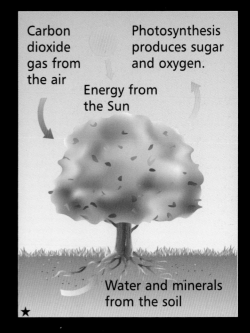

Carbon dioxide gas from the air

Photosynthesis produces sugar and oxygen.

Energy from the Sun

Water and minerals from the soil

★

Flowering plants

The largest group of plants are flowering plants. They include trees as well as flowers. Their main parts are the leaves, stem and roots.

Leaves have a green chemical inside which helps to make food.

The stem supports the plant. Water and food travel inside it.

Roots hold a plant upright and take in water and minerals.

Internet links

- Scan the code to see bees collect pollen and take it to their hive.
- For more links, go to www.usborne.com/quicklinks

Many flowers have bright colors and a strong smell. These attract insects to the sweet liquid called nectar inside.

Inside a flower

Flowers contain parts that can make seeds which will grow into new plants. To make the seeds, a yellow dust, called pollen, has to be carried from one flower to another. The wind and small animals do this job.

Pollen rubs off on a hummingbird's head as it feeds on nectar.

Pollen sticks to a bee's body as it drinks nectar. This will rub off on the next flower it visits.

How plants grow

Many plants start off as seeds. Each seed has tiny parts inside that will grow into a new plant, as well as a store of food for the baby plant.

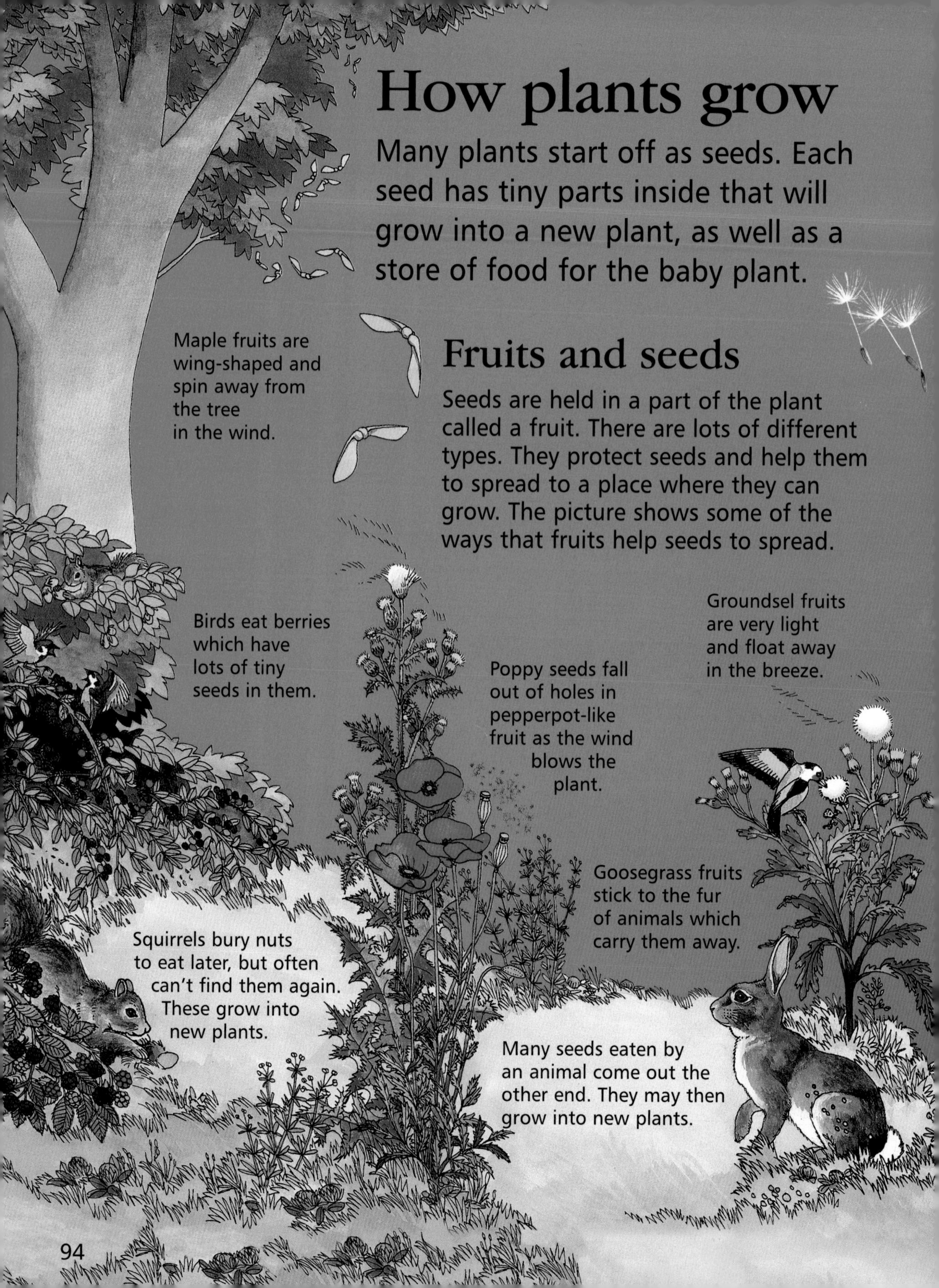

Maple fruits are wing-shaped and spin away from the tree in the wind.

Fruits and seeds

Seeds are held in a part of the plant called a fruit. There are lots of different types. They protect seeds and help them to spread to a place where they can grow. The picture shows some of the ways that fruits help seeds to spread.

Birds eat berries which have lots of tiny seeds in them.

Groundsel fruits are very light and float away in the breeze.

Poppy seeds fall out of holes in pepperpot-like fruit as the wind blows the plant.

Squirrels bury nuts to eat later, but often can't find them again. These grow into new plants.

Goosegrass fruits stick to the fur of animals which carry them away.

Many seeds eaten by an animal come out the other end. They may then grow into new plants.

Starting to grow

To start growing, a seed needs water, warmth and oxygen. When it is warm enough, roots and a tiny shoot will push their way out. A plant at this stage is called a seedling.

Seed

A root pushes down.

A shoot pushes up.

From seedling to plant

A seedling lives off the food stored in its seed until it grows leaves to make its own food. The plant grows and has flowers and seeds of its own. The seeds grow into new plants, and so on.

These dandelion fruits are being carried away by the wind.

Life and death

The changes that happen to a living thing during its life are called its life cycle. Different types of plants have life cycles of different lengths.

Foxgloves live for many years, making seeds for new plants.

Snapdragons grow, flower, make seeds and die within one year.

Internet links

- Scan the code to watch a video of dandelions.
- For more links, go to www.usborne.com/quicklinks

Grow a bean plant

You will need:
a glass jar; paper towels; dried kidney beans; a pot; some compost.

1. Line a glass jar with damp paper towels. Put some dried kidney beans next to the glass.

2. After a few days, look for shoots growing up and little roots growing down.

3. To grow plants, put the seedlings in pots of compost and water them.

Trees and leaves

A tree is a plant with a thick, woody stem called a trunk. Most trees can grow for hundreds of years. Some trees are small, but many are taller than a house.

Tree bark

As a tree grows, its outer layers become harder. When they die, they form a tough layer called bark. There are many different types.

A beech tree has smooth, thin bark. ★

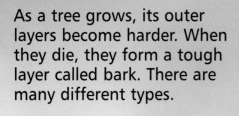

An English oak has cracked, ridged bark. ★

Cypress trees are evergreen, which means they don't lose their leaves all at once.

Getting bigger

Look at the rings in a tree stump. You can count these to find out the tree's age.

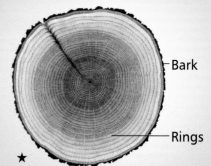

Bark

Rings

★

A tree grows from its middle out. One ring of new wood builds up each year, making the trunk thicker.

Tree roots

A tree uses its roots to take in water from the soil. They also act as an anchor. Tall trees, such as the cypress trees below, could not stay standing without their strong roots.

Looking at leaves

Leaves contain a green chemical which absorbs sunlight to help make food (see Making food on page 92). When leaves die, the green chemical fades away and they change color.

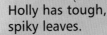

Holly has tough, spiky leaves.

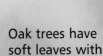

Horse chestnut leaves have seven separate parts, called leaflets.

Losing leaves

Many types of trees lose all their leaves every fall. They are called deciduous trees. Trees that don't lose their leaves all at once are called evergreens.

Atlas cedars have bunches of thin, sharp leaves.

Oak trees have soft leaves with a wavy edge.

Internet links

- Scan the code for a fun guide to trees.
- For more links, go to www.usborne.com/quicklinks

Green leaves turn beautiful shades of red and gold before they fall from the tree.

Seeds and fruits

All trees produce flowers, which grow into fruits. Fruits contain seeds which can grow into new trees.

This acorn is the fruit of an oak tree.

An apple has several seeds in its core.

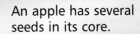

Fungi

Fungi are not plants because they can't make their own food. Instead, they feed on living or once living things.

Types of fungi

Fungi come in thousands of different shapes and sizes.

★ Mushrooms and toadstools are fungi. You can eat some types but others are deadly poisonous.

★ The green furry blobs you sometimes see on fruit or cheese are a type of fungus known as mold.

These inkcap toadstools are growing and feeding on an old, moss-covered log.

Spores

Fungi don't make seeds or pollen. Instead, they shed clouds of tiny specks, called spores. These are scattered all around by the wind, and grow into new fungi.

Fungus spores seen using a microscope ★

Useful fungi

Some types of fungi are very useful. A fungus called yeast is used to make bread and wine. Some medicines are made from fungi, too.

Internet links
- Scan the code to see amazing photos of fungi.
- For more links, go to www.usborne.com/quicklinks

How your body works

Your body

Have you ever wondered what's inside you? Your body is made up of lots of separate parts. They all do different jobs to help you stay alive.

Organs

Organs are important body parts such as the heart, lungs, stomach and brain. Most of them are in the upper body and head. You can see some of the main organs in this picture.

Each organ has a special job to do. For example, your stomach holds the food you eat, and your lungs take air into your body.

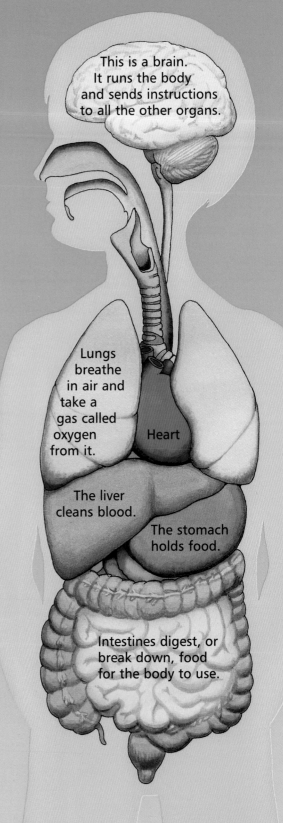

This is a brain. It runs the body and sends instructions to all the other organs.

Lungs breathe in air and take a gas called oxygen from it.

Heart

The liver cleans blood.

The stomach holds food.

Intestines digest, or break down, food for the body to use.

How much air do your lungs hold?

You will need: a plastic bottle with a lid; a bendy straw; a bowl of water

 ★ **1.** Fill the bottle with water and put the lid on. Hold it upside down in the bowl and take off the lid.

 ★ **2.** Push the straw into the neck of the bottle. Breathe in deeply, then blow gently into the straw until your lungs are empty.

 ★ All the air you breathe out will be trapped at the top of the bottle. This is how much air your lungs can hold.

Blood

As well as organs, a human body contains up to nine pints of blood. The heart pumps blood around the body along thousands of tubes called blood vessels. As it flows along, blood delivers oxygen and food to every part of the body.

Blood is made of cells (see page 56) floating in a liquid called plasma. This picture shows different types of blood cells.

Platelet (part of a blood cell)

White blood cell

Red blood cell

Feel your pulse ★

To feel your blood being pumped around your body, press two fingers on the inside of your wrist. The beating you feel is called your pulse.

Internet links

• Scan the code to watch a video clip about your skin.

• For more links, go to www.usborne.com/quicklinks

Safe in your skin

Your skin gives your whole body a waterproof covering, and protects your insides from dirt and germs. Skin is made up of two main layers.

This close-up photograph shows the layers in human skin.

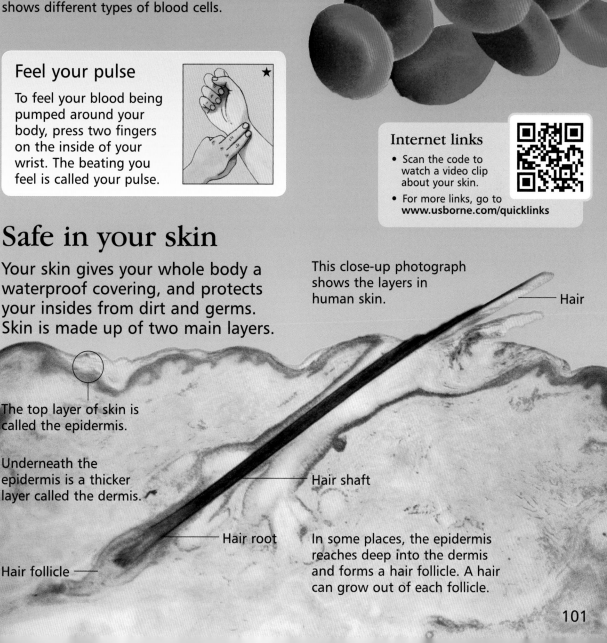

Hair

The top layer of skin is called the epidermis.

Underneath the epidermis is a thicker layer called the dermis.

Hair shaft

Hair root

Hair follicle

In some places, the epidermis reaches deep into the dermis and forms a hair follicle. A hair can grow out of each follicle.

Bones and muscles

Bones and muscles are your body's support system. They hold you up and let you move around. Without them, you'd be nothing but a helpless blob.

Your skeleton

Together, your bones make up your skeleton, which acts as a framework for your whole body. Bendable joints where bones meet let you move into different positions.

Bones protect your insides too. For example, rib bones in your chest stop the organs inside from getting squashed.

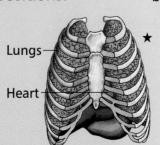

Lungs

Heart

★

Soft skeletons

A baby's bones are partly made of a flexible material called cartilage. As the baby grows, most of the cartilage slowly turns into hard bone.

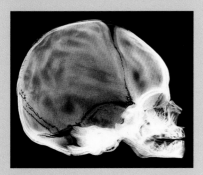

This is an X-ray picture of a newborn baby's skull. As the baby grows, the gaps in its skull close up and the skull hardens.

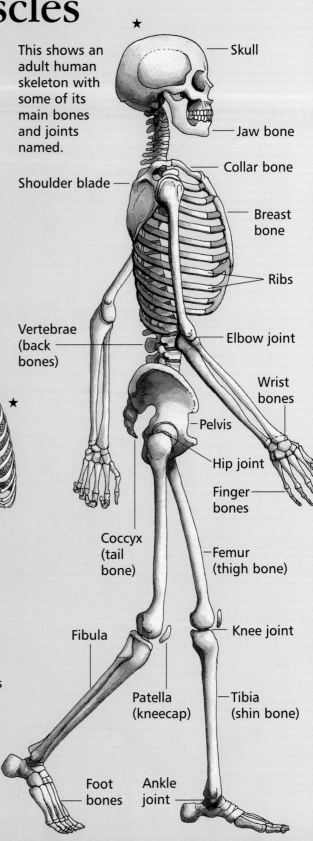

★

This shows an adult human skeleton with some of its main bones and joints named.

Shoulder blade

Vertebrae (back bones)

Coccyx (tail bone)

Fibula

Foot bones

Skull

Jaw bone

Collar bone

Breast bone

Ribs

Elbow joint

Wrist bones

Pelvis

Hip joint

Finger bones

Femur (thigh bone)

Knee joint

Patella (kneecap)

Tibia (shin bone)

Ankle joint

Muscles

The bones of your skeleton are moved by muscles. These help you move in all kinds of ways, from walking or swimming to playing the recorder or using a computer.

You also have other muscles (in your heart, for example) that work without you even thinking about them.

Internet links

- Scan the code for a video clip about the human skeleton.
- For more links, go to **www.usborne.com/quicklinks**

There are over 600 muscles in the human body. This picture shows some of the main ones.

Trapezius

Triceps

Deltoid

Biceps

Gluteus maximus

Rectus abdominis

Quadriceps

Gastrocnemius

Gracilis

Moving muscles

Muscles work by getting shorter. This is called contracting. As a muscle contracts, it pulls on the bones it's joined to, and they move. These little pictures show how muscles contract to bend and straighten your arm.

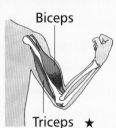

Biceps

Triceps ★

To bend your arm, the biceps muscle contracts, pulling up the lower arm.

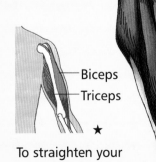

Biceps

Triceps

★

To straighten your arm, the triceps muscle contracts, pulling the lower arm down.

What happens to food?

The food you eat gives you the energy you need to live. But to get this energy, you have to turn food into chemicals in your body. This is called digestion.

Your food's journey

As food travels into and through your body, it gets turned into smaller and smaller bits. Follow the steps on the big picture to find out how this happens.

Teeth

Salivary glands (where saliva is made)

Throat

Esophagus

1. When you chew food, your teeth cut and mash it up.

2. Saliva (spit) mixes with the food, making it soft, mushy and easy to swallow.

3. When you swallow, food is forced down your throat into a tube called the esophagus.

4. Muscles in your esophagus squeeze the food down into your stomach.

Did you know?

- An adult's salivary glands make over a quart and a half of saliva (spit) each day.

- Your stomach can hold up to one gallon of food and stretch to the size of a melon.

- Your small intestine is coiled up, but if it were stretched out it would be almost 30ft long.

- Food takes between 18 and 48 hours to make its complete journey through your body.

Internet links

- Scan the code to try an online quiz about digestion.

- For more links, go to www.usborne.com/quicklinks

Food for your cells

After food has been broken down into chemicals, it is carried all around your body in your blood. Some food is used to give your cells the energy they need to work – for example, to make muscles move. Some food is used to build new cells and repair injuries.

If you eat more food than you need, your body stores it as fat. This is why you get fatter if you eat a lot and don't exercise much.

Waste

Most food contains bits that can't be digested, such as seeds and fruit skin. They go into your large intestine and collect into lumps, which end up in the toilet.

Millions of tiny bacteria, like these E. coli bacteria, live inside your intestines. They help themselves to your food, but are usually harmless.

5. Your stomach squeezes the food and mixes it with acid, making a thick liquid.

7. The food chemicals are taken to your liver, ready to be sent around your body.

Liver

Stomach

Large intestine

Large intestine

Large intestine

Large intestine

Small intestine

6. Your small intestine takes food chemicals from the liquid food mixture.

8. The large intestine collects food that can't be digested. It takes water out of it, leaving lumps of waste called feces.

Rectum

9. The lumps of waste from your large intestine are squeezed out of your rectum when you go to the bathroom.

Your brain and senses

Your brain controls your body. Your five senses – sight, hearing, touch, taste and smell – tell your brain what's going on around you, so it can make decisions.

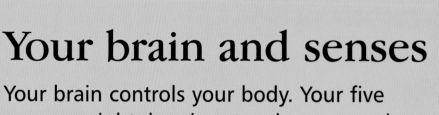

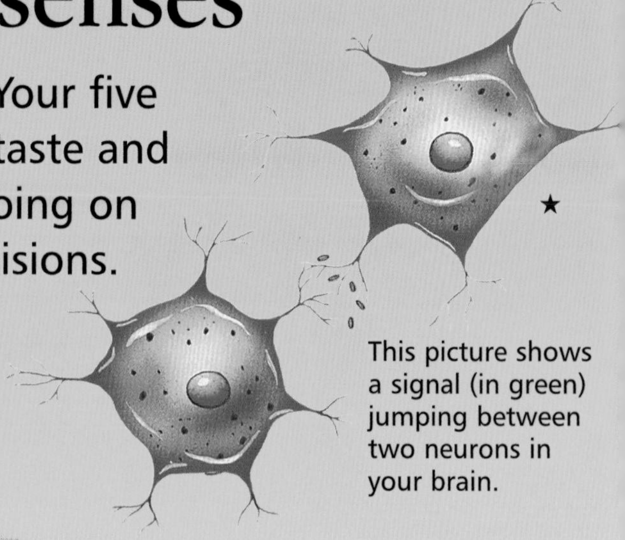

Brain bundle

Your brain is made of a big bundle of cells called neurons. When you think, your neurons are passing signals to each other. Neurons also link your brain to your sense organs and to other parts of your body.

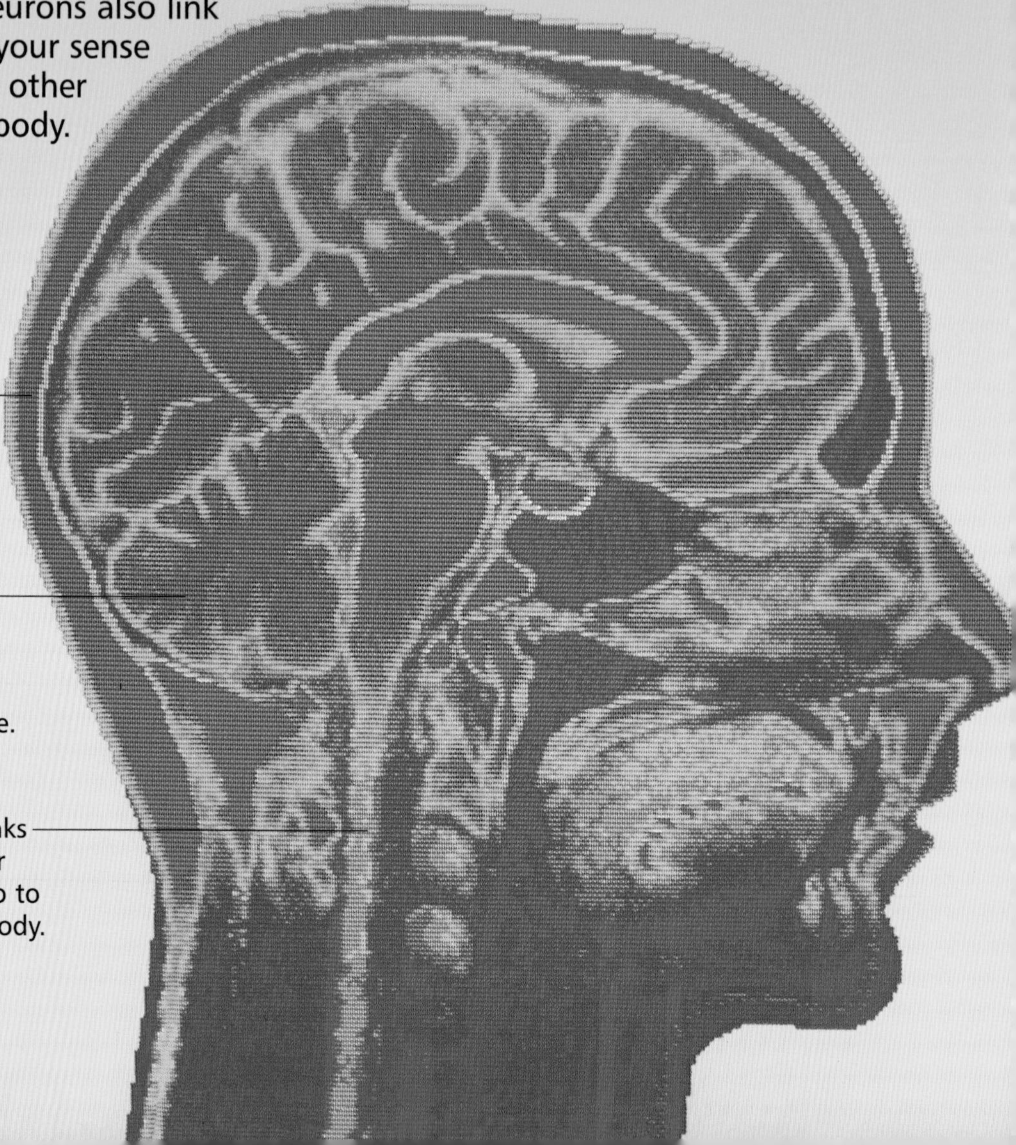

This picture shows a signal (in green) jumping between two neurons in your brain.

This scan of a person's head shows the brain inside the skull.

The skull, shown here in blue, protects your brain.

The brain is this blue and yellow area. The yellow lines are folds in the brain's surface.

The brain stem links your brain to your spinal cord and so to the rest of your body.

Seeing things

You see things because light bounces off them and goes into your eyes. Your eyes collect the light patterns and turn them into signals your brain can understand.

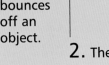
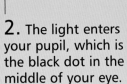

4. The optic nerve (made of neurons) carries signals to your brain.

1. Light bounces off an object.

3. Patterns of light hit your retina, an area of light-sensitive cells on the inside of your eye.

2. The light enters your pupil, which is the black dot in the middle of your eye.

Internet links

- Scan the code to watch a video about your eyes.
- For more links, go to **www.usborne.com/quicklinks**

How you hear

Sounds make tiny particles in the air vibrate (move to and fro). You hear when these vibrating particles hit your ears. The vibrations are turned into signals that are sent to your brain.

1. Sounds make vibrations travel through the air.

2. The vibrating air hits a patch of skin called the eardrum.

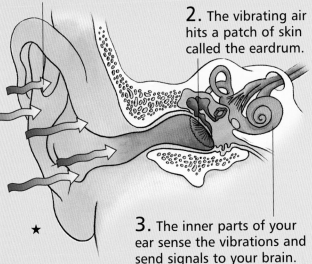

★

3. The inner parts of your ear sense the vibrations and send signals to your brain.

Taste and smell

Sensitive spots called taste buds on your tongue can detect a few simple tastes. Sensitive cells in your nose detect different smells, and also help you tell the difference between flavors.

★

Tiny pink bumps on your tongue have taste buds in them. The bumps are easier to see after a drink of milk.

Touch

There are millions of sensitive nerve endings in your skin. They can feel heat, cold, pressure and pain.

Some blind people use their fingers to read Braille writing, which is made up of tiny bumps.

Babies

Babies come from inside their mothers. After growing there for about nine months, they are big enough to live in the outside world.

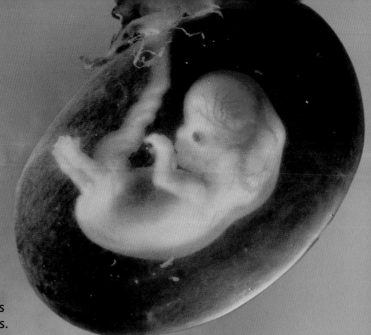

This unborn baby has been growing inside its mother for eight weeks.

Making a baby

To make a baby you need a grown-up man and a grown-up woman. The woman has little eggs inside her body. The man makes tiny swimming cells called sperm inside his body.

The sperm swim into the woman's body. When one sperm joins up with an egg, a baby starts to grow.

★

One sperm is joining with this egg to make a baby start to grow.

Egg

Sperm

Inside the mother

The baby grows inside the mother's womb. This is filled with a watery liquid which helps keep the baby safe. A tube joins the baby to its mother. It carries oxygen, food and drink from the mother's body to the baby.

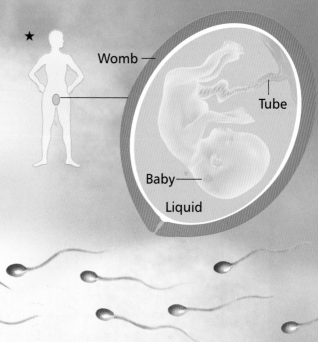

★

Womb

Tube

Baby

Liquid

Growing and moving

After about four months, the baby has grown so much that it makes a bump in its mother's tummy. Sometimes, the mother can feel the baby kicking and wiggling inside her.

Internet links
- Scan the code to find out more about babies.
- For more links, go to www.usborne.com/quicklinks

Unborn baby at four months

Unborn baby at six months

At nine months, the baby is ready to be born.

This baby boy is four days old.

Being born

When the baby is ready to be born, the mother's womb starts to squeeze. The baby comes out of an opening between the mother's legs. It can take many hours for the baby to be born. It makes the mother tired.

Like Mom or Dad?

The baby may look like its father, its mother, or a mixture of both. Who it looks like depends on its genes. These are instructions in the baby's cells that tell the body how to grow. A baby's genes come from the father's sperm and the mother's egg.

Each sperm has half the genes needed to make a baby. The rest of the genes come from the mother's egg.

Staying healthy

When your body isn't working properly, you might feel ill. There are lots of ways to take care of yourself and help your body stay healthy.

Eating well

You need to eat different types of food to stay healthy. The picture below is a guide to how much of each type of food you should eat every day.

Eat only small amounts of fatty or sugary foods, such as butter, cake, sweets and sugary drinks.

Eat two servings of foods from the milk group, for example milk, yogurt and cheese.

Eat three servings of vegetables, such as carrots, peas and broccoli.

Keeping clean

Keeping clean helps to stop harmful germs from building up on and in your body and making you ill. Washing your hands after using the restroom and before eating helps stop germs from spreading. Brushing your teeth helps get rid of the germs that make holes in your teeth.

Eat two servings of foods from the meat group. This includes fish, eggs, nuts and beans as well as meat.

Eat two servings of fresh, dried, canned or juiced fruit.

Eat six servings from the grain group each day. This group includes bread, pasta, rice and cereals.

Keeping fit

Exercising is an important way of taking care of your body, and can be great fun too. Different types of exercise can help your body in different ways.

Jogging and skipping strengthen your heart and lungs, so you can be active for longer.

Canoeing and rowing make your muscles stronger so they work better without straining.

Gymnastics and dancing help you to bend and stretch more easily, and keep you from getting stiff.

Swimming is a good way to exercise and keep your body healthy.

Sleeping

It is very important to get enough sleep. While you are asleep, your body tissues have the chance to grow and repair themselves. Children need more sleep than adults because there is more growing to do.

Internet links

- Scan the code to find out how to do some simple yoga poses.
- For more links, go to www.usborne.com/quicklinks

Doctors and medicine

When you are ill, you might visit a doctor.
A doctor's job is to find out what is wrong
and tell you what to do to feel better.
Doctors also give people advice
on how to stay healthy.

Finding out

The doctor asks how you
are feeling and checks
your body for signs of
illness. You may need
to have some tests
done to find out
what is wrong.

X-rays are used
to take pictures of
the bones inside
your body. This
picture shows
a broken arm.

Making it better

The pictures below show several
ways the doctor might help you
get better. Sometimes she may
just tell you to rest a lot or
change what you eat.

You may have to take
medicine, either by
drinking it in a liquid or
by taking some pills.

A doctor may put a
needle into your body
to give you medicine.
This is an injection.

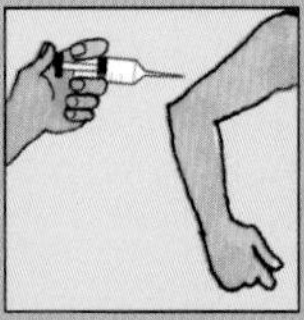

A broken bone may need
a plaster cast. This holds
the broken ends together
so that the bone mends
straight, not crooked.

Internet links

• Scan the code
  to find out more
  about doctors.

• For more links, go to
  www.usborne.com/quicklinks

History

Dinosaur world

There were animals on Earth long before there were any people. Different kinds of animals lived at different times. At one time, the biggest and fastest animals on Earth were the dinosaurs.

There were many kinds of dinosaurs. Here you can see one of the biggest and one of the smallest compared with a person.

What were dinosaurs?

Dinosaurs belonged to a group of animals called reptiles (see page 70). All reptiles have scaly skin. Birds also have some scaly skin, and experts think they are probably a kind of dinosaur too.

All dinosaurs lived on land. Some hunted other animals for food, but many of them ate plants. Most dinosaurs died out 65 million years ago, long before the first people appeared. Only the birds survived.

Internet links
- Scan the code to explore a dinosaur factfile.
- For more links, go to www.usborne.com/quicklinks

Baby dinosaurs grew inside eggs laid by their mothers. These babies have just broken out of their eggs. This is called hatching.

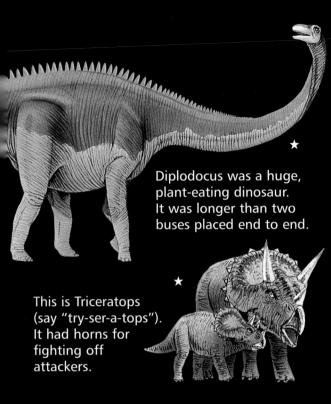

Diplodocus was a huge, plant-eating dinosaur. It was longer than two buses placed end to end. ★

Sea and sky

At the time of the dinosaurs, there were also lots of flying reptiles in the sky. They were called pterosaurs (say "terra-sors"). Other huge reptiles swam in the sea.

This sea reptile is called an ichthyosaur (say "ick-thee-oh-sor"). It was a powerful swimmer.

Pterosaurs had big, leathery wings. This is a pterosaur called Pteranodon (say "ter-ran-oh-don").

★ This is Triceratops (say "try-ser-a-tops"). It had horns for fighting off attackers.

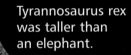

Tyrannosaurus rex was taller than an elephant.

This fierce dinosaur is called Tyrannosaurus rex (say "tie-ran-oh-saw-russ rex"). It was a meat-eater.

This dinosaur had long, sharp teeth for tearing up meat.

Claws for holding onto food

The first people

The first people lived by hunting animals, catching fish and gathering plants to eat. As the seasons changed, they moved around from place to place looking for food.

In the summer, people lived in tents that they made from branches and animal skins.

In the winter, when it was cold, they sometimes sheltered in caves.

Finding food

People spent a lot of time looking for food. They hunted deer, horses, bison and wild pigs for meat. They also ate whatever plants and small animals they could find.

These are some of the things that the first people ate.

Berries

Fish

Snails

Mushrooms

Dandelion leaves

Nuts

Crabs

Birds' eggs

Lizards

Shellfish

These animals
were painted on the wall
of a cave at Lascaux, in France. Can
you guess what kinds of animals they
are meant to be? (Answers on page 320.)

Cave paintings

Inside the deepest, darkest caves,
people painted pictures of the
animals they hunted. They may
have thought that the pictures
were magical and would help
them with their hunting.

Internet links

- Scan the code
  to see prehistoric
  cave paintings.
- For more links, go to
  www.usborne.com/quicklinks

Stone tools

The first people used tools
made from a kind of stone
called flint. They used
spears tipped with a
sharp, flint point for
hunting. They also made
flint axes and knives for
cutting up meat.

Later, people made arrows
with flint tips like this.

117

The first farmers

Farming began when people learned how to plant seeds to grow food. They also tamed animals, such as sheep and cows. This meant that people could stay in one place, instead of moving around to find food.

This clay pot was made by early farmers in Turkey.

Growing food

Around 12,000 years ago, people in the Middle East began growing wheat and barley. They ground the grain into flour for making bread.

These are wheat plants. You can see the grains at the top of each stalk.

Making things

Farmers didn't need to spend all day looking for food, so they had time to learn new things. They made clay pots for storing and cooking food. They also learned how to make cloth by spinning and weaving wool.

This is part of a farming village in the Middle East. It has a wall around it to keep out wild animals.

This man is offering gifts to a statue of the village goddess.

New tools

The first farmers made tools from stone, bone and wood. Later, people learned how to make things from metal. The first metal tools were made of copper.

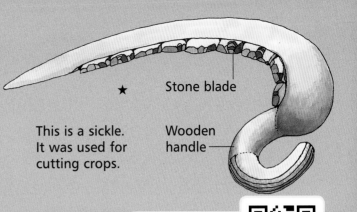

This is a sickle. It was used for cutting crops.

Stone blade

Wooden handle

Internet links

- Scan the code for a video about early farmers.
- For more links, go to www.usborne.com/quicklinks

Women carry water from the stream.

People use tools called sickles to cut the crops.

These men are making mud bricks to mend the wall.

The roofs of the houses are covered with straw.

Cows are kept for their meat, milk and skins.

Ancient Egypt

The Ancient Egyptians were farmers who lived along the banks of the Nile. They used water from the river to help them grow food. The Egyptians were ruled by a powerful king called a pharaoh.

A gold mask from the tomb of the pharaoh Tutankhamun

Internet links

- Scan the code to watch a video clip of how mummies were made.
- For more links, go to **www.usborne.com/quicklinks**

Pharaohs and pyramids

Some pharaohs were buried inside huge, stone pyramids on the edge of the desert. The pharaoh's body was placed in a secret room in the middle of the pyramid. There are still about 80 pyramids in Egypt, and each one took at least 20 years to build.

These are the pyramids at Giza. Three pharaohs and their wives were buried here.

A pharaoh called Menkaure was buried inside this pyramid.

This is the Great Pyramid. It is made up of over two million stone blocks.

Menkaure's three wives were buried in these smaller pyramids.

Mummies and coffins

The Egyptians tried to stop dead people's bodies from rotting away. They thought this would allow them to have another life after they died. They took out the person's insides, dried the body out and wrapped it in bandages. Bodies kept like this are called mummies.

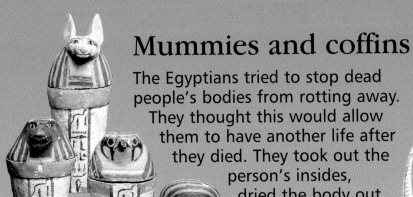

The insides of the body were kept in jars like these.

Mummies were put inside painted wooden coffins like this one.

Picture writing

Egyptian writing was made up of lots of small pictures, or symbols, called hieroglyphs (say "hi-ro-gliffs"). There were over 700 different symbols. Here are just a few of them:

B   D

H   I   K

N

R   T

See if you can spot the symbols for "I", "N", "R" and "T" in this Egyptian painting.

Ancient Greece

In ancient times, Greece wasn't all one country like it is today. Instead, each city had its own rulers. The greatest of these cities was Athens, which was famous for its learning and plays.

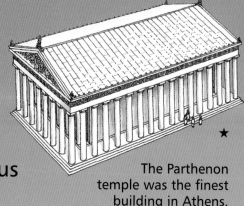

The Parthenon temple was the finest building in Athens.

Big buildings

In every city in Greece, people built huge, stone temples for their gods and goddesses. Greek temples usually had a triangular-shaped roof held up by rows of tall pillars.

These are the ruins of the Parthenon temple. It stands on a hill high above the city of Athens.

Spot the pillar

The Greeks used three types of pillars in their buildings. Can you spot which type they used for the Parthenon?

A Doric pillar

An Ionic pillar

A Corinthian pillar

The walls and pillars are made from a stone called marble.

This is how big people look compared with the Parthenon.

The first plays

The first great plays in the world were written by the Ancient Greeks. They believed that performing the plays would please their gods. People put the plays on at festivals which lasted several days. There was a prize for the best play.

Internet links
- Scan the code to see images of athletes on Ancient Greek pots.
- For more links, go to www.usborne.com/quicklinks

Actors playing gods can fly through the air on this crane.

Musicians

★ Here you can see Greek actors putting on a play at a festival.

Scenery

Stage

The Olympic Games

The Greeks loved athletics and they organized competitions all over the country. The most famous was the Olympic Games, which took place every four years at Olympia.

This Greek painting shows an athlete training for the long jump.

The actors wear masks and costumes to show which parts they are playing.

These actors are called the chorus. They perform songs and dances to explain what is happening on the stage.

Ancient Rome

About 2,000 years ago, Rome was one of the biggest cities in the world. At that time, the Romans ruled all the lands around the Mediterranean Sea. These lands were called the Roman Empire.

On this map, all the lands shown in red were once part of the Roman Empire.

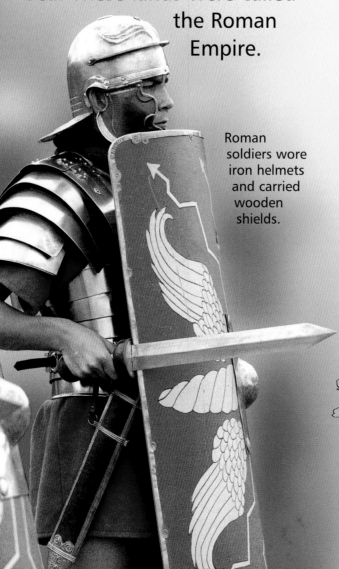

Roman soldiers wore iron helmets and carried wooden shields.

The Roman army

The Romans had a huge army of well-trained soldiers. They used their army to fight for new lands and to protect the Empire from enemies. Most soldiers fought on foot using a spear, a sword and a dagger.

Roman soldiers built long, straight roads linking towns all over the Empire.

Internet links

- Scan the code to find out how to dress like a Roman soldier.
- For more links, go to **www.usborne.com/quicklinks**

Home comforts

In Rome, rich people lived in comfortable houses with large gardens. Some houses even had toilets, running water and a kind of central heating.

This is a Roman house. Parts of it have been cut away so you can see inside.

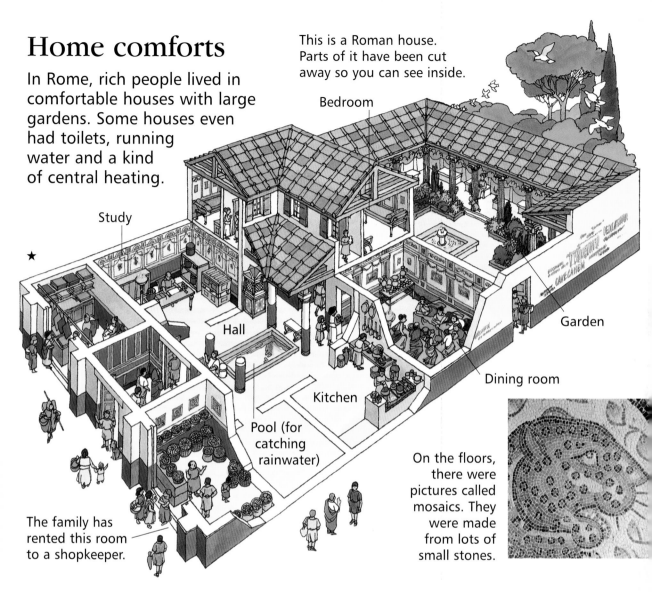

Bedroom

Study

Hall

Kitchen

Pool (for catching rainwater)

Garden

Dining room

The family has rented this room to a shopkeeper.

On the floors, there were pictures called mosaics. They were made from lots of small stones.

Roman pastimes

The Romans loved watching chariot races. These took place at a huge racetrack called a circus.

People also enjoyed watching gladiators fight each other. Gladiators often died in these brutal fights.

Most Romans went to the public baths every day to relax, exercise, meet friends – and to get themselves clean.

Viking raiders

The Vikings came from Norway, Sweden and Denmark. They were great sailors and traders, but they were also fierce warriors. They attacked and robbed villages all around the coasts of Europe.

This man is dressed as a Viking warrior.

Greenland
Iceland
North America
British Isles
France
Spain
Italy
The Vikings lived here.

The Vikings sailed to all these places.

A Viking longship

Viking ships

The Vikings made their attacks in fast boats, called longships. The ships were strong enough to sail across rough seas. They weren't very deep, so they could also travel up shallow rivers.

This carved dragon's head is meant to scare enemies.

The Vikings in this ship are on their way to launch a raid.

There's a big oar at the back for steering the ship.

Viking homes

Viking chiefs lived in large homes called longhouses. Each longhouse had only one big room, where everyone ate, worked and slept. There weren't any windows, so it must have been very dark inside.

Part of this longhouse has been cut away so you can see inside.

The roof is covered with straw.

The walls are made of logs.

A hole in the roof lets out smoke from the fire.

The chief's bedroom

This woman is weaving cloth using a wooden frame called a loom.

Toilet

Most people sleep on benches at the sides of the room.

In the winter, farm animals are kept inside.

Internet links

- Scan the code to watch an animated movie about Viking raiders.
- For more links, go to www.usborne.com/quicklinks

Viking crafts

The Vikings made beautiful brooches, arm rings and belt buckles from gold, silver and bronze. They also carved spoons and combs from pieces of animal bone and horn.

Women used brooches like this to fasten their clothes.

127

Living in a castle

In the Middle Ages (between 500 and 1,000 years ago) kings and lords in Europe often fought each other for land. They built castles with strong, stone walls to protect themselves from their enemies.

Inside a castle

A lord lived in a castle with his family and all his soldiers and servants. It must have been very cold inside, because the first castles had no glass in the windows.

This picture shows part of a castle. Some of the walls have been cut away to let you see inside.

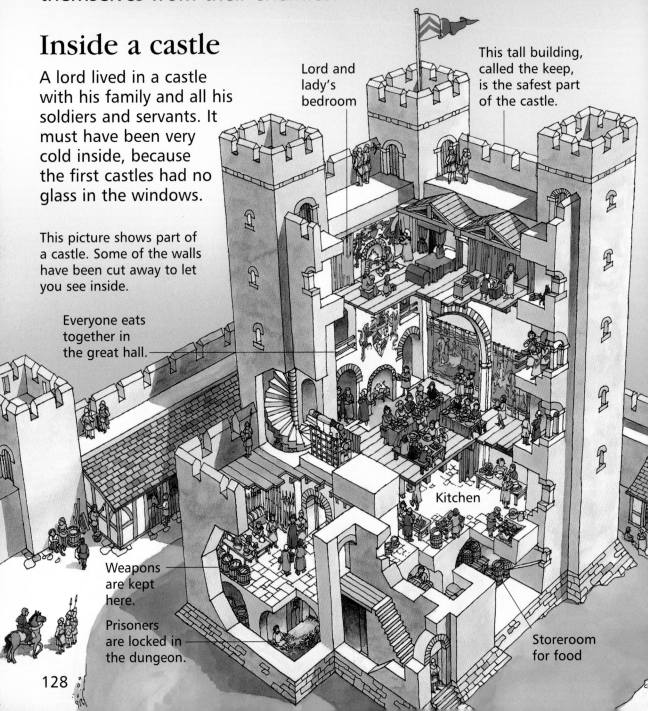

Lord and lady's bedroom

This tall building, called the keep, is the safest part of the castle.

Everyone eats together in the great hall.

Kitchen

Weapons are kept here.

Prisoners are locked in the dungeon.

Storeroom for food

Noble knights

Knights were soldiers who fought on horseback. Only boys from noble families could train to be knights. A good knight had to be strong and brave. He also had to promise to fight only for his lord.

This picture from the Middle Ages shows two knights taking part in a contest called a joust.

Painted shield

Chainmail shirt made from lots of metal rings

This knight is being knocked off his horse.

This long spear is called a lance.

Internet links

- Scan the code to see inside a castle from the Middle Ages.
- For more links, go to www.usborne.com/quicklinks

This wall keeps enemies out.

Guards look out for enemies.

Fun feasts

Feasts took place in the great hall of the castle. The guests ate lots of rich food, such as roast swan, spiced beef, squirrel stew and sugared mackerel. For dessert, there might be apple pie or honey cakes.

A jester told jokes to make the guests laugh.

Musicians, called minstrels, played their instruments and sang.

These people are acting out an old Inca festival at the city of Cuzco, in Peru.

Inca cities

The Incas lived in the Andes mountains of South America. Most of them were farmers, but they were also great builders. They were ruled by an emperor called the Inca.

Cities of stone

The Incas built huge cities from massive blocks of stone. They used stone hammers to shape the blocks so they would fit together perfectly. Each city had temples, palaces, and observatories for watching the stars.

Machu Picchu is 7,700ft above sea level.

This is the ruined Inca city of Machu Picchu, high up in the Andes mountains.

On the road

The Incas built stone roads to link their cities together. Teams of runners used the roads to carry messages from city to city. The roads were also used by soldiers, traders, and farmers taking food to market.

Llamas were used for carrying heavy loads.

The Incas made bridges out of reeds, so people could get across valleys and rivers.

Food and drink

Inca farmers grew corn, potatoes, peppers, beans, tomatoes and squash. They kept guinea pigs for their meat. Women made a drink called chicha by spitting chewed fruit into warm water.

Peppers

★ Squash

★ Tomatoes

★ Beans

★ Corn

Internet links

- Scan the code to watch a video about Machu Picchu.
- For more links, go to **www.usborne.com/quicklinks**

Farmers grew food on wide ledges, called terraces, that they dug into the mountainside.

Ming China

Around 500 years ago, China was ruled by a family of emperors called the Ming. The Ming emperors made Beijing their capital city. They lived there in a huge palace, called the Forbidden City.

The Chinese invented gunpowder. They used it for making fireworks, as well as weapons.

The Forbidden City

The Forbidden City was made up of great halls, temples, courtyards and gardens. It was surrounded by a wall and a moat (a big ditch filled with water). Only the emperor's family and servants were allowed inside.

In this picture, you can see a royal procession outside the Hall of Supreme Harmony in the Forbidden City.

The buildings are made of wood and bricks glued together with steamed rice and egg whites.

The palace has 9,999 rooms and is as big as 74 soccer fields. It took a million workers 14 years to build.

Officials and soldiers

Made in China

In Ming times, the Chinese made many beautiful things. They are especially famous for making a kind of fine pottery, called porcelain. They also made a very expensive kind of cloth, called silk.

Porcelain jar

This wooden box is covered with a shiny varnish called lacquer.

This picture was painted on silk. It shows two Chinese officials.

Internet links

• Scan the code to see how porcelain pots were made in Ming times.

• For more links, go to www.usborne.com/quicklinks

Time for tea

The Chinese started growing tea about 1,700 years ago. At first, they used the leaves to make medicines. Later, tea became a very popular drink. The Chinese made their tea in teapots and drank it out of little bowls.

Chinese workers picking leaves from tea plants

The emperor rides in a coach pulled by elephants.

Tudor England

The Tudors were a family of kings and queens. They ruled England for over a hundred years and made the country rich and powerful.

This is a painting of King Henry VIII. He divorced two of his wives and had two of them beheaded.

These coins came from the wreck of a Tudor warship.

Henry VIII

Henry VIII became king when he was 17 years old. He married six times, but only had three children. Henry also had an argument with the Pope (the head of the Church in Europe) and set up his own English Church.

Internet links

- Scan the code to find out about Henry VIII's clothing.
- For more links, go to **www.usborne.com/quicklinks**

Explorers and pirates

In Tudor times, many explorers sailed to North and South America. They brought back new foods, such as potatoes. Some English explorers were pirates too. They stole treasure from Spanish ships on the coast of America.

Elizabeth I

Queen Elizabeth was the last and greatest of the Tudors. She ruled England for 45 years. During her reign, England fought off an attack by a group of Spanish ships, called the Spanish Armada.

This is a portrait of Elizabeth. She loved clothes and owned 260 different dresses.

Plays and playhouses

In Elizabeth's time, people loved going to see plays. In London, actors performed in playhouses such as the Globe. The most popular plays were written by William Shakespeare.

Here you can see actors performing a play at the Globe.

A flag is flown during the play.

This roof keeps the actors dry if it rains.

The roof is covered with straw.

The walls have been cut away to let you see inside.

Oak beams

Stage

Rich people watch from seats around the sides.

Poorer people stand in the yard around the stage.

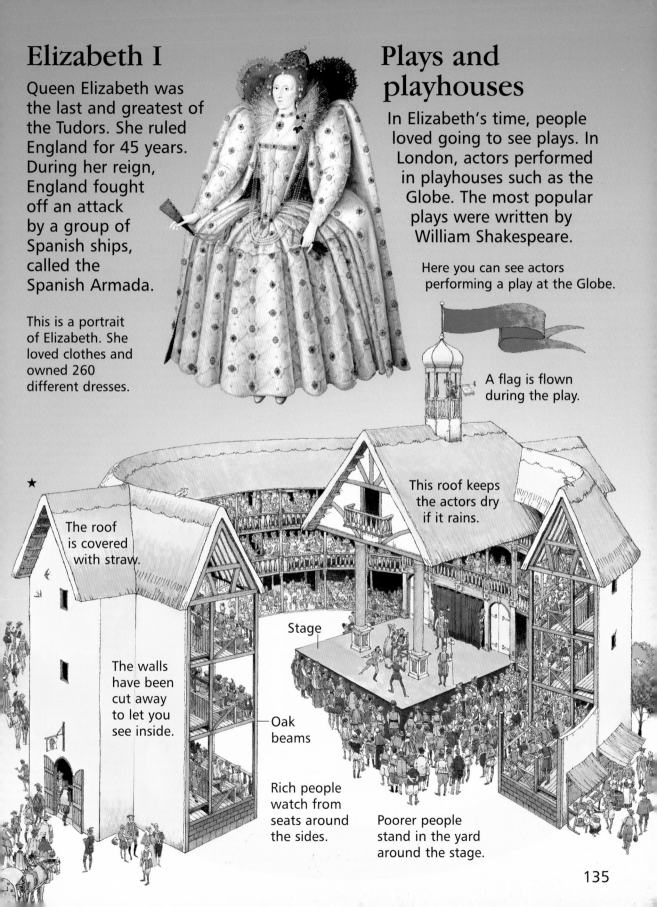

Living in America

In 1620, a group of English people, called the Pilgrims, went to settle in North America. The Pilgrims were very religious. They wanted to be free to worship God in a way they weren't allowed to in England.

The Pilgrims sailed to America on a ship called the *Mayflower*. This is a copy of their ship.

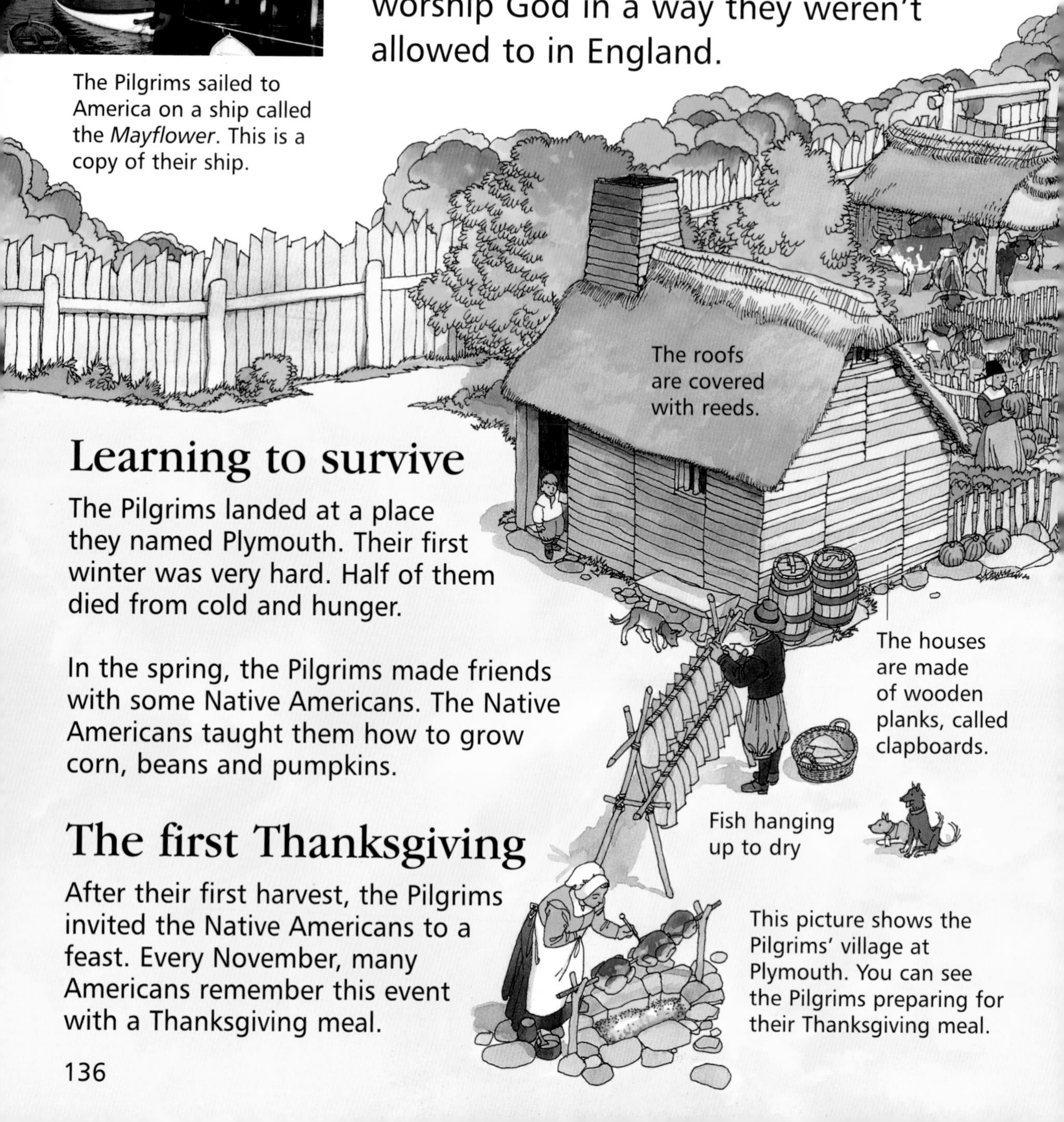

Learning to survive

The Pilgrims landed at a place they named Plymouth. Their first winter was very hard. Half of them died from cold and hunger.

In the spring, the Pilgrims made friends with some Native Americans. The Native Americans taught them how to grow corn, beans and pumpkins.

The first Thanksgiving

After their first harvest, the Pilgrims invited the Native Americans to a feast. Every November, many Americans remember this event with a Thanksgiving meal.

The roofs are covered with reeds.

The houses are made of wooden planks, called clapboards.

Fish hanging up to dry

This picture shows the Pilgrims' village at Plymouth. You can see the Pilgrims preparing for their Thanksgiving meal.

Internet links

- Scan the code to find out about the Pilgrims' first Thanksgiving.

- For more links, go to **www.usborne.com/quicklinks**

This fence keeps wild animals out of the village.

The gardens are planted with beans, onions, turnips and squash.

These women are plucking wild turkeys.

This boy is grinding corn to make bread.

These Native Americans are bringing a deer for the feast.

This woman is stewing pumpkins to put in a pie.

A new country

More and more Europeans came to settle in North America. At first, all the settlers who lived on the east coast of America were ruled by Britain.

In 1783, the settlers won a war against the British and began ruling themselves. They called their new country the United States of America.

This is George Washington, the first President of the United States of America.

137

French finery

Around 350 years ago, the most powerful ruler in Europe was King Louis XIV of France. Louis became king when he was just five years old and he reigned for 72 years. He was fabulously rich and lived a life of luxury.

This is the Hall of Mirrors in the palace at Versailles. One of its walls is covered with 17 huge, arched mirrors.

The king's palace

Louis built a magnificent new palace at Versailles, near Paris. He filled it with priceless furniture, paintings and statues. Louis lived there with his family, his advisers, and over 1,500 servants. Lots of rich French nobles lived in the palace too.

Internet links

- Scan the code to see the magnificent palace of Versailles.
- For more links, go to **www.usborne.com/quicklinks**

Inside the palace, there are 700 rooms and 67 staircases.

This is Louis XIV's palace at Versailles. It took 47 years to build.

The fountains used so much water they could only be turned on for three hours at a time.

French fashions

In the 1700s, rich nobles at Versailles wore the most fashionable clothes in Europe. Their clothes were made of the finest silk and were decorated with beautiful embroidery, jewels, lace and ribbons.

Here you can see what rich French nobles were wearing in the 1770s.

Lace cravat

Women had very tall hairstyles, up to 3ft high.

Men wore wigs made of human, horse or goat hair.

Silk breeches

Silk stockings

Rich and poor

In 1789, the poorer people of France rebelled against the rich. They killed the king, the queen and hundreds of nobles, and began ruling the country themselves. This was called the French Revolution.

Some skirts were so wide that women had to go through doors sideways.

The American West

At first, Europeans who settled in North America stayed near the east coast. Then, explorers found ways to the West. Later, families began to cross America looking for land to farm.

Most families started their journey in Missouri, in the United States. These are the routes they took to the West.

This is Chimney Rock, one of the landmarks on the Oregon Trail.

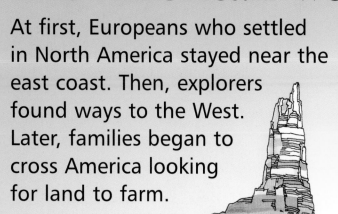

On the move

Families who went to live in the West were called pioneers. They made the long, hard journey in wagons pulled by oxen. Sometimes, they were attacked by Native Americans.

Here you can see some pioneers on their way to the West.

The pioneers have to cross mountains, rivers and deserts.

The wagons are covered with cloth stretched over wooden hoops.

Inside the wagons, there is plenty of food for the journey, as well as farm tools and furniture.

Going for gold

In 1848, gold was discovered in California, on the west coast. Thousands of people rushed there hoping to get rich. This was called the Gold Rush.

These men are looking for gold at the bottom of a stream.

★

Internet links

• Scan the code to watch a video about cowboys.

• For more links, go to www.usborne.com/quicklinks

Cowboys and cattle

The grassy plains of the West were good for farming cattle. Men called cowboys herded the cattle across the plains. They loaded them onto trains to be sold in the East.

This is what a cowboy wore.

Bandana to keep dust out of his mouth and nose

Lasso for catching cows

Hat with a wide brim

Leather leggings, called chaps, to protect his legs

★

Fighting for land

As farmers moved west, they took land away from the Native Americans who lived there. The Native Americans fought hard to keep their land, but they lost most of it in the end.

This is Sitting Bull, a famous Native American chief.

Farm animals follow behind.

Barrel of water

Lots of families travel together for safety.

Victorian times

The time when Queen Victoria ruled Britain is called the Victorian period. By then, there were lots of factories in Britain. Towns grew bigger, as people moved there to work in the factories.

Steam trains like this carried passengers and goods cheaply from town to town.

Living in a town

Rich people owned grand houses at the edge of the town. Factory workers lived in rows of tiny houses, with no running water or inside toilets. The air was full of smoke from the factories, and the streets were filthy. People often got sick and died.

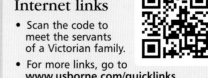

Internet links
- Scan the code to meet the servants of a Victorian family.
- For more links, go to **www.usborne.com/quicklinks**

Here you can see part of a Victorian town. Can you spot a policeman catching a thief in the street?

People work long hours in cloth factories like this one.

The streets are lit by gas lamps.

Up to 20 people live in each tiny house.

People burn coal to keep warm. Chimneys let out the smoke.

Victorian children

Boys from rich families went to school. Girls were usually taught at home.

Children from poor families had to work in coal mines and factories.

Homeless children were sent to live in a harsh place called a workhouse.

Victorian fashions

In the 1850s and 1860s, women wore dresses with very wide skirts. The skirts were held out by a circular frame called a crinoline. To make their waists look smaller, women wore a kind of tight underwear called a corset.

Victorian women's underwear looked like this.

The ideal waist size was only 18ins.

Corset

Crinoline

This picture from a Victorian fashion magazine shows what women were wearing in 1859.

Bonnet tied under the chin

The First World War

The First World War began in 1914. On one side were Britain, France, Belgium and Russia, who were called the Allies. On the other side were Germany and Austria. Later, many other countries joined in too.

The poppies that grew on the battlefields became a symbol for remembering the war.

Internet links
- Scan the code to listen to letters written by a First World War soldier.
- For more links, go to www.usborne.com/quicklinks

In the trenches

A lot of the fighting happened in northern France. Soldiers on both sides dug rows of deep ditches, called trenches, to protect themselves from enemy bullets.

The soldiers lived in the trenches for weeks at a time. During a battle, they climbed out and charged at the enemy. Millions of men died in these terrible battles.

Here you can see some British soldiers in a trench.

The men rest in holes dug into the sides of the trench.

Wooden walkways, called duckboards, stop the soldiers from sinking into the mud.

Officers live in underground shelters, called dug-outs.

The men's feet are always wet and often get sore.

New weapons

Both sides tried new ways of fighting to win the war. The Germans were the first to use poison gas, while the British invented tanks.

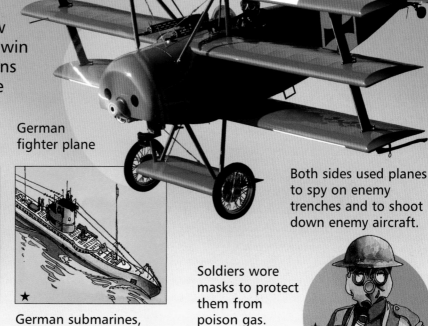

German fighter plane

Both sides used planes to spy on enemy trenches and to shoot down enemy aircraft.

Tanks could run over barbed wire and machine guns, but they often broke down.

German submarines, called U-boats, attacked ships on their way to Britain and France.

Soldiers wore masks to protect them from poison gas.

German trench

A soldier called a sentry keeps watch.

Machine gun

Barbed wire

Sandbags

The trenches are full of rats, fleas and lice.

The war ends

In 1917, the United States of America joined the war on the side of the Allies and helped them to win. The war finally ended at 11 o'clock on November 11, 1918. It had killed over 16 million people.

On November 11 every year, many people around the world remember those who have died in wars.

The Second World War

The Second World War started in 1939, when Germany attacked Poland. Later, Japan attacked the United States. Lots of countries joined together to fight the Germans and the Japanese.

There wasn't much to eat during the war. This British poster is telling people to grow their own food.

The Blitz

In just a few months, the Germans took over most of western Europe. Then they began bombing cities in Britain. This was called the Blitz. The bombs wrecked buildings and killed thousands of people.

Later in the war, the British dropped bombs on German cities. These are the ruins of the city of Cologne.

In Britain, children from big cities were sent away to the countryside to keep them safe from the bombs.

Internet links

- Scan the code to watch a video about children sent out of the cities during the war.
- For more links, go to **www.usborne.com/quicklinks**

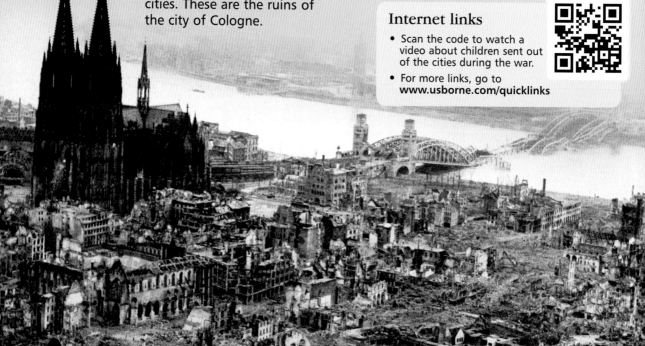

Pearl Harbor

In 1941, Japanese planes attacked Pearl Harbor, in Hawaii, killing over 2,000 Americans. The United States joined the war, and the fighting spread to the Far East and the Pacific Ocean.

American soldiers landing on an island in the Pacific Ocean

American ships on fire in Pearl Harbor. Many ships and planes were damaged or destroyed.

The Holocaust

The German leader Adolf Hitler wanted to kill all the Jewish people in Europe. During the war, he had six million Jews murdered. This terrible crime is called the Holocaust.

The war ends

Germany and Japan didn't have enough soldiers or weapons to win the war. The Germans were forced to stop fighting in May 1945.

These Russian soldiers are flying their country's flag in Berlin, the capital city of Germany.

In August, the Americans dropped two huge bombs on Japan. The Japanese finally gave up. The war was over, but it had killed more than 50 million people.

The bombs dropped on Japan were a new kind of bomb, called an atom bomb.

The modern world

On this page, you can read about some of the discoveries and inventions that have changed people's lives since the end of the Second World War.

1952 The first passenger jet began flying.

1957 The first nuclear power station began working in the United States.

1958 The microchip was invented. Microchips are an important part of computers.

1961 Yuri Gagarin was the first person to travel into space.

1962 Live TV pictures were sent from the United States to Europe for the first time.

1967 A doctor named Christiaan Barnard carried out the first heart transplant.

1969 Neil Armstrong was the first person to walk on the Moon.

1969 The jumbo jet flew for the first time.

1972 A game called Pong was the first computer game.

1975 The first home computers were sold in the United States.

This is the space rocket that took Neil Armstrong to the Moon in July 1969.

1976 Concorde began flying. It was the first passenger plane to travel faster than the speed of sound.

1979 The first mobile phones, or cell phones, went on sale in Japan.

1981 The first PC, or personal computer, was made.

1981 The American space shuttle made its first flight.

1982 The first compact discs, or CDs, went on sale.

1982 A patient was given an artificial heart for the first time.

1989 The World Wide Web was invented. The Web allows people to get information from the Internet quickly and easily.

1990 A huge telescope, called the Hubble Space Telescope, was sent into space.

1994 The Channel Tunnel opened between Britain and France.

1997 A sheep called Dolly was the first large animal to be cloned. A cloned animal is an exact copy of another animal.

How
people
live

People around the world

There are more than six billion people living in the world today. No two of us are the same, as nobody looks, thinks or feels exactly the same as anybody else.

Each of the 13.5 million people living in Shanghai, China, is different in the way he or she looks, thinks and feels.

What is a person?

Humans are probably the most intelligent creatures on Earth. We can make things, solve problems and create beautiful works of art. Most scientists believe that it took an extremely long time for us to develop into the amazing people we are today.

The way we look

Everyone looks different from everyone else in the world. For example, some people are taller or shorter than others, with darker or lighter skin or eyes of a particular shape. Even identical twins don't look exactly alike.

★   ★   ★
These children have different skin and hair color and different shaped eyes, noses and mouths.

Internet links

- Scan the code for a day in the life of an Egyptian boy.
- For more links, go to www.usborne.com/quicklinks

What we think

People have many different beliefs about the world around them. These beliefs are often called a religion. You can find out more about the religions of the world on pages 178-179.

These Aboriginal boys from Australia are taking part in a ceremony to mark their change into adults. The patterns painted on their skin are believed to help them grow.

What we say

Today, there are at least five thousand languages. Some are used by only a few people. Others, such as Mandarin Chinese, are spoken by many millions.

Six month old babies could learn to speak any language.

What we do

People in each part of the world have their own ways of doing things. These are called traditions and customs. Along with beliefs, they affect how people behave, including what they wear, what they eat and how they celebrate important times in their lives.

For example, the way we greet other people varies from place to place.

In countries such as Germany, people usually shake hands when they meet.

French people often greet each other with several kisses on the cheeks.

In India, people put their hands together and bow their heads to greet each other.

Houses and homes

Homes have many uses. These include being places where we eat, sleep and keep our things. Any type of building, such as a house, a hut or a tent, can be someone's home.

Building homes

In some countries, builders make houses, often using wood, stone or bricks. In other places, people build their own homes. They use materials that are easy to find, such as wood, mud or grass.

These round homes in the Kalahari Desert in Botswana are built from woven sticks covered with mud. The roofs are made from grasses.

Beating the weather

Houses have to be built in a style that protects the people who live in them from the weather.

In hot countries, many houses have shutters to keep out the sun, so the house stays cool inside.

Snow settles on the sloping roof of this Swiss chalet and helps to keep the heat inside the house.

In places where floods often happen, many houses are built on stilts to keep them dry.

What's in a house?

A house has areas where you can sleep, prepare food, eat and relax. In some homes, everything is done in one room, but many houses have a different room for each activity. Most have a bathroom too.

Internet links

- Scan the code to see how a yurt is erected.
- For more links, go to **www.usborne.com/quicklinks**

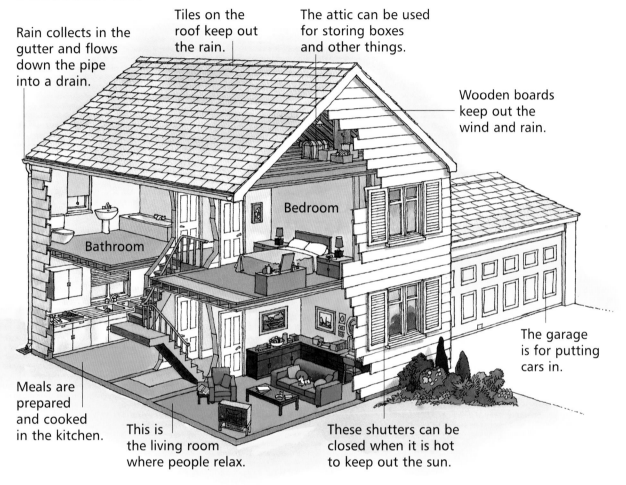

Rain collects in the gutter and flows down the pipe into a drain.

Tiles on the roof keep out the rain.

The attic can be used for storing boxes and other things.

Wooden boards keep out the wind and rain.

Bedroom

Bathroom

The garage is for putting cars in.

Meals are prepared and cooked in the kitchen.

This is the living room where people relax.

These shutters can be closed when it is hot to keep out the sun.

On the move

Some people, who are known as nomads, don't live in one place all the time. They move from place to place, taking their homes with them. They might travel to find work, or to find food and water for their herds of animals.

This family from central Asia travels from one place to another, living in a tent called a yurt.

Cities and towns

A city is a big, busy town where many people live and work. About half of all the people in the world live in a town or city. Many cities have tall buildings because of the shortage of land.

Living together

People living in towns and cities need houses, schools, hospitals and stores. They also need places where they can enjoy themselves, such as parks and theatres. There must be work for people to do, too, so they can afford to live there.

As in many cities, these buildings in New York, USA have many floors on top of each other to use less land. Most cities have parks for people to enjoy. This is New York's Central Park.

★ In the middle of a city, there are often large and well-known stores as well as many smaller ones.

★ Cities have restaurants, museums and theatres where people can enjoy themselves.

City problems

Many people like living in a city. There is plenty to do, and stores and schools are nearby. But city life is not always easy. For example, it can sometimes be hard to find a job, or a home that you can afford to live in.

There are often too many cars in cities. They jam the roads and fill the air with fumes.

Sinking city

Around 19 million people live in Mexico City. So much water has been pumped from underground lakes beneath the city to provide for them that now the streets are sinking a little more each year.

Internet links

- Scan the code to take a walking tour of New York's Central Park.
- For more links, go to www.usborne.com/quicklinks

How a country is run

The way a country is run and the people who lead it are very important for the people who live there. The leaders decide what laws are made and how much money can be spent, for example on schools and roads.

Who's in charge?

The people who run a country are called the government. A government that people choose, or vote for, is called a democracy.

If one person or a group of people rules a country without giving anyone a choice, it is called an autocracy.

Bill Clinton was President of the USA from 1993-2001. The President is the head of the government.

In 1994, for the first time, all South African people were allowed to vote for their government. People lined up for hours waiting to vote.

Making a choice

In a democracy, people choose their government in an election.

On election day, adults cast a vote, by putting a mark or a number on a paper by the name of the person they want to support.

Without showing anyone who they voted for, they put their paper into a locked ballot box.

After an election, all the votes on the ballot papers are counted. The person with the most support wins.

Nelson Mandela worked hard to bring democracy to South Africa. In 1994, he was elected President.

Ballot paper

Ballot box

Divided power

In 1783, the people of America decided to divide power three ways. America has an elected President. Americans in each state also vote for people to work with the President in Congress. Judges in the Supreme Court make sure their decisions are fair.

This is the White House in Washington, DC, where the US President makes decisions.

At the top

In the past, many countries were ruled by kings, queens or emperors. When a ruler died, the power to rule was usually passed on to a son or daughter. Today, there are not many really powerful royal families.

This sceptre belongs to the British king or queen. It is a symbol of his or her power.

Internet links

- Scan the code for facts about Nelson Mandela.

- For more links, go to www.usborne.com/quicklinks

Food and cooking

The food people eat and the way they cook is very different around the world. Everyone needs food, but at least 800 million people in the world do not have enough.

A healthy diet can include brown bread, nuts and eggs, and plenty of fruit and vegetables.

Growing and buying

The main food of a country is called its staple food. Rice is the staple food of about half the world. Other staples include corn, wheat and potatoes. Some people grow their own staple foods. Others buy them in stores and markets, along with many other foods such as fruit and vegetables.

A vegetable market in Hong Kong, China

How people cook

Cooking food can make it taste better and keep longer. It helps kill germs that might make you ill too. Cooked food is also easier to digest (see page 104). There are many different ways of cooking.

This Indian woman is cooking meat in a clay oven called a tandoor.

In China, food is often cooked in round metal pans, called woks.

Internet links

- Scan the code to find out how to use chopsticks.
- For more links, go to www.usborne.com/quicklinks

A famous Spanish dish is called paella. It is cooked in a shallow pan, sometimes over a wood fire.

Mealtime customs

There are many different ways of eating across the world. Some people kneel on the floor to eat, and some sit at high tables. Many people use their hands to eat, while others use chopsticks, or a knife and fork.

In China, even young children use wooden sticks, called chopsticks.

Feasts and festivals

When people celebrate, food is often a big part of the festival. It is important in several religions too. For example, during the holy month of Ramadan, Muslims eat nothing during the day until sunset. When Ramadan ends, they hold a feast to celebrate.

Clothes and fashion

People may have first worn clothes to protect them from the weather. Over time, clothes became a way of showing where you came from, what job you did and how rich you were. Today clothes can say a lot about you.

Women wearing traditional dresses in western Tibet

What is fashion?

A fashion is a style that is only popular for a short time, so fashions change all the time. Some of the clothes on sale in stores are based on styles first seen at big fashion shows in New York, Paris and Milan.

Internet links

- Scan the code to watch a video clip of Masai women.
- For more links, go to www.usborne.com/quicklinks

Following fashion

People who want to be fashionable wear the latest styles however unusual they may be. Things such as huge wigs and skirts, that were once very popular, often look strange to us now.

These Japanese girls have dyed their hair and wear bright clothes to look fashionable.

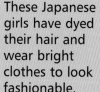

160

Traditional clothes

In some places, people still wear the style of clothes they have worn for centuries. They follow tradition rather than fashion. A country's traditional dress is called its national costume.

This young Masai woman is wearing traditional bead necklaces.

This Japanese woman wears a gown called a kimono.

This Moroccan water carrier is wearing a traditional hat.

This Indian woman wears a sari over a small top.

Clothes for climates

People usually wear clothes that suit their way of life. This means dressing for the climate where they live and for the work they do. Find out more about work clothes on page 162.

In cold climates people wear many layers of clothes. Air trapped between the layers keeps out the cold.

People who live in hot, damp places, such as rainforests, often wear very little. This helps to keep them cool.

In hot, dry, desert climates, people wear loose robes to shield them from the scorching sun.

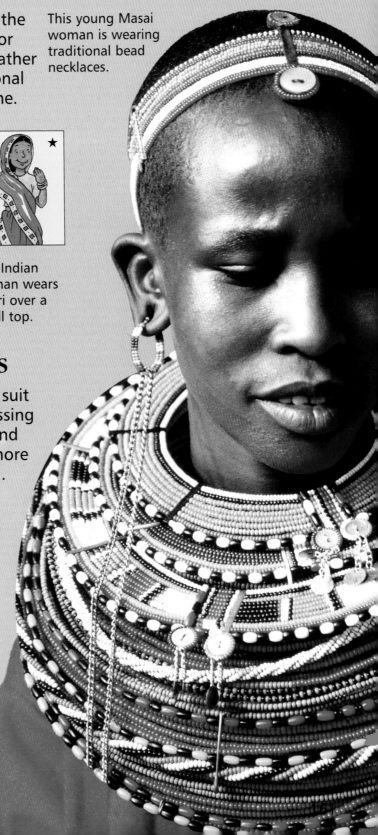

Jobs and work

The main reason people work is to earn money for themselves and their families. Many people enjoy their work. For others, it means earning just enough to survive.

Changing times

In the richer parts of the world, the way people work has changed through the ages.

For centuries, most people farmed a small piece of land.

About 200 years ago, people began working in factories.

Now many people work in an office, or at home, using a computer.

This boy has a part-time job before school each day. He delivers newspapers to people's homes.

Surgeons

Working clothing

For some jobs, people have to wear special clothes. This may be a uniform that makes them easy to spot. It may be things such as hard hats and goggles that help protect them while they work.

A chef's hat stops hairs from dropping into the food while he is cooking. His apron protects his other clothes.

Motorcycle courier

Welder

Can you guess why all these people wear special clothes?

Builder

Police officers

Teamwork

Many people work as part of a team. Each person in the team has a different job to do. This team of workers is building a brick house.

A roofer fixes the tiles to the roof.

Bricklayers stick the bricks together with a mixture called mortar.

In this picture, parts of the walls and roof of the house have been cut away, so you can see inside.

A carpenter builds the wooden parts of the house and fits the doors and windows.

These men are digging a hole to put pipes in. The pipes will bring clean water into the house and take dirty water away.

A plumber puts in the water pipes inside the house.

This man is mixing the mortar for the bricklayers.

Children at work

In many countries, children start work at 16 or 18, after they have left school. In other places, children start work much younger. Over 150 million of the world's children do some kind of work.

Farming

Farmers grow crops and keep animals to feed people. Some farmers produce food just for their own family. Others sell their food to stores for other people to buy.

These farmers in Thailand are planting rice shoots by hand.

On big farms, machines help farmers to plant and gather, or harvest, crops.

This machine is called a combine harvester. It is cutting wheat.

Growing crops

The type of crop a farmer can grow depends on the soil, the type of land and the weather in the place where he lives. Rice needs hot, wet weather. Wheat grows best in cooler, drier places.

A tractor is a very useful farm machine. This one is pulling a trailer to collect the wheat grains.

Internet links

- Scan the code to watch a combine harvester at work.
- For more links, go to **www.usborne.com/quicklinks**

164

Keeping animals

Keeping animals is called livestock farming. Animals give us milk, wool, eggs and leather, as well as meat. Some farmers keep just one kind of animal.

Farmers keep sheep for meat, wool and milk.

Hens are kept for their eggs as well as their meat.

Goats are kept for their milk, meat and skin.

Cows give us milk, meat and leather. One cow can make over 3,000 gallons of milk each year.

Using chemicals

Some farmers need to produce as much food as they can in a short time. They use machines to spray crops with chemicals to help them grow and to kill pests and diseases.

These sunflowers are being sprayed with fertilizer to help them grow. Some people worry that these chemicals are bad for us.

Organic farming

Farming without chemicals is called organic farming. It is harder to produce lots of food this way, but many people think organic foods are healthier than other kinds.

Many farmers are now growing organic fruit and vegetables to sell in local markets.

165

Going to school

Children go to school to learn the things they need to know when they grow up. Only about half of the children in the world go to school.

Skills to survive

In poorer countries, many children do not have time to go to school. They have to work to help their family survive. They do not learn to read or write, but are taught other skills they need, such as hunting and farming.

The young girl on the left is helping to prepare palm fruit for her family to eat. She is from the Kpelle tribe in Liberia, Africa.

Kinds of schools

Schools and ways of learning can be very different around the world. Some schools do not have walls, chairs or even books.

These children in a mountain village in Nepal sit outside on the ground to learn.

This Australian boy lives far from a school. He learns at home, using the Internet.

These children at a school in the USA work at desks inside a classroom.

What can you learn?

All schools teach basic skills such as reading, writing and using numbers. As you get older, you can learn more and more different subjects. There are other things you can do at school too, such as playing sports or using a computer.

At some schools you can learn to play a musical instrument and join a band or orchestra.

Older children may do chemistry experiments in a school laboratory.

Computers are useful for many subjects. Computer skills are often called ICT (Information and Communication Technology) skills.

Some schools have team sports, such as softball, baseball or basketball.

Taking tests

In most schools, you have to take important tests called exams. These show how well you understand the things you have learned. You need to pass these tests if you want to go to college or a university.

Internet links

- Scan the code to find out about going to school in different parts of the world.
- For more links, go to www.usborne.com/quicklinks

Sports and games

People play sports and games for fun, to keep fit, because they want to win, or as part of a festival. There are hundreds of sports. Many need fitness and skill.

Internet links
- Scan the code to discover different sports and activities you could try.
- For more links, go to www.usborne.com/quicklinks

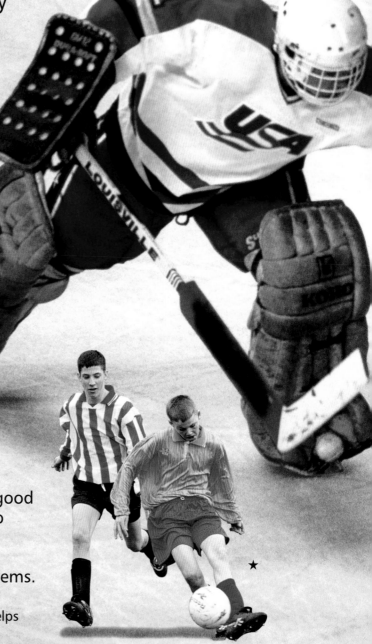

Playing together

Some games and sports, such as archery, are played by just one person. Others, such as baseball and hockey, are played in teams. In a team sport, everyone has to work together to succeed.

In a team game, such as ice hockey, each player has his own job to do. Here a goalkeeper tries to stop another player from scoring.

Useful sports

Sports and games can be very good for you. Playing a sport helps to keep you fit and healthy. Even computer games can teach you to think quickly and solve problems.

Playing a team sport, such as soccer, helps to keep you fit and can be fun.

168

The Olympic Games

The world's main sporting event is the Olympic Games. The first Games were held in the town of Olympia, in Ancient Greece. Athletes showed off their skills at many sports, such as running and wrestling. The Games are now held every four years, in different cities around the world.

The winners of the Ancient Olympics were given a garland of laurel leaves as a prize.

Today, Olympic winners get gold medals. Runners-up get silver and those in third place get bronze.

Sports for all

Anyone can enjoy sports. For instance, athletes with disabilities often have specially designed racing wheelchairs. The main sporting event for wheelchair athletes is the Paralympics.

These athletes are taking part in time trials to qualify for the Paralympics.

169

Communicating

There are many different ways of telling each other things. This is called communicating. We can use noises, such as sirens, or signs, such as flashing lights. The main ways we communicate are by talking, pictures and writing, though.

Some signs and symbols can be understood by people who speak different languages. Can you guess what these symbols mean?

Keeping in touch

Televisions, telephones and the Internet allow us to share information quickly and easily. People thousands of miles apart can get in touch in seconds by picking up the phone or sending an email or text message. TV allows us to find out what is happening all over the world.

:-) Happy   l-O Yawning

:-o Wow!   :-D Laughing

:-(Sad   ;-) Winking

These symbols are called smileys or emoticons. You can add them to e-mails to show how you are feeling.

A Masai farmer in Kenya using his mobile phone

170

Writing it down

To record what they said, early people made marks that stood for words. This is how writing began. The first types of writing were rows of pictures. These then became letters, which stood for sounds.

In Ancient Egypt, men called scribes kept records.

In Europe, the printing press was first used in about 1450.

Now most writing is done on computers.

Internet links

- Scan the code to write your name in Egyptian hieroglyphs.
- For more links, go to **www.usborne.com/quicklinks**

Spreading the word

Writing a book or newspaper is a way of sharing facts, news, ideas and stories with many people. Books were first printed in China over 1,000 years ago. In Europe, until about 550 years ago, the only way to make a book was to write it all out by hand.

A German man named Johannes Gutenberg invented the first printing press in Europe. This machine could print many copies of the same book. Now if a book is popular, millions of copies are made and people all around the world can read it.

This boy is choosing books to borrow from a library. Libraries hold thousands of books on different subjects.

Art and painting

Every work of art is different. Artists may try to create something which is beautiful, or shocking, or shows people how they feel. Whoever sees their work usually feels something, too; they may like it, or they may hate it.

What is art?

People often disagree about what is a work of art and what is not. Many artists say that anything at all can be art. In some cases a work of art can be hard for anyone but the artist to understand.

This painting is by a famous French artist named Paul Gauguin who died in 1903. It shows a mother and daughter in Tahiti and is called *When will you marry?*

Making art

Not every work of art is painted. Art can be made in many ways, using stone, clay, wood, metal or other things. Pieces of art which are not flat are often called sculptures.

This bronze sculpture by Rodin is called *The Thinker.* There are over 20 casts, or versions, made from the same mold, in cities around the world.

172

Different styles

There are many styles of art. Some artists work from real life and try to copy what they see. Others don't try to show real things. They use colors, lines and shapes instead.

Aboriginal art, from Australia, is usually painted on tree bark or rocks. It is used to tell stories. This shows a crocodile and a fish called a barramundi.

Traditional art

Some types of art are traditional. This means artists have worked in the same style for thousands of years. There are many kinds of traditional art around the world.

Is it art?

Artists are always trying out new ways of making art, but other people don't always accept them. Many people think photos and movies can be art. Some artists use computers to help them create art. Others use leaves, lights or even old cars.

Internet links

- Scan the code to explore a famous painting.
- For more links, go to www.usborne.com/quicklinks

A group of artists half-buried ten cars in a field in Texas, USA in 1974. They called their sculpture *Cadillac Ranch*. You can still see it there.

All over the world people act and dance to entertain each other. They might use acting and dancing to celebrate an event, tell a story, communicate a message or to show feelings.

These people are making a movie. The cameramen are filming the actors. Actors in movies may have to repeat a scene many times before it is right.

On the stage

A story which is acted out is called a play. A person who writes plays is known as a playwright. Some plays tell true stories, but others are made up. Plays performed in front of other people are 'live', so each performance is a little different. Plays are often performed in theatres.

Movies

Movies are stories that are acted out and recorded on film, so we can watch the same performance over and over again. People can go to the theatre to watch movies, or see them at home on video or DVD.

These stage actors are performing in a famous comedy called *A Midsummer Night's Dream* by William Shakespeare.*

On stage, clothes, makeup, masks, scenery, lights and music may be used to create different feelings.

*See page 135

Ways of dancing

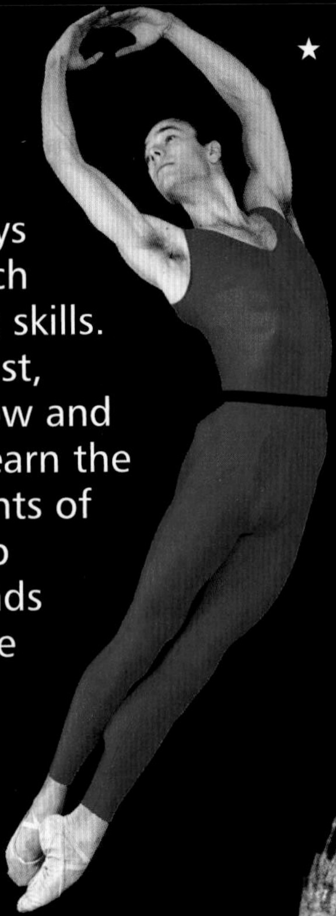

There are many ways of dancing, and each one needs different skills. Some dances are fast, while others are slow and graceful. You can learn the steps and movements of a dance or make up your own. Most kinds of dancing are done with music.

Ballet dancing uses many carefully-planned movements. Some take years of training to do well.

Why do we dance?

We don't really know why people dance or how dancing began. It may have started as a way of celebrating something, worshipping gods or telling a story. Today, many people dance to keep fit or just for fun.

Dancers in Bali use every part of their body in their dance, including their eyes, face, neck and hands.

Internet links

- Scan the code to watch ballet dancers in a performance of *The Nutcracker*.
- For more links, go to www.usborne.com/quicklinks

Music

Music is a pattern of sounds put together to make a tune or rhythm. People have many different ideas about what music should sound like.

Musical sounds

You can make music just with your body by singing, clapping, whistling or humming. Musical instruments, such as the ones below, can help you make all kinds of other musical sounds. Here are some groups of instruments.

These are string instruments. You pluck their strings or stroke them with a bow.

These are wood-wind instruments. You blow into them to make a sound.

Percussion instruments make sounds when you hit, shake or scrape them.

These are brass instruments. You play them by buzzing your lips on the mouthpiece.

These boys are making music with cymbals, drums, horns, clapping and singing, during Bahag Bihu, an Indian spring festival.

Why make music?

Music can make us want to dance, sing, or even cry, and people often use it to show how they feel about something. It may be used to celebrate big events such as weddings, and in religious ceremonies.

In West African music, rhythms are usually more important than tunes. These Gambian women are dancing to the rhythm of a drum.

Types of music

There are two main types of music: classical and popular. Each type contains many musical styles and traditions.

Jazz is a style of popular music. It began early in the last century in New Orleans, USA. This jazz musician is playing a saxophone.

Playing together

Some types of music can be performed by one person. Many types are played or sung by people in groups. A group of musicians playing together is often called a band.

A large group of musicians playing different instruments is called an orchestra.

Internet links
• Scan the code to watch musicians in an orchestra.
• For more links, go to www.usborne.com/quicklinks

Religions

A religion is a belief in something greater than any person. It may be a belief in one God, or in several gods. For some people, religion is more to do with the way they live their life. There are many religions in the world.

Like many boys in Buddhist countries, this boy is spending time as a monk, learning about his religion.

Buddhism

Buddhism teaches people to think deeply about life and what is really important. This thinking is called meditation. Buddhism is based on the ideas of a south Asian prince who became known as the Buddha.

Christianity

People who follow Christianity are called Christians. They believe that God watches over them and wants them to be good. Christians believe that a man named Jesus was the Son of God. The Christian holy book is the *Bible*.

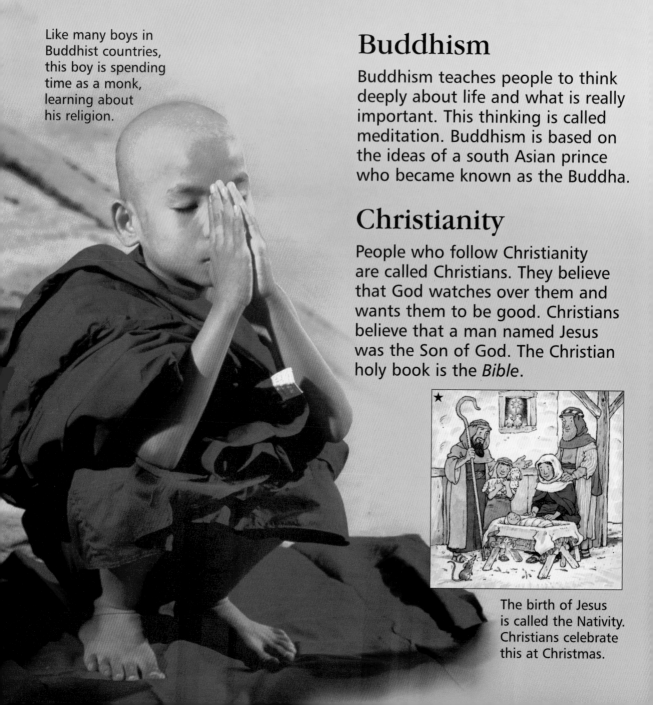

The birth of Jesus is called the Nativity. Christians celebrate this at Christmas.

Hinduism

Hinduism has many gods and beliefs. The main god is Brahman. Hindus believe that people have many lives, one after the other. This pattern only ends when the believer becomes close to Brahman.

★ The Hindu god Krishna is usually shown with blue skin. Here he is playing his flute.

Islam

Followers of the religion of Islam are called Muslims. They obey the laws of God, who is called Allah. A man named Muhammad taught Allah's laws. These were written down in the Muslim holy book, the *Qur'an*.

This Muslim girl is praying to Allah.

Judaism

Followers of Judaism are called Jews. They worship God in a building called a synagogue. The Jewish holy day, or Shabbat, is from sunset on Friday to sunset on Saturday.

This boy is in a synagogue, reading from the Jewish holy writings. He is wearing a cap and shawl to show that he respects God.

Sikhism

A person who follows Sikhism is called a Sikh, which means "learner". Sikhs believe in one God, whom they worship in a building called a gurdwara. There, they listen to readings from the Sikh holy book, the *Guru Granth Sahib*.

This is a symbol of Sikhism. It is called the khanda. ★

Internet links

- Scan the code to watch a video about Buddhist monks.
- For more links, go to **www.usborne.com/quicklinks**

179

Myths

Myths are stories filled with strange creatures, gods and goddesses and amazing happenings. They are often tales of good and evil.

Neptune was the Roman god of the sea. He could control the oceans.

Myths and gods

People may have made up myths to explain why puzzling things happened before science gave us the answers. For instance, the Romans believed that tidal waves and earthquakes happened when the sea-god Neptune was angry.

Myths and monsters

There are many incredible monsters described in the world's myths.

The yeti is an ape-like creature that lives on snowy mountains. People disagree whether the yeti is real or mythical. ★

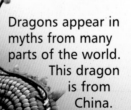

Dragons appear in myths from many parts of the world. This dragon is from China.

Creation myths

Every country has its own myths, but they are often about the same things. For instance, there are many different creation myths explaining how the world began.

Internet links

- Scan the code to see mythical creatures from around the world.
- For more links, go to www.usborne.com/quicklinks

Science

What is science?

Science is what we know about the world around us. Why do volcanoes erupt? What is gravity? Is there life on other planets? How do our brains work? Science tries to answer all these questions and many more.

Scientists have found out why leaves turn red or brown in the fall.

Being a scientist

People who do science are called scientists. They study things by looking at them closely, asking questions, and doing experiments to find out how they work.

Scientists can use their scientific knowledge to help them invent things, like this cell phone.

Scientists who study animals, such as this macaw, are called zoologists.

Scientists have found 17 different species (types) of macaws in the wild.

Studies of macaws have shown that their bright feathers may help them to find a mate.

Internet links

- Scan the code to see how science can explain why flamingos are pink.
- For more links, go to **www.usborne.com/quicklinks**

Branches of science

There are hundreds of different kinds, or branches, of science, and many different kinds of scientists. Here are just a few of them.

Biologists study living things.

Botanists study just plants.

Chemists study chemicals.

Technology

Scientists can use their understanding of the world to design or invent new things. Without science, we wouldn't have many of the machines and medicines we have today. Using science in this way is called technology.

Medical scientists use X-ray machines to look inside people's bodies. The picture above is an X-ray photo of a foot. Can you see the bones?

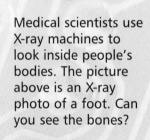

This is a machine called a robot. It can move around and make its own simple decisions.

Some types of robots can do dangerous jobs instead of humans.

183

What scientists do

To find out about things, scientists do experiments. These are tests that show how living things, objects or substances behave.

Internet links

• Scan the code for a video about scientists who study penguins in the Antarctic.

• For more links, go to www.usborne.com/quicklinks

Asking questions

Scientists use experiments to help them answer questions. For example, a scientist might ask, "does music make plants grow faster?"

As an experiment, she could take two groups of plants and play music to just one of them, to see which grew faster.

These pictures show a simple experiment on plants.

A scientist grows two similar groups of plants.

Music is played to only one of the groups.

Later, the two groups can be compared.

Theories

Scientists think up theories that might explain how things work. For example, they might have a theory that penguins travel to a certain area because there is more food there. Then they do experiments to test their theories.

Scientists write down their results and repeat their experiments to make sure they work.

— Transmitter

This penguin is part of an experiment. Scientists have fitted it with a jacket containing a transmitter. (It doesn't hurt the penguin at all.)

The transmitter will send signals that the scientists can collect. From this, they can track the penguin's movements.

Observing

Observing means watching and measuring things very carefully. It's an important part of being a scientist.

Scientists often use tools to help them observe things. For example, astronomers (space scientists) use powerful telescopes to study planets, stars and galaxies.

Telescopes make far away things look closer. There is a huge telescope in this building that a team of astronomers uses to watch the night sky.

This is a comet. Comets are balls of ice and dust that zoom through space. By observing the path of a comet, astronomers can work out where it will go next.

Do your own experiment

Find out if adding salt to water will make a difference to how things float in it. You will need:
2 half-full glasses of water; 2 fresh eggs; 10 heaped teaspoons of salt

1. Stir the salt into one glass of water until it has dissolved and is invisible.

2. Put an egg in each glass. Do both eggs float? Do they both behave the same way?

You can find out more about floating on pages 200-201.

Atoms and molecules

Scientists have found out that everything is made out of tiny particles called atoms. Atoms can join together in groups called molecules.

Internet links
- Scan the code for an animation about the size of atoms.
- For more links, go to www.usborne.com/quicklinks

What is an atom?

An atom is like a tiny ball. It has a center, or nucleus, and outer layers called shells. There are about 100 types of atoms.

Atoms are so tiny that you can't see them. A piece of paper, such as this page, is about a million atoms thick.

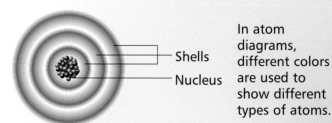

Shells
Nucleus

In atom diagrams, different colors are used to show different types of atoms.

Atoms are made up of even smaller particles. You can see some of them in the nucleus of the atom above.

Hydrogen atom
Iron atom
Gold atom
Oxygen atom

Making molecules

Atoms sometimes join together to make bigger units called molecules. This joining together is called bonding.

These pictures show two types of atoms bonding to make water molecules.

Did you know?

- Most of an atom is empty space.

- Some types of atoms, such as francium, do not exist naturally. They can only be made by scientists in a science lab.

- Atoms constantly move around, even in solids. They jiggle, vibrate and bump into each other.

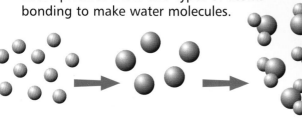

Hydrogen atoms

Oxygen atoms

Water molecules

Water

Water is made up of lots of water molecules.

Materials

All the things around us – rocks, air, water, sand, glass, wood, plastic, and even our bodies – are made of atoms and molecules. Scientists call all these different types of stuff "materials".

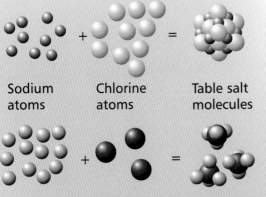

Sodium atoms + Chlorine atoms = Table salt molecules

Hydrogen atoms + Carbon atoms = Methane gas molecules

Molecules are often shown as balls (the atoms) and sticks (the bonds between them). This shows parts of two molecules of aspirin.

Materials hunt

Can you find things made of these materials in your home or classroom?

★ Paper   ★ China

★ Plastic   ★ Wood

★ Glass   ★ Metal

Chemists mix materials together in glass beakers and flasks like these.

Chemistry

Different materials behave in different ways. For example, if you heat butter, it melts, but if you heat an egg, it gets harder. Salt dissolves quickly in water, but sand doesn't.

Scientists called chemists study how materials behave, change, and bond together. This kind of science is called chemistry.

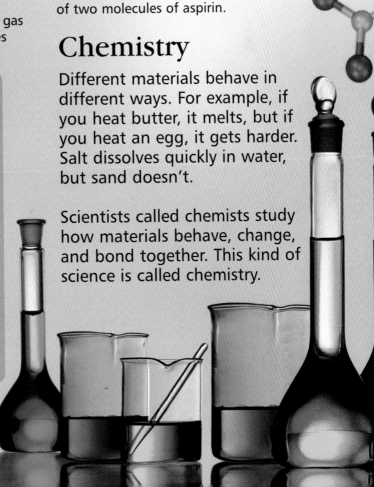

Solids, liquids and gases

Most materials can exist in three different forms: solids, liquids and gases. In solids, molecules are packed together. In liquids and gases, they're more spread out.

Internet links
- Scan the code to watch an experiment about water in its solid and liquid states.
- For more links, go to **www.usborne.com/quicklinks**

Gold is a solid.

Solids

The molecules in solids are firmly attached to each other and don't move around much. Because of this, most solids stay the same shape.

Molecules in solids are squashed tightly together.

Liquids

The molecules in liquids are not so squashed together. They can move around more and are not as firmly fixed to each other. This is why liquids can flow, splash and be poured.

Molecules in liquids are not squashed together.

Drinks are liquids. They flow into every part of a container.

Gases

The molecules in gases are not attached to each other at all and move around all the time at high speeds. This means that gases quickly spread out to fill the space they are in. They have no shape of their own.

Gas molecules don't stick to each other at all.

Many gases are invisible. You can only see this gas because it is burning.

Make a gas

You can make carbon dioxide gas and blow up a balloon with it. You will need:

a narrow-necked jar; some baking soda; some vinegar; a balloon; a teaspoon

1. Fill a quarter of the jar with vinegar. Put the soda into the balloon, using the teaspoon.

 ★

2. Stretch the neck of the balloon over the top of the jar. Don't let any soda spill into the jar.

 ★

3. Quickly lift the balloon up to tip all of the soda into the jar. The vinegar will react with the soda, making bubbles.

 ★

When the vinegar and soda react (see page 191), they make carbon dioxide gas which fills the balloon, blowing it up a little.

Three forms

The same material can exist as a solid, a liquid or a gas. For example, water exists as a liquid, as solid ice, and as a gas called water vapor.

There is water vapor (water gas) in the air. As it cools, it forms clouds and may turn into rain.

Ice is frozen water. It is a solid.

Water in rivers and seas is a liquid.

189

How materials change

Materials can change all the time. They can grow, shrink and change between a solid, a liquid and a gas. They can also combine to make new materials.

Changing state

Materials can change between solid and liquid, or between liquid and gas. These changes are called changes of state. They often happen when materials heat up or cool down.

★  When juice gets very cold, it turns from a liquid to a solid. This is called freezing.

★ Wax turns from a solid into a liquid as a candle burns. This is called melting.

★ When you heat water, it turns from a liquid into a gas. This is called boiling.

★ When water vapor cools, it turns into a liquid – rain. This is called condensing.

Inside a freezer, it's cold enough for water to freeze into ice.

Getting bigger

Water expands (gets bigger) when it freezes. Most materials, however, shrink as they get colder and expand as they get hotter. For example, a thermometer* contains a liquid that expands as the temperature rises.

A thermometer contains liquid in a narrow tube. (In this photo, the liquid is black.) As the liquid warms up, it gets bigger and fills more of the tube.

Make water get bigger

Here's what you will need:

a plastic bottle (don't use a glass bottle); a piece of foil; a freezer

1. Fill the bottle to the top with water. Cover the top with the foil.

2. Stand the bottle upright in the freezer. Leave it there overnight.

3. The water pushes the foil upward as it freezes and gets bigger.

Mixing materials

Materials can be mixed together to make new materials. If you mix sand, cement, broken stones and water, you get concrete. Concrete is useful for building, because it is stronger than any of the ingredients by themselves.

Internet links

- Scan the code for a quiz about changing states.
- For more links, go to www.usborne.com/quicklinks

The Catedral Metropolitana in Brazil is made of 16 curved concrete columns.

Reactions

In a mixture, materials are combined but their molecules do not change. Sometimes, however, materials react with each other. This means that when they are mixed, their molecules change and they turn into different materials.

  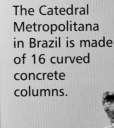

Rusting happens to iron when it is left out in the rain or in damp air.

Molecules of iron react with oxygen atoms and water molecules.

The reaction makes a new type of molecule called iron oxide, or rust.

These rocks formed in Mono Lake in California, USA because of a reaction between two different chemicals in the lake.

Energy

Energy is the power that makes things happen. You can't see it, but it's all around you, making all kinds of objects move and work.

Electrical energy flows into lights and changes into heat and light energy.

All kinds of energy

Energy comes in many types, or "forms". For example, heat, light, electricity and sound are all forms of energy.

Internet links

• Scan the code for a video about rollercoasters.
• For more links, go to www.usborne.com/quicklinks

People shouting and machines moving release a lot of sound energy.

The same energy

You can't destroy or make energy. This means the amount of energy in the Universe* is always the same. But one form of energy can change into another form.

Plants change light energy from the Sun into food energy.

*For more about the Universe, see page 212.

Movement energy

Whenever something moves, it has energy. The energy of something that is moving is called kinetic energy.

To fly, these birds change energy stored in their bodies into kinetic energy.

At the top of the roller coaster, the car contains stored energy.

As the car goes down the hill, stored energy changes into kinetic energy.

These flags have kinetic energy as they flutter in the breeze.

These children have a lot of kinetic energy because they are running fast.

Stored energy

Potential energy is energy that is stored, ready to use. When it's used, it turns into another form of energy, such as kinetic energy or heat.

As the hammer is lifted up, it gains a store of potential energy.

Food turns into stored energy in our bodies. A candy apple will give this boy enough energy to walk for 20 minutes.

This boy's video camera uses electrical energy that's stored in a battery.

193

Forces

A force is a push or a pull that makes an object do something. For example, if you kick a ball, the force of your kick makes the ball move. Forces can also make things change their direction, speed and shape.

Direct forces

Some forces work by touching the object they are pushing or pulling on. These are called direct forces. Kicking a ball, lifting a pen or pulling your sock off are all examples of direct forces.

Pushing a sled is a direct force.

Pulling a sled uphill on a rope is a direct force.

From a distance

Some forces don't have to touch the things they work on. For example, gravity* pulls you down when you jump off a wall. A magnet pulls paperclips toward it. Scientists are still not sure how these distant forces work.

Forces can stop things too. This snowdrift has a force that has stopped this sled.

Gravity is a distant force. It is pulling the sleds downhill, but not touching them.

Internet links

- Scan the code to watch a video clip about forces and gravity.
- For more links, go to **www.usborne.com/quicklinks**

*For more about gravity, see pages 198-199.

Balanced forces

When something isn't moving, you might think that there are no forces working on it. In fact, there are, but they are balanced against each other, and cancel each other out.

These two tug-of-war teams are not moving, because the forces they make are balanced. To win, one of the teams must use more force.

Using forces

We use forces all the time to move things, lift things and travel around. Machines help us to use forces to do things we can't do on our own. They turn our energy, or other forms of energy such as electricity, into the right kinds of force to do different jobs.

An excavator turns electrical energy into a pulling force to scoop up a heavy load of soil.

Scissors are simple machines. Their sharp blades use the force of your fingers to cut things.

Hot and cold

Heat is a form of energy.
Whenever you heat
something up, you are
giving it more energy.

Heating up

When many materials heat
up, their molecules spread
out. This makes them expand,
or get bigger. When they cool
down, they contract, or get smaller,
again. As air heats up, it expands a
lot, making it much lighter than cold
air. This is why hot-air balloons float.

The hot air inside these
balloons is lighter than
the air they float in. For
more about floating, see
pages 200-201.

Moving around

Heat moves from hotter to colder places.
For example, hot food gets cold because
its heat moves into the cooler air around
it. You can't usually see heat, but it can be
photographed with an infrared camera.

This picture was taken using an infrared
camera. The red areas show where the
buildings are giving out the most heat.

The Golden
Gate Bridge in
San Francisco, USA

Bridge gaps

Bridges often get slightly
longer as they heat up in the
sun. Large bridges have special
joints with gaps in them, so that
there's room for them to expand.

This is an expansion joint.
Joints like these allow
bridges to expand and
contract. Without them,
bridges could break and
collapse.

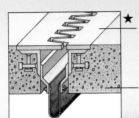

★ When a bridge expands in
hot weather, these plates
are pushed together.

— Bridge

Expansion and contraction

You can do an experiment to see
how air expands when it is heated
and contracts when it cools down.
This is what you will need:

a bowl; a bottle; a balloon

1. Ask an adult to hold the
empty bottle under hot water
for a minute. Stretch the
balloon over its neck.

 ★

2. Half-fill the bowl with cold
water and stand the bottle in
it. The air cools and shrinks,
pulling the balloon inside.

 ★

3. Empty the bowl and ask
an adult to add hot water to
it. The expanding warm air
pushes the balloon out again.

 ★

Internet links

• Scan the code to see heat
given off by a reindeer's body.

• For more links, go to
www.usborne.com/quicklinks

Measuring hotness

Temperature means how hot
something is. It is measured in
degrees Centigrade (°C) or
degrees Fahrenheit (°F).
Normal room temperature is
about 20°C (68°F).

Temperature is measured
using a thermometer.
Can you see what the
temperature is on
this thermometer?

 ★

Gravity

When you jump up in the air, you drop back down again. This is because there's an invisible force pulling you down to the ground. This force is called gravity.

Mars

Pulling together

All objects have gravity and make a slight pull on other objects. With small objects, this force is too weak to have an effect. But huge objects like planets have enough gravity to pull other things toward them.

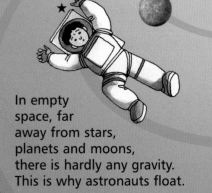

Mercury

In empty space, far away from stars, planets and moons, there is hardly any gravity. This is why astronauts float.

Gravity on other planets

The bigger an object is, the stronger its gravity is. Very big planets, like Jupiter, have much stronger gravity than Earth. Small planets and moons have weaker gravity than Earth.

Jupiter's gravity is more than twice as strong as Earth's. If you could visit Jupiter, you wouldn't be able to move because its gravity is so strong.

Jupiter

Jupiter's moon Io is quite small and its gravity is much weaker than the Earth's. You could jump many times higher on Io than you can on Earth.

This is Io, one of Jupiter's many moons.

The Sun

Venus

The Earth is in
orbit around
the Sun.

The Moon is in
orbit around
the Earth.

Testing gravity

Gravity pulls objects at the same speed,
even if they have different weights. Try
testing this yourself. You will need:

tissue paper; a coin; two identical boxes (such as
camera film boxes or food containers with lids)

1. Carefully tear a piece of
tissue paper the same size
as the coin. It will be lighter
than the coin.

 ★

2. Drop the paper and the
coin from the same height.
The paper falls more slowly
because air gets in its way.

 ★

3. Now put the coin in one
box and the paper in the
other. Put the lids on and
drop both boxes together.

 ★

4. The boxes have the same
air resistance and land at the
same time, even though they
are different weights.

★

Internet links

- Scan the code to
calculate your weight
on other planets.

- For more links, go to
www.usborne.com/quicklinks

In orbit

In space, large objects orbit,
or travel around, each other.
Planets orbit the Sun. Moons
orbit planets. This happens
because of gravity.

Gravity doesn't pull planets
and moons right together,
because they're moving too
fast. This diagram shows
how orbits work.

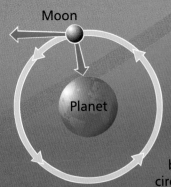

Moon

Planet

Moons move very fast. A
moon is always trying to
fly away from its planet
in a straight line.

Meanwhile, the planet's
gravity pulls the moon
toward it. The two forces
balance out and the moon
circles around the planet.

Floating

If you throw a stone into a pond, it will sink to the bottom. But if you put a balloon in some water, it will float. Why do some things float and others sink?

Weight and size

Floating is all about density – how heavy something is for its size. For example, a cork is light for its size. A piece of iron the same size as a cork is much heavier, because iron is denser than cork. Objects that are denser than water sink in water. Objects that are less dense than water float in water.

Internet links

- Scan the code to watch a video clip about floating in salt water.
- For more links, go to www.usborne.com/quicklinks

These inflatable rings are light for their size and float well.

If you try to push an inflatable ring under water, you'll feel the water pushing back.

Does it float?

Guess which things will float in water and then see if you were right. You will need:

a bowl of water; solid things, such as a cork, a candle, a coin, an apple, a raisin, a plastic toy, an eraser.

1. Make a chart to compare your guesses with what actually happens.

2. Try floating different objects and write down which of them really float.

	Will it float?	
	Guess	Actual
Cork	✓	☐
Coin	✓	☐
Candle	✗	☐
Apple	✗	☐

Upthrust

Things float because water pushes up on them more than they push down. This upward force is called upthrust. If an object is denser than water, the water cannot provide enough upthrust, so the object sinks.

How do ships float?

Some ships are so huge, it seems amazing that they float – but they do. Even if a ship is made of heavy iron, it has a lot of air inside it. This makes the ship less dense than water, so it floats.

This big cruise ship is light for its size because it has lots of air inside it.

This floating red buoy is used to warn boats that this stretch of water is dangerous.

Floating in air

Floating in air is just like floating in water. Anything that is less dense than air will float in it. But because air is very light itself, not many other things are light enough to float in it.

These balloons are filled with a gas that's less dense than air. It makes them float.

People are almost the same density as water, and just barely float. Air-filled life belts can help people to float better.

Salty sea

Salty water is denser than pure water. This makes it easier for people to float in it. A lake in Israel called the Dead Sea has water that's so salty, it's very easy to float in.

This woman is floating in the very salty water of the Dead Sea.

201

Friction

Whenever an object tries to slide across a surface, it is slowed down by the two surfaces gripping each other. This force is called friction.

Internet links
- Scan the code to watch a video clip about friction.
- For more links, go to www.usborne.com/quicklinks

The rough...

Friction slows things down because objects have rough surfaces. The rougher the surface, the more friction there is, and the more the object slows down.

This snowboarder can move very fast because there's not much friction between the smooth snow and the smooth snowboard.

...and the smooth

Very smooth surfaces don't have much friction and often feel slippery. If you are on a smooth surface, you can move fast without being slowed down very much.

Getting a grip

As well as slowing down moving things, friction helps things stay still. If it weren't for friction, we wouldn't be able to grip onto anything, or even stand up without slipping.

The soles of walking boots are molded into rough ridges. This makes lots of friction to keep the walker from slipping.

Hot friction

Wherever there is friction, there is heat. This is because as objects rub together, friction turns kinetic, or movement, energy into heat energy. There's more about energy on pages 192-193.

When a Space Shuttle comes back to Earth, it glows red hot because of friction between its surface and the air.

Coin warmer

To see how friction heats things up, try to warm up a metal coin using friction. You will need:

a coin; a pad of paper

1. Hold the coin flat on the paper with one finger on top of it, like this:

2. Press down and rub the coin very fast from side to side about 50 times.

The coin warms up because there is lots of friction between it and the paper. The friction turns the energy of the coin's movement into heat energy.

Streamlining

Even air and water cause friction when things move through them. Cars, planes and boats are built so that water or air can move past them in smooth lines to reduce friction. This is called streamlining.

Dolphins have streamlined bodies which help them to move fast in water.

Magnets

A magnet is a piece of metal that can pull some other types of metal toward it. Magnetism is a force. It happens because of the way atoms are arranged inside the metal.

Iron filings (tiny bits of iron) stick to the parts of this horseshoe-shaped magnet where its magnetic force is strongest.

Pushing and pulling

Magnetic forces are strongest at the two ends of a magnet. These ends are called the north pole and the south pole. If you try to put two magnets' poles together, they will either stick to each other or push each other away.

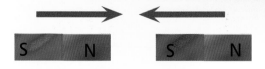

A north pole and a south pole always pull toward each other. This is called magnetic attraction.

Two poles of the same type always push each other away. This is called magnetic repulsion.

Magnetic fields

The area of force around a magnet is called its magnetic field. Our planet is magnetic and has its own magnetic field. It pulls compass needles so that they always point north.

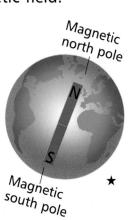

Magnetic north pole

Magnetic south pole

Like all magnets, the Earth has magnetic north and south poles. They are near the North Pole and South Pole you can see on a globe*.

*See page 13.

204

Magnets at work

You might use magnets to stick notes on your refrigerator. They are also used inside motors, DVD players and watches. Because magnets only attract some metals, such as iron, they are also used to separate materials from each other.

Which metals?

Try testing different metal things around your house with a magnet. You will need:

a magnet; metal objects, such as pins, coins, scissors or jewelry

Will it stick?	Guess	Actual
Tin can	✓	☐
Coin	✓	☐
Bottle	✗	☐
Ball	✗	☐

1. Guess which objects the magnet will attract.

2. Now test them by seeing if the magnet sticks to them.

The objects the magnet sticks to probably contain some iron, steel or nickel.

This huge magnet is being used to separate different types of metal so that they can be reused.

"Maglev" trains use magnetic repulsion to make them float just above a rail. This allows them to move very smoothly.

Internet links

- Scan the code to try a quiz about magnets.
- For more links, go to **www.usborne.com/quicklinks**

Light and color

Light is a form of energy. Most of the light on our planet comes from the Sun. Light comes from other places too – electric lights, candle flames and even some types of animals.

Lines and shadows

Light always travels in straight lines. If light hits an object that's not see-through, it can only shine past it, not around it. This makes a shadow where the light can't reach.

Light can turn a corner if it reflects (bounces) off a surface, such as a mirror.

★ Light shines in straight lines. Shadows happen because rays of light cannot bend around objects.

★ You can make light turn a corner. If you shine a lamp at a mirror, the light will bounce off it.

Fireflies can make light as bright as the display lights on a stereo.

The speed of light

When you flick a light switch, light seems to fill the room instantly. This is because light travels very fast. It moves at 186,000 miles per second.

It takes eight minutes for light to travel from the Sun to the Earth.

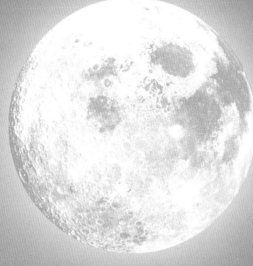

Seeing light

We see things because our eyes are designed to collect and sense light (there's more about eyes on page 107). When we see an object, we're really seeing light reflecting off it.

We see the Moon because light from the Sun reflects off it.

Colors

Bright white light is made up of different colors of light mixed together.

We see colors because some objects only reflect one color of light. For example, a green leaf only reflects green light, so it looks green.

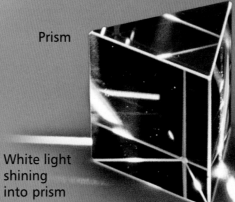

Prism

A piece of shaped glass called a prism can split white light into all its colors.

White light shining into prism

Separate colors of light shining out of prism

Sometimes raindrops act like mini-prisms. They split sunlight into lots of colors, making a rainbow.

Did you know?

• Most people can detect more than 10 million different shades of color.

• Some people are "colorblind". They can see some colors, but find it hard to tell the difference between red and green.

• Many animals see only in shades of gray, not in color.

• Scientists think it's impossible for anything in the Universe to travel faster than light.

Sound

Sound is a form of energy. It is made of vibrations (back-and-forth movements) that can move through air, solid things and liquids, but not through empty space.

Sound vibrations

When you hit a drum, speak or clap, molecules in the air vibrate. We hear sounds because the vibrations travel through air, or other substances, and hit our ears. (Read more about ears on page 107.)

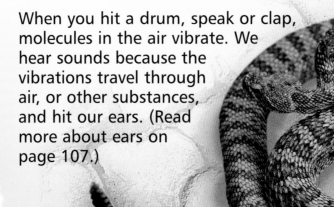

The loudest sounds, such as a rocket lift-off (180 decibels), will damage your ears.

A rattlesnake can make a rattling sound with its tail to scare enemies. The movement of rings on its tail makes molecules in the air vibrate.

Loud and soft

The volume (loudness) of a sound depends on how big the vibrations are. Volume is measured in units called decibels. This chart shows how loud different sounds are in decibels.

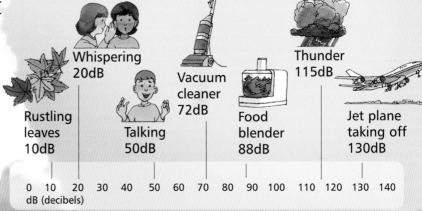

Rustling leaves 10dB

Whispering 20dB

Talking 50dB

Vacuum cleaner 72dB

Food blender 88dB

Thunder 115dB

Jet plane taking off 130dB

0 10 20 30 40 50 60 70 80 90 100 110 120 130 140
dB (decibels)

High and low

Fast sound vibrations make high sounds. Slower sound vibrations make lower sounds. The highness or lowness of a sound is called its pitch. Some animals can hear pitches we can't hear.

Internet links

- Scan the code to watch a video clip of an experiment with high and low sounds.
- For more links, go to **www.usborne.com/quicklinks**

This farmer's whistle makes a very high sound. Dogs can hear it, but people can't.

Elephants can make sounds so low that people can't hear them.

Scientists know that blue whales make the lowest, loudest sound of any animal.

Making music

Musical instruments have parts that vibrate to make sounds. When someone plays an instrument, they make different notes by changing the speed of the vibrations.

On a violin, shorter strings vibrate faster and make higher-pitched notes. Violin players make the strings shorter or longer with their fingers.

Feel sound vibrations

You can't normally feel sound vibrations in the air, but you can in this experiment. You will need:

a radio; a blown-up balloon

Turn the radio on and hold the balloon next to its speaker. The vibrations travel through the balloon and into your fingers.

Electricity

Electricity is a very useful form of energy. It can easily be changed into other forms of energy, such as light and heat. It makes lights, televisions and computers work. Most of the electricity we use comes from power stations.

Lightning is a kind of static electricity that's made when water molecules inside clouds rub together during storms.

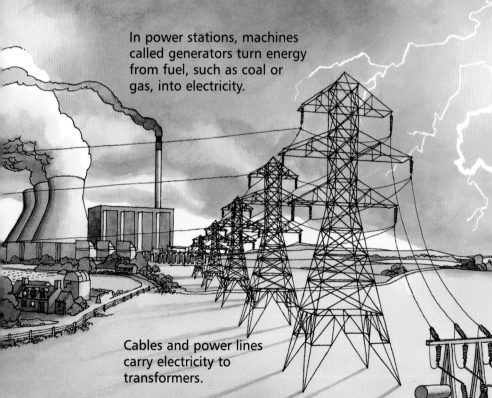

In power stations, machines called generators turn energy from fuel, such as coal or gas, into electricity.

Cables and power lines carry electricity to transformers.

Transformers, like this one, make electricity safe for us to use.

Getting electricity

Electricity travels from power stations to homes along underground cables, or wires attached to high towers. They are kept out of reach, because if electricity touches you, it can give you a dangerous shock.

Here, the cables go underground.

Using electricity

When an appliance, such as a toaster, is plugged in, it is connected to the electricity supply. Electricity flows into it and gives it the energy to work. Plastic does not conduct, or carry, electricity well, so it is used to cover electrical appliances. This stops you from getting a shock.

Can you guess which of these uses the most electricity in one minute?

Answer: the hairdryer

Internet links

- Scan the code to watch a video clip about static electricity.
- For more links, go to www.usborne.com/quicklinks

Static electricity

Static electricity is a form of electricity that builds up in some substances when they are rubbed together. It can make objects stick to each other. Do you ever feel a small shock when you touch metal? This is caused by a small build-up of static in your body as you move around.

Make static electricity

You will need:
a balloon; a sweater

1. Blow up a balloon, and rub it up and down on a sweater a few times.

2. Gently put the balloon on the wall. Static electricity makes it stick there.

Transformer

The orange and yellow lines show the route the cables take underground.

Electricity flows from the underground cables into homes.

Science words

atom one of the very tiny units that everything is made of.

chemical reaction a change that sometimes happens when two materials are mixed together.

contract get smaller.

density how heavy a material is for its size.

electricity a form of energy which is used to make machines work.

energy the power that makes things work. Heat, light, movement and electricity are all forms of energy.

expand get bigger.

experiment a scientific test to find out about how something works.

force a push or a pull. Forces can make things move, stop, speed up, slow down or change shape.

friction a force that slows things down as they rub or slide against each other.

gravity a force that pulls objects toward other objects. (Usually smaller objects to larger objects.)

heat a form of energy which we can feel. It flows from warmer objects into cooler ones.

kinetic energy the kind of energy that something has when it moves.

light a form of energy that we can sense with our eyes.

magnet a piece of metal that pulls some types of metal toward it.

materials the different kinds of stuff all around us, such as water, metal, wood, glass and plastic.

molecules tiny particles made up of atoms. Everything is made of them.

nucleus the central, most important part of an atom.

observe look at something carefully.

particle a very small piece or part.

pitch how high or low a sound is.

poles the parts of a magnet where its pulling power is strongest.

potential energy energy that's stored up and ready to use.

robot a machine that can do a job in a similar way to a person.

science what we know about the Universe and how things work.

technology using science to invent machines and other useful things.

temperature how hot something is.

theory an idea about how something works or why it is the way it is.

Universe everything that exists in space.

upthrust a pushing force that makes things float.

Internet links
- Scan the code to try a science quiz.
- For more links, go to **www.usborne.com/quicklinks**

How things work

Clocks

Most clocks have two or more hands that move around the clock face to show the time. But how does this happen?

Internet links

- Scan the code to see the levers and wheels inside an old clock.
- For more links, go to **www.usborne.com/quicklinks**

What's the time?

To show the right time, the hands on a clock have to move at different speeds from each other. Each time the minute hand moves all the way around the clock face, the hour hand just moves to the next number.

In this picture, parts from the inside of a wind-up clock are all stretched out, so you can see them clearly.

Spring power

A part called the mainspring makes a clock's hands move. This is a curled-up strip of metal that unwinds slowly.

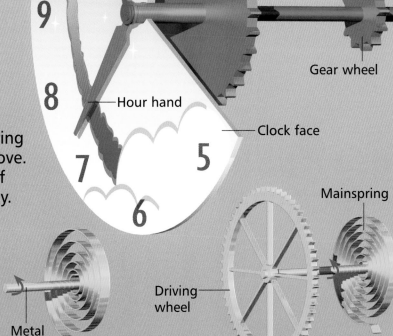

Minute hand

Gear wheel

Gear wheel

Hour hand

Clock face

Mainspring

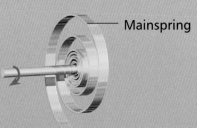

Mainspring

Metal pole

Driving wheel

When you turn a knob on the back of the clock, it winds the spring into a tight roll.

The spring starts to unwind. As it unwinds, it turns a metal pole attached to its middle.

The pole is attached to a driving wheel. As it turns, it makes the driving wheel turn.

214

The lever and escape wheel

The mainspring would unwind all at once without a part called the lever. The lever moves back and forth at the same speed all the time. This controls how fast the mainspring unwinds, as shown here.

Lever

Escape wheel

Lever

Escape wheel

Driving wheel

Escape wheel

As the lever moves forward, it pushes the escape wheel forward one notch.

The lever moves back again, catching the next notch of the escape wheel.

The escape wheel is joined to the driving wheel. Each time the escape wheel moves forward one notch, it lets the driving wheel and mainspring move a little too.

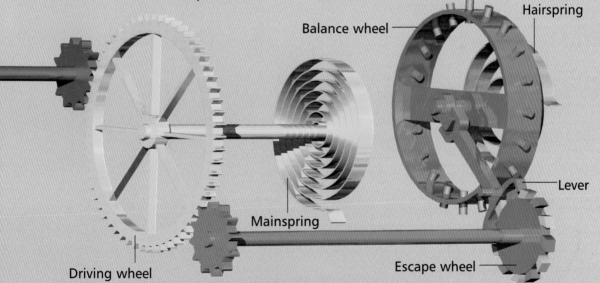

Balance wheel

Hairspring

Lever

Mainspring

Driving wheel

Escape wheel

Gears and teeth

The driving wheel turns little wheels called gears, which make the hands move at different speeds. They are locked together by teeth, so as one moves, it moves the others. The fewer teeth a gear has, the faster it moves.

A tooth

The small gear moves around faster than the big one, because it has fewer teeth.

215

Cameras

Cameras are small machines used for taking photos. Many digital devices, from mobile phones to tablets, have built-in cameras.

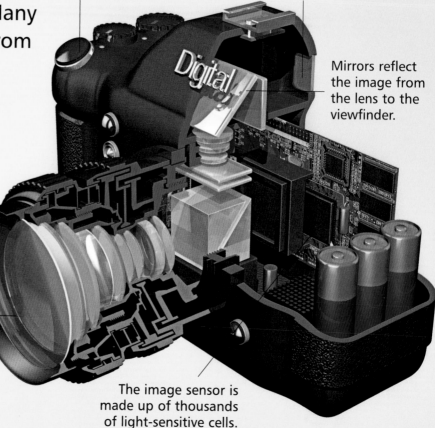

You push this button to take a photo.

This is the viewfinder. You look through it to see your subject (what you're taking a picture of).

Mirrors reflect the image from the lens to the viewfinder.

In this picture, parts of an SLR camera have been cut away, so you can see inside.

This glass lens lets light into the camera.

The image sensor is made up of thousands of light-sensitive cells.

Taking pictures

When light shines on things it reflects, or bounces, off them. This allows you to see them. A camera also uses light reflecting off things to take pictures. A sensor in the camera detects reflected light to create a photo of what you're seeing.

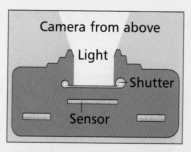

Inside the camera, a flap called the shutter covers the sensor. It stops any light from touching it. If you press the button, the shutter opens...

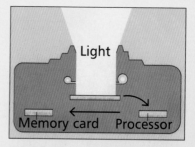

Light enters the lens and hits the sensor, which captures the photo. A processor stores the photo on a memory card as a digital image file.

Browsing

Most cameras have a screen where you can see your stored photos and decide which to keep and which to delete. For many cameras, the screen also functions as a viewfinder.

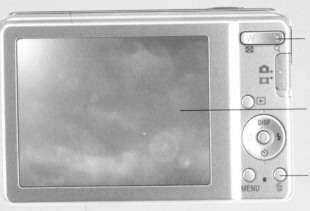

The zoom button lets you see your photos up close.

Screen/viewfinder

The trash button lets you delete your photos.

Internet links

- Scan the code to hear how digital cameras make photos.
- For more links, go to **www.usborne.com/quicklinks**

Uploading photos

Pictures from digital cameras can be loaded directly onto a home computer so that you can see them on a larger screen. Photos can be printed out, uploaded to a website, or sent to other computers or phones by email.

Digital photos are made up of tiny squares called pixels.

Movies

A movie is made from a sequence of photos, called frames, shown very quickly one after another. Movies used to be shown using film projectors. Today, digital projectors are used instead.

This small digital projector is for watching movies at home. Projectors in movie theaters are much larger, with powerful cooling fans to keep them from overheating.

Digital

A lamp inside the projector sends a strong beam of light across a liquid crystal display (LCD). The display is covered in thousands of color cells, which make up the frames. The light leaves through a lens and projects the frames onto a screen.

Cooling fans

The light exits the projector through the lens.

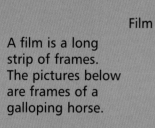

Reel

Film

Lens

A film is a long strip of frames. The pictures below are frames of a galloping horse.

Film

A film projector has two big wheels, called reels. The reels turn, winding the film off the top reel and onto the bottom one. Each frame of the film passes in front of a bulb, which shines a bright light through it.

Moving pictures

Most projectors show 24 frames every second. This is much too fast for you to be able to see one frame changing to the next. This makes it look like one, moving picture.

When the light hits the movie screen, it makes a much bigger copy of the frame in the projector.

Internet links

- Scan the code to watch a video clip about how to make a simple animation.
- For more links, go to www.usborne.com/quicklinks

Make your own flipbook movie

A flipbook works in the same way as a movie. Here's how to make a mini-movie of somebody jumping up and down:

1. Get a notebook and draw a stick person, like the one here, on the last page.

2. On the page before, draw another person, just starting to jump up in the air.

3. Keep doing this until you have pictures of the person jumping up and down.

4. Flip through the pictures quickly. It will look like a film of the person jumping.

Televisions

Have you ever wondered where television programs come from and how they reach your screen? And if you could look inside a television screen, what would you see?

Flat-screen television

Screens

Most televisions made today use either a plasma or LCD (liquid crystal display) screen. Both work by charging thousands of tiny cells with electricity to create a picture. The cells in a plasma screen are made from pockets of gas. The cells in an LCD screen are made up of 'liquid crystals'.

Glass panels

These red, blue and green cells are pockets of gas. Each block of red, blue and green cells is called a pixel.

Here, the layers of a plasma screen have been separated so you can see them.

Pictures

Televisions work like movies by showing lots of pictures quickly, one after another. Each picture on a television is made up of tiny lines.

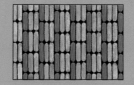

The cells on a television screen create a grid of tiny red, blue and green lines.

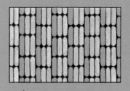

When you turn the television on, electricity charges the cells, making them glow.

The lines are so tiny that the colors seem to mix, making all the colors you see on the screen.

Getting the pictures

TV programs are made in TV studios. Then they are turned into invisible signals called radio waves and sent into the air (see page 223). Below, you can see how the radio waves get to your TV set.

(see page 223)

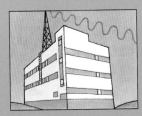

A TV station sends radio waves out to a transmitter tower. They travel quickly through the air.

Transmitter towers pick up the radio waves and send them in all directions. This is called broadcasting.

Radio waves from a transmitter tower can travel a long way to reach lots of TV sets.

Antenna

Antennae collect waves and pass them to televisions by a cable. TVs turn them back into programs.

Satellite TV

Some TV signals come from spacecraft called satellites. Satellites orbit (travel around) the Earth. They can cover a much bigger area than transmitter towers.

Satellite TV sets pick up radio waves from space using a kind of antenna called a satellite dish.

This satellite in space picks up radio waves and broadcasts them back to Earth.

A TV station sends radio waves into space.

Sound systems

Sound systems are devices used for listening to music or the radio. Some have lots of different parts.

Internet links

- Scan the code for a video clip that shows how speakers work.
- For more links, go to **www.usborne.com/quicklinks**

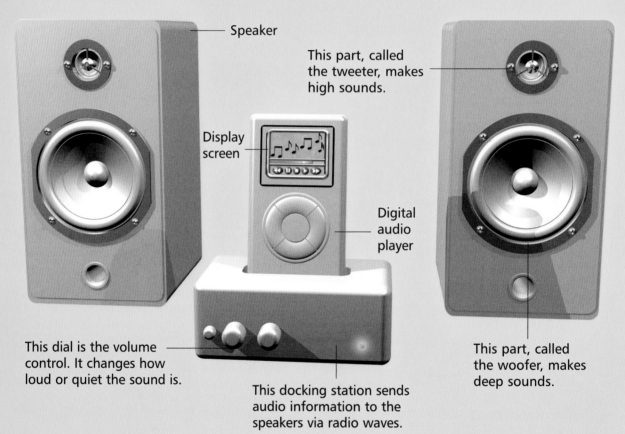

Speaker

This part, called the tweeter, makes high sounds.

Display screen

Digital audio player

This dial is the volume control. It changes how loud or quiet the sound is.

This docking station sends audio information to the speakers via radio waves.

This part, called the woofer, makes deep sounds.

Digital audio players

Digital audio players play files such as MP3s, downloaded from the internet or copied from CDs. Audio files store sound in code, which is read by software and broadcast through headphones or speakers.

Speakers

Most sounds are made by making air move quickly.* Parts inside a speaker shake to make the air around them move. This turns audio signals sent from an audio player into sounds you can hear.

*Find out more on pages 208-209.

CD players

CDs have sound stored on them in code. Inside a CD player, a CD spins around very fast. A thin beam of light, called a laser beam, shines onto the CD and reads the code.

Speaker

CDs go on a tray, which slides in and out of the CD player.

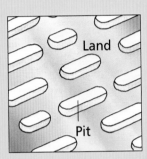

Land

Pit

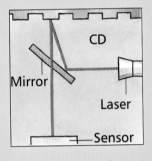

CD

Mirror

Laser

Sensor

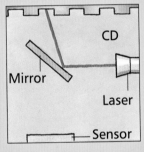

CD

Mirror

Laser

Sensor

The coded sound is on the underside of a CD. The code is made of flat parts, called land, and dips, called pits.

A laser beam reflects off a mirror onto the spinning CD. If it hits land it bounces off, and hits a sensor.

If the beam hits a pit, it doesn't bounce off. The sensor can tell from this that the beam has hit a pit.

The CD player turns the sound information from the sensor into another code, which it sends to the speaker.

Radios and radio waves

Radio stations make programs and send them into the air as radio waves. Radio waves are invisible signals that can carry information. Radios pick up the signals and play the programs.

Some radio waves 'bounce' between the earth and the atmosphere.

Some radio waves travel in straight lines.

223

Telephones

Telephones all over our planet are
linked together, so people can talk
to each other wherever
they are in the world.

This telephone has some
of its plastic case cut
away, so you can see the
electrical parts inside.

The part you listen to
is called the speaker.

The plug fits into a
socket in the wall.
Wires in the wall give
it power and link the
phone to others.

The part you
speak into is
called the
mouthpiece.

Sending signals

If you call a friend, your phone
sends a signal to his or her phone.
This only takes a few seconds, even
if your friend lives a long way away.

1. When you dial,
it sends a signal
out of your phone
and down a wire.

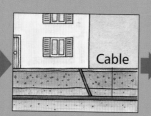

Cable

2. The wire carries
the signal out of your
home to a bigger
wire, called a cable,
under the ground.

3. The cable carries
the signal to a
telephone exchange –
a building full
of computers.

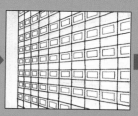

4. The computers at
the exchange read the
number you dialed.
It tells them where
to send the signal.

Cell phones

Cell phones send signals called radio waves (see page 223) to connect to other phones. The waves travel through the air, so cell phones can be used almost anywhere.

To make a call, a cell phone sends out radio waves. The waves are picked up by the nearest transmitter tower.

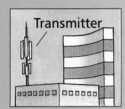

Radio waves

There are transmitter towers all over the world. They are linked to switching stations, full of computers.

Transmitter

To make a cell phone ring, a station sends out radio waves to lots of towers. The phone picks them up from the nearest one.

This is a smartphone: a cell phone with extra features, such as internet access and a camera.

This is the speaker.

This shows how much power is left in the battery.

This screen shows what your phone can do, such as make calls or write messages.

This is the camera button. You press it to take a photo.

This button accepts calls.

This button ends calls. It is also the power button.

Radio waves

5. Signals are sent along cables. For very long distances, they are sent via satellites as radio waves.

6. The signal travels to the exchange nearest your friend's home. There are exchanges all over the world.

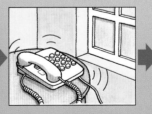

7. This exchange sends the signal to your friend's home. It travels to the phone and makes it ring.

8. Your friend picks up the phone. This connects the two phones, so you can talk to each other.

225

Computers

Computers can help people to do all kinds of things, from writing letters to flying space rockets. They can store information and do complex calculations very fast.

This is called the systems unit. In this picture, parts have been cut away so you can see inside.

You can put CDs in the CD drive to play games or get information.

The monitor shows information as words and pictures.

This is the central processing unit (CPU). It has a fan on top which keeps it cool.

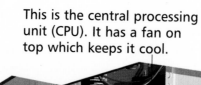

This fan keeps the unit cool.

This is the hard drive. It has hard disks inside which store information.

★

You use the keyboard, together with the mouse, to tell the computer what to do.

Mouse

Computer brain

Inside the systems unit, the part of the computer called the CPU, or the central processing unit, is like the computer's brain. It works things out and tells all the other parts what to do.

Computer programs

Computers can't actually think for themselves. People have to write sets of instructions for them, called programs. These are stored inside the systems unit in the hard disks. The computer uses these instructions to carry out tasks.

Using a program called Microsoft® Paint, you can draw pictures using a computer.

Sending messages

The different parts of a computer are used for doing different tasks. To work, the computer sends messages between the different parts.

You press a key on the keyboard. This sends a message down a wire into the systems unit.

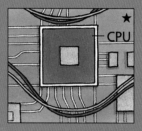

Inside the systems unit, a message is sent to the CPU. The CPU works out what to do.

A message is sent to the monitor. The screen shows you what the computer has done.

Useful robots

Robots have computers inside them that make them work a little like people or animals. They can be used in factories to make cars or other things. Scientists are now trying to create robots that can learn things by themselves, like people can.

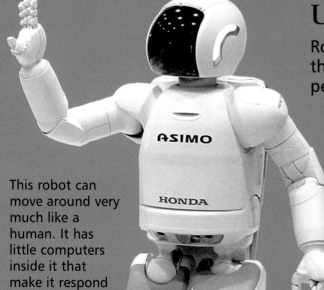

This robot can move around very much like a human. It has little computers inside it that make it respond to different commands.

Internet links

• Scan the code to watch a video clip about robots.

• For more links, go to www.usborne.com/quicklinks

227

The Internet

Computers can be linked together to share information. A group of linked computers is called a network. The biggest network in the world is called the Internet.

Some computers send messages to satellites in space. Satellites send them to other computers.

Computers can be attached to telephone lines. Information travels along these lines.

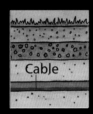

Cable

Some computers are connected by cables. Cables go under the ground or under the sea.

Websites

Part of the Internet is called the World Wide Web. The Web is made up of websites, which are pages of information. There are all kinds of different websites - some provide services to people, while others are created just for entertainment. They are stored on powerful computers called servers.

Emails

Some servers can send messages called emails between computers. Emails can be sent and received within seconds, allowing people to exchange information quickly.

An email message

Social networking

Many people use social networking websites to connect with their friends online. The websites allow people to share their interests and activities with each other, and interact via the Web.

Internet links
- Scan the code to hear how computers share information.
- For more links, go to www.usborne.com/quicklinks

Addresses

There are millions of websites on servers all over the world. To help you find the one you want, each site has its own Web address.

This is a website address.

http:// www.usborne.com

"www" stands for World Wide Web.

Finding a site

To find and show you a website, a computer uses a program called a browser, and a device called a modem. Most computers have a modem inside them. They help computers get and send information down a phone line. Follow the numbers to see how.

Your computer

1. You type the website address into a browser on your computer.

4. Your computer's modem turns the information back into a Web page.

A server

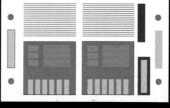

3. The server finds the Web page. It sends the information to your computer.

2. The modem turns the address into information that can travel down a phone line, and sends it to a server.

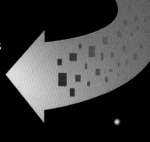

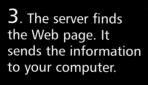

Refrigerators

Food stays fresh longer if it is kept in a refrigerator. A refrigerator stays cool by pumping liquid refrigerant through pipes.

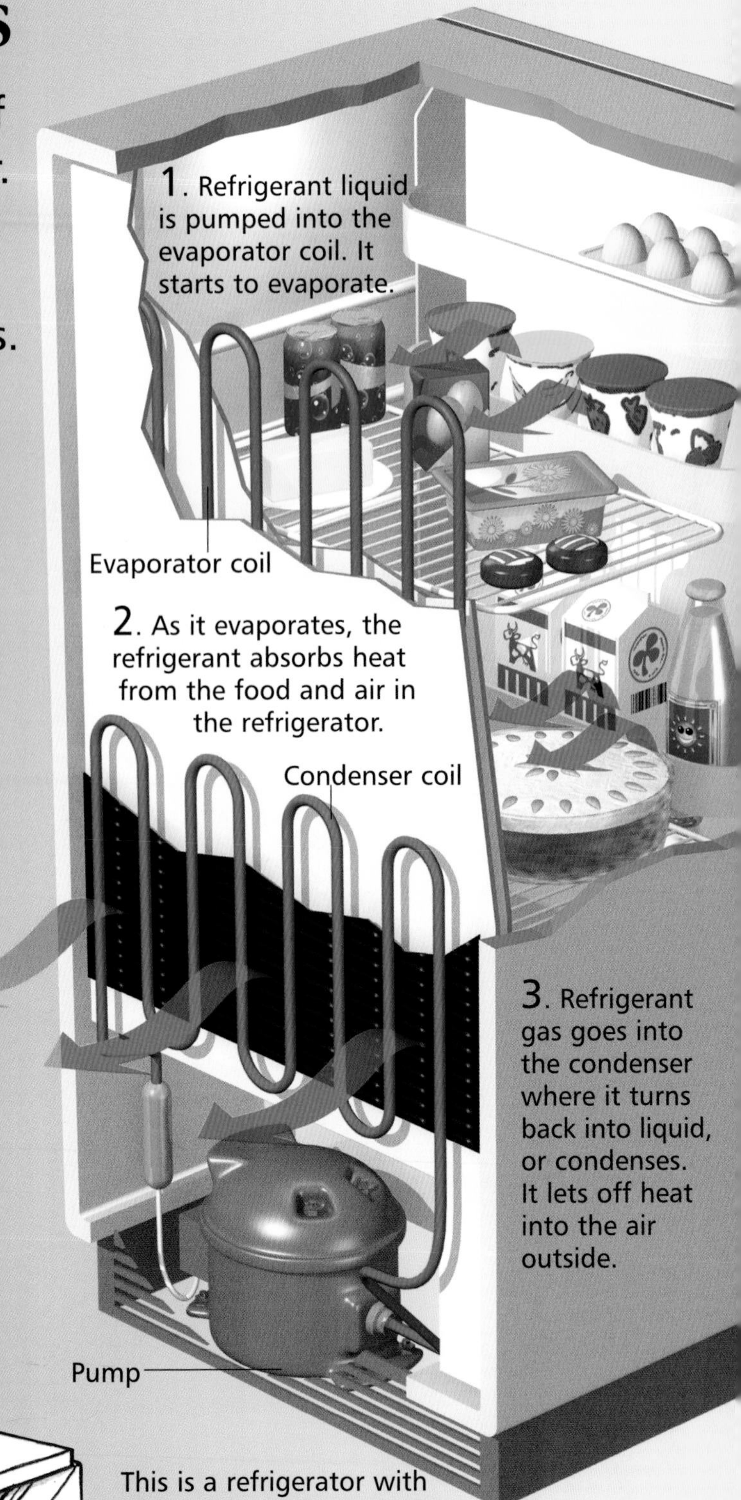

Keeping cool

When you get wet, your skin cools down as it dries. This is because the water turns into a gas, or evaporates. As liquid evaporates, it absorbs heat, and this is also what keeps a refrigerator cool. Follow the numbers on the big picture on the right to see how.

Red arrows show heat.

The light inside

The light inside a refrigerator comes on whenever you open the door. When you shut the door, it presses against a switch, turning the light off.

When the refrigerator door opens, the switch pops up and the light comes on.

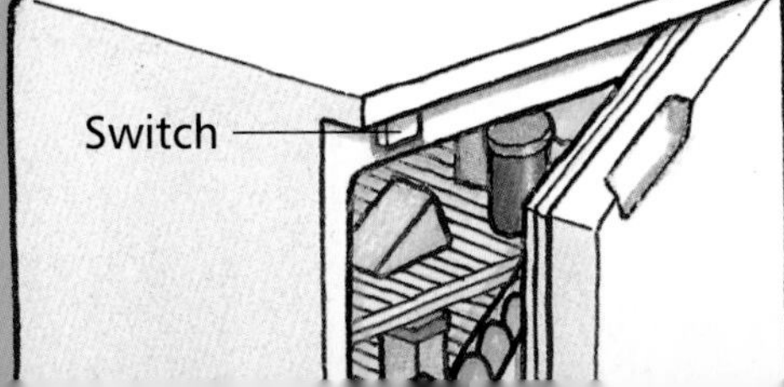

Switch

1. Refrigerant liquid is pumped into the evaporator coil. It starts to evaporate.

Evaporator coil

2. As it evaporates, the refrigerant absorbs heat from the food and air in the refrigerator.

Condenser coil

3. Refrigerant gas goes into the condenser where it turns back into liquid, or condenses. It lets off heat into the air outside.

Pump

This is a refrigerator with parts cut away so you can see how it works.

★

Microwave ovens

A microwave oven can heat up food much more quickly than a normal oven can. To do this, it uses invisible waves called microwaves.

Internet links

• Scan the code to see how a microwave oven works.

• For more links, go to www.usborne.com/quicklinks

Hot and cold

Everything in the world is made up of very tiny parts called atoms.* They are much too small to see, but when something gets hot, it's because the atoms in it are moving quickly.

When something is cold, the atoms in it move slowly.

In something hot, the atoms move more quickly.

Bouncing waves

A microwave is a kind of radio wave (see page 223). Microwaves can travel through the air and through water, too. Food contains water, so microwaves can travel through it. When they do this, they make all the atoms move around more quickly. This heats the food up.

Microwaves are invisible but the red arrows show how they travel.

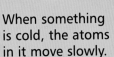

Magnetron – this makes the microwaves.

★

Part of this microwave oven has been cut away, so that you can see inside.

This plate turns around so the microwaves go into all parts of the food.

Microwaves bounce off the oven's metal walls.

*Find out more on pages 186-187.

Toilets and faucets

The water you use in your home probably comes from a place called a reservoir. Linked-up water pipes carry it to toilets, faucets and showers around the house. This is called plumbing.

1. A main service pipe brings water into a house.

Water tank

2. The water is stored in a tank. Two pipes come out of it.

Toilet

Sink

Shower

3. One pipe goes to this tank, called a cylinder, which heats the water.

4. Dirty water leaves through pipes called drainpipes.

Main service pipe

Drainpipe

Reservoirs are enormous man-made lakes. Water is stored in them until it is needed.

Down the drain

Dirty water and waste from toilets flows through underground pipes to places called sewage stations. At a sewage station, all the dirt and waste is removed, so that the water can be used again.

The picture on the right shows a sewage station from the air. The dark circles are enormous tanks of dirty water.

232

Around the bend

Water for flushing a toilet is stored in a tank called a cistern. Here's what happens when you flush:

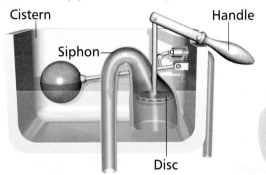

When you push the handle, the disc lifts up. This pushes water over the top of the siphon. As the water falls, it sucks the rest of the water with it.

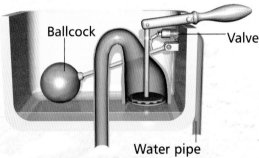

As the cistern empties, the disc drops, and a float, called a ballcock, drops too. This pulls a valve out of the pipe so more water flows into the cistern.

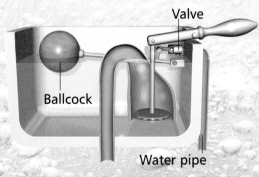

As the cistern fills again, the ballcock rises. When it is full, the ballcock pushes the valve back into the pipe. This stops any more water from getting in.

Internet links

- Scan the code for fun facts about toilets.
- For more links, go to **www.usborne.com/quicklinks**

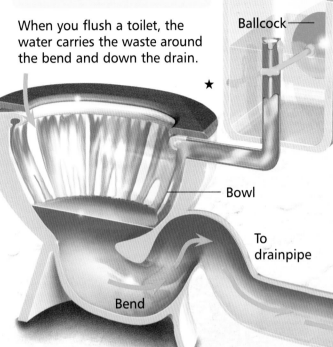

When you flush a toilet, the water carries the waste around the bend and down the drain.

★

Turning a faucet

Inside a faucet, there is a long screw with a disc, called a washer, on the end. When you turn the faucet handle, it turns the screw. This moves the washer up to turn the faucet on, or down to turn it off.

★ The washer plugs the hole to turn the faucet off.

233

Cars and motorcycles

Cars and other vehicles, such as trucks, vans and motorcycles, have engines in them to make them go. They need fuel to make the engines work.

This is the engine.

There are four of these cylinders inside this engine. Each cylinder has a piston inside it.

Spark plug

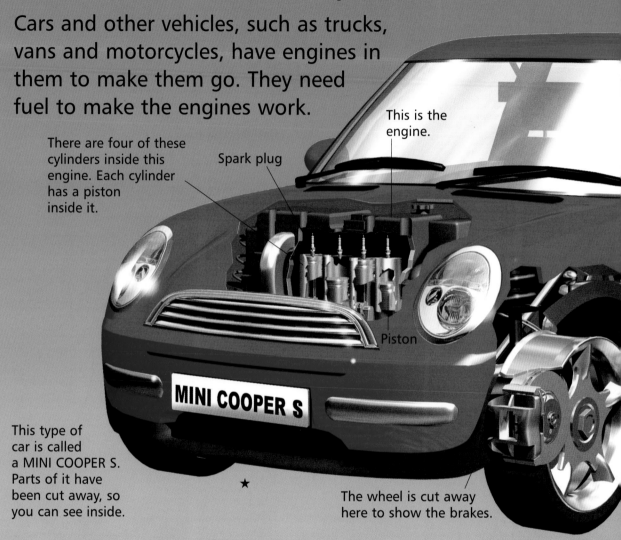

Piston

MINI COOPER S

This type of car is called a MINI COOPER S. Parts of it have been cut away, so you can see inside.

★

The wheel is cut away here to show the brakes.

How does the engine work?

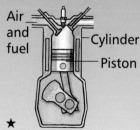

Air and fuel

Cylinder

Piston

★

A piston inside the cylinder moves down, sucking air and fuel into the cylinder.

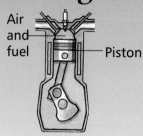

Air and fuel

Piston

The piston then moves up again. This squashes the air and the fuel together.

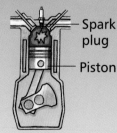

Spark plug

Piston

The spark plug lights the fuel. It burns with a bang, pushing the piston down.

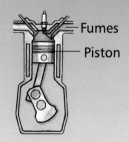

Fumes

Piston

There are fumes left. The piston moves up, pushing them out of the cylinder.

Internet links
• Scan code to see a motorcycle rider.
• For more links, go to
www.usborne.com/quicklinks

An exhaust pipe takes fumes away from the engine.

How the wheels turn

The pistons in an engine are connected to a pole called the crankshaft. As they go up and down, they turn the crankshaft, which makes the driveshafts turn. The driveshafts make the front wheels go around.

The whole car is pulled along by the front wheels.

Piston

Driveshaft

Crankshaft

Fuel tank

Exhaust pipe

Motorcycles

Motorcycles work in a similar way to cars. They have smaller engines than cars, but can accelerate (speed up) much quicker. A driver twists the handles on a motorcycle to accelerate.

Disc brakes

Cars and motorcycles have kinds of brakes called disc brakes to make them slow down or stop.

When you press a car's brake pedal, a liquid called brake fluid is pushed down a pipe to the brake pads.

A rider makes the bike lean all the way over to go around bends.

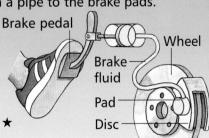

Brake pedal

Wheel

Brake fluid

Pad

Disc

★

The pads push on the discs. The discs grip the wheels which stops them from turning.

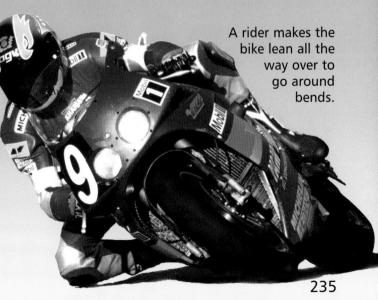

235

Excavators

An excavator is a machine for digging large holes. The kind of excavator you can see here is called a backhoe excavator. It uses a metal bucket, called a backhoe, to dig into the ground.

Internet links

- Scan the code for facts on excavators and other machines.
- For more links, go to www.usborne.com/quicklinks

These parts move the excavator's arm.

These hinges allow the arm to move.

The excavator's body can spin around.

This is the excavator's arm.

When it's muddy, these crawler tracks help the excavator to grip.

Teeth

The backhoe's metal teeth cut into the earth, helping it to dig.

Moving the arm

An excavator's arm moves using metal discs, called pistons, inside oil-filled tubes, called cylinders. These are attached to different parts of the arm by metal rods. The driver can move the pistons up and down in the cylinders, making parts of the arm move. Here's how the driver moves the backhoe:

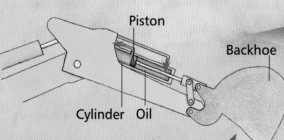

Piston

Backhoe

Cylinder   Oil

The driver pulls a lever. Oil pumps into the bottom and out of the top of a cylinder. This pushes the piston up, pulling the backhoe up.

Oil   Piston

Cylinder

Pushing the lever makes oil pump into the top and out of the bottom of the cylinder. This pushes the piston down, which pushes the backhoe down.

Backhoe

Tractors

Tractors' big engines are extremely powerful. This makes them useful for lifting and pulling heavy things.

This shows a tractor with part of the front cut away, so you can see inside.

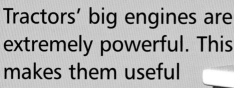

Tractors move slowly, so their engines don't use much fuel.

The part where the driver sits is called the cab.

Large wheels with tough tires help tractors to keep their grip in mud.

Tools can be attached to these metal links at the back of a tractor.

Power tools

At the back of a tractor there's a metal pole called a power take-off, or PTO. Tools connected to the PTO get power from the tractor's engine. Below are two of the tools that a farmer can attach to a tractor to do different jobs.

This is the PTO (power take-off). It is connected to the tractor's engine.

Post driver

Hay baler

A post driver bangs fence posts into the ground. The farmer moves it to where he wants to put a post.

When the farmer presses a button, a big weight rises and falls, hammering the post into the ground.

A hay baler collects up dried grass, called hay. Tubes inside it spin, rolling the hay into a cylinder called a bale.

When the baler is full, it opens, and the new bale rolls out. The hay can be used for feeding farm animals.

Trains

Trains move along specially
built tracks to take people
and things from one place to
another. They often travel
huge distances: the longest
train track in the world
is over 5,500 miles long.

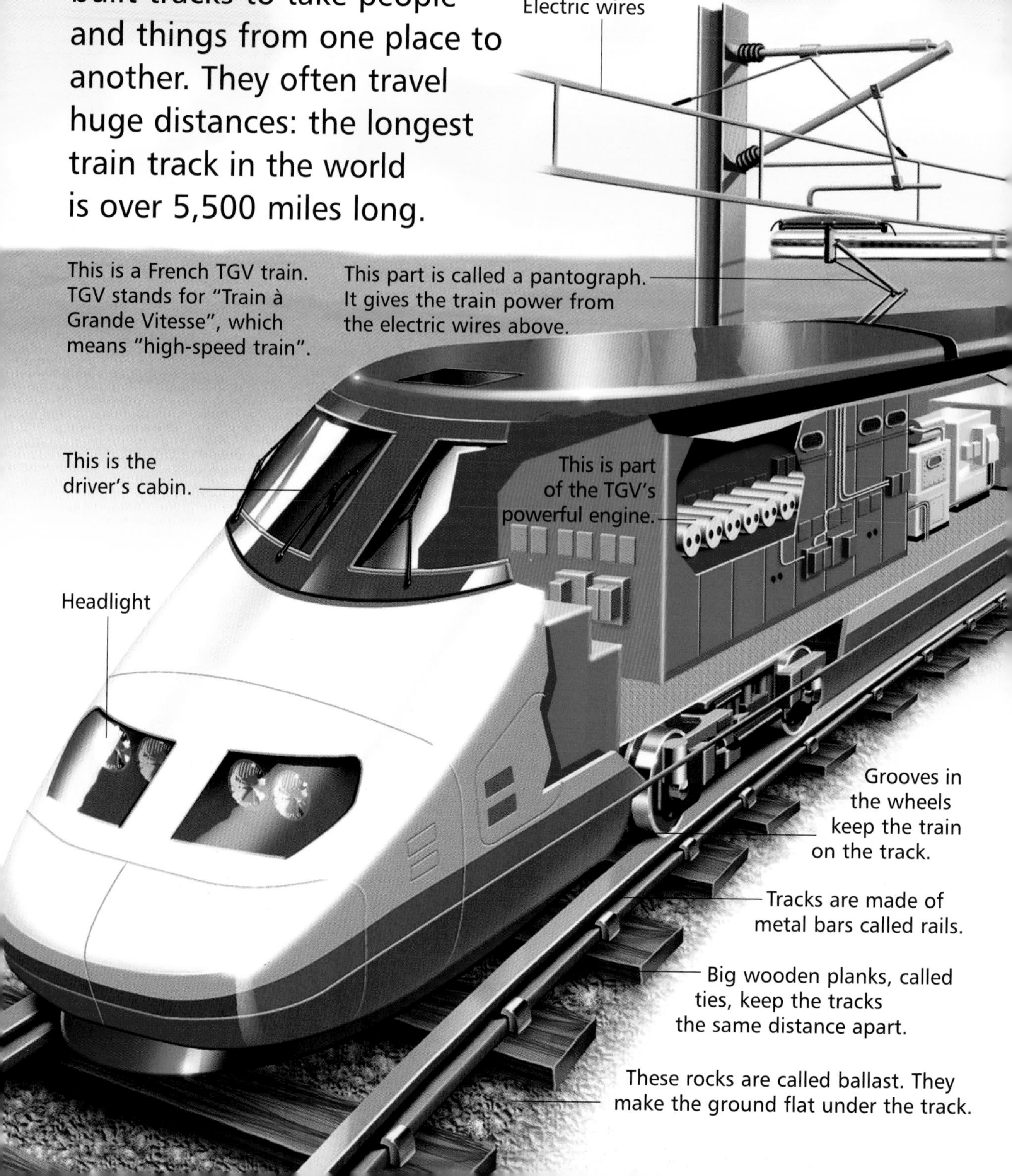

Electric wires

This is a French TGV train.
TGV stands for "Train à
Grande Vitesse", which
means "high-speed train".

This part is called a pantograph.
It gives the train power from
the electric wires above.

This is the
driver's cabin.

This is part
of the TGV's
powerful engine.

Headlight

Grooves in
the wheels
keep the train
on the track.

Tracks are made of
metal bars called rails.

Big wooden planks, called
ties, keep the tracks
the same distance apart.

These rocks are called ballast. They
make the ground flat under the track.

Getting faster

Scientists are always looking for ways to make faster trains. This train, called a maglev, doesn't even touch the rail. It uses magnets to push it through the air.

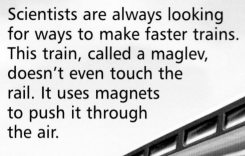

Magnets on the sides of the train push it along very quickly.

Magnets on the bottom of the train pull it toward the rail.

A Japanese Bullet Train can travel at more than 180mph.

The sections of a train are called cars.

Most TGV cars have seats for up to 60 passengers.

In the driver's seat

The train driver sits in a cabin, called the control cabin, at the front of the train. The picture below shows the controls inside the cabin of a TGV train.

This button stops the train very quickly in an emergency.

This lever controls the speed of the train.

This shows how fast the train is going.

The driver can talk to the controller on this radio.

★

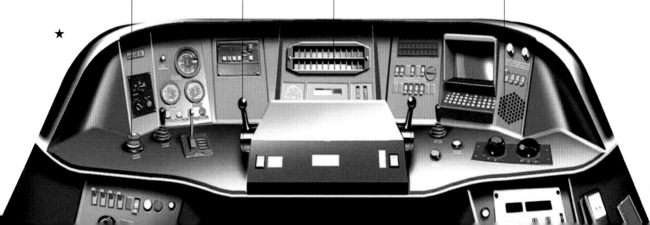

Planes

Flying in a plane is the fastest way you can travel. Planes are able to fly because they have powerful engines and specially shaped wings.

Internet links
- Scan the code to watch a plane take off and fly.
- For more links, go to www.usborne.com/quicklinks

Take-off

A plane's wings are more curved on the top than on the bottom. This shape is called an airfoil. Follow the numbers below to see how it helps a plane to take off and fly.

The tip of this plane's wing shows the airfoil shape.

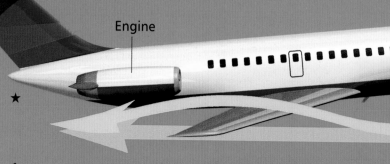

Engine

These arrows show how the air flows.

1. The plane's powerful engines make it go forward very quickly. Air rushes past the wings.

2. Because of the airfoil shape, air flows faster over the tops of the wings than underneath them.

3. The air under the wing pushes up more than the air on top of it pushes down. This lifts the plane up.

Make a wing

See how air flowing fast over one side of a piece of paper makes it lift, like a plane's wing. You will need:

a piece of thin paper, 2in x 6in

1. Hold the short side of the paper to your lips, letting it hang down.

2. Blow across the top of the paper. It will lift up into the air.

Concorde planes could fly at supersonic speed (faster than the speed of sound), but they aren't in use any more. They had very pointed noses, which let the air flow past smoothly so they could travel faster.

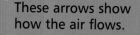

These arrows show how the air flows.

Steering the plane

Planes have parts on their wings and tails that can move. To make the plane go in different directions, the pilot uses the controls to move these parts.

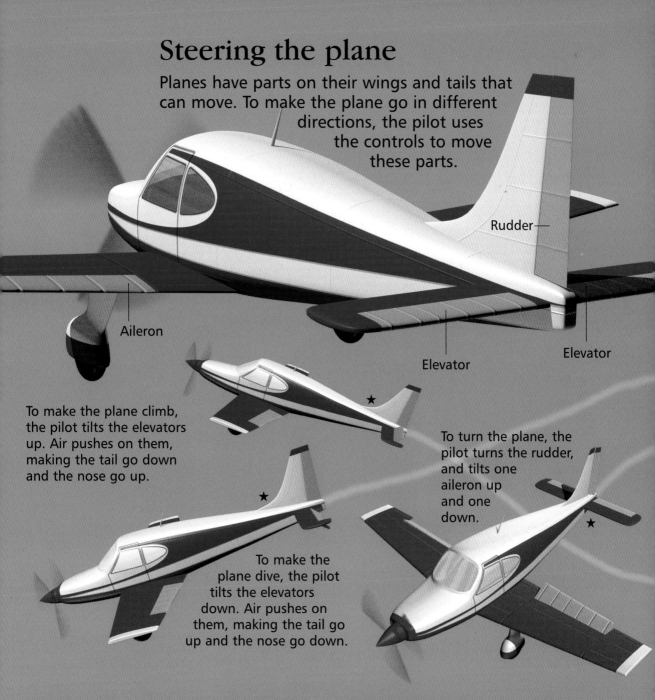

Rudder

Aileron

Elevator

Elevator

To make the plane climb, the pilot tilts the elevators up. Air pushes on them, making the tail go down and the nose go up.

To turn the plane, the pilot turns the rudder, and tilts one aileron up and one down.

To make the plane dive, the pilot tilts the elevators down. Air pushes on them, making the tail go up and the nose go down.

Flight control

The pilot controls the plane from the cockpit at the front. Inside the cockpit, the control panel of a small plane looks like this.

This dial shows how high in the sky the plane is flying.

This dial shows the direction in which the plane is flying.

The pilot moves these controls to steer the plane.

Ships and boats

Ships and boats are often used for carrying people or heavy things around the world. Big boats are called ships. Some, like this cruise ship, can hold up to two thousand passengers.

In this picture of a cruise ship some parts have been cut away, so you can see inside.

Lifeboats like this can be used in emergencies.

The back of a ship is called its stern.

Four propellers push the ship forward.

Four engines power the propellers.

Internet links
- Scan the code to see some of the world's biggest cruise ships.
- For more links, go to www.usborne.com/quicklinks

How do boats float?

If you could put an enormous lump of metal that weighed the same as a boat into the sea, it would sink. A boat can float because it is hollow, and because of its special shape. You can find more about how things float on pages 200-201.

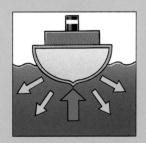

When a boat is in water, it pushes downwards. The water pushes back, which makes the boat float. This is called upthrust (see page 200).

Make your own boat

Try this to see how a boat's shape makes it float. You will need:

a large bowl of water; a lump of modeling clay

1. Take the clay and roll it into a ball. Put it in the bowl of water. It will sink.

2. Cup the clay in one hand. Use your thumb to make it into a boat shape.

3. Put the clay in the water again. This time its shape will help it to float.

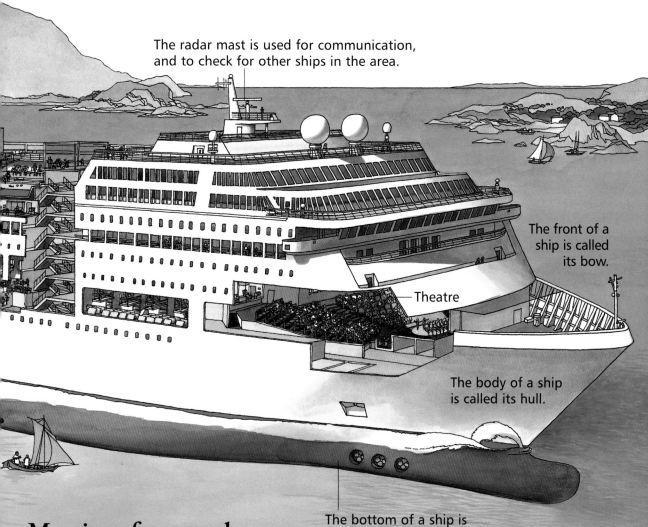

The radar mast is used for communication, and to check for other ships in the area.

The front of a ship is called its bow.

Theatre

The body of a ship is called its hull.

The bottom of a ship is called its keel. It keeps the ship steady in the water.

Moving forward

Boats need power to move through the water. Here are some of the different ways they can get it.

Engine

Oar

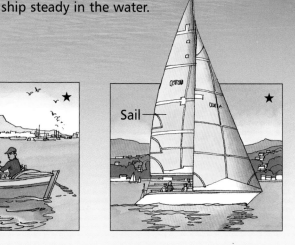

Sail

Some boats have engines attached to propellers. The propellers spin around and push the boat forward.

Rowboats have oars with flat ends. The rower pulls the oars through the water. This pushes the boat along.

A sailboat, or yacht, has tall sails. The wind blows against them and pushes the boat through the water.

Submersibles and submarines

Submarines are machines that people can use to travel underwater. Small submarines, called submersibles, are used for exploring the oceans. Below is a submersible called Deep Flight.

This picture shows the Deep Flight submersible in use.

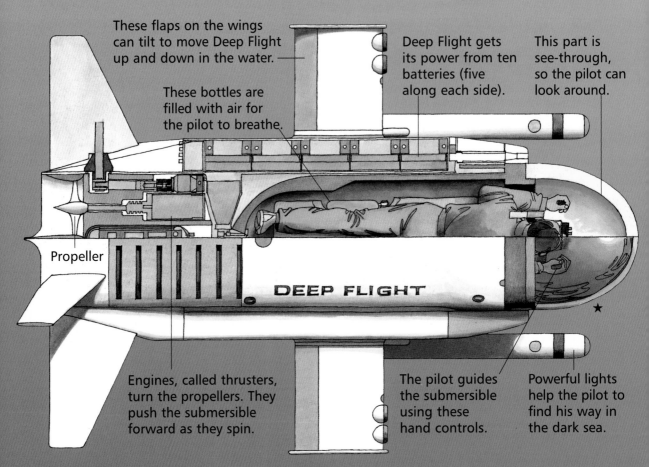

These flaps on the wings can tilt to move Deep Flight up and down in the water.

These bottles are filled with air for the pilot to breathe.

Deep Flight gets its power from ten batteries (five along each side).

This part is see-through, so the pilot can look around.

Propeller

DEEP FLIGHT

Engines, called thrusters, turn the propellers. They push the submersible forward as they spin.

The pilot guides the submersible using these hand controls.

Powerful lights help the pilot to find his way in the dark sea.

Going down

Deep Flight uses its wings to go up and down, but big submarines rise and sink in a different way.

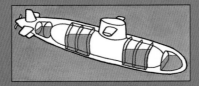

To dive down, tanks inside a submarine fill with water. This makes it heavy, so it sinks.

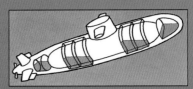

To come up, the water is pumped out. This makes the submarine lighter, so it rises.

Space

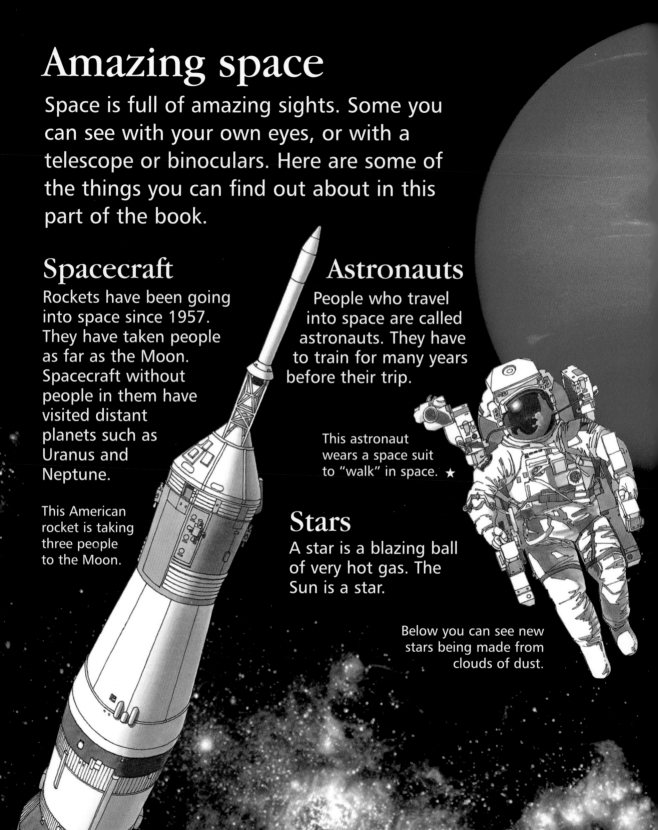

Amazing space

Space is full of amazing sights. Some you can see with your own eyes, or with a telescope or binoculars. Here are some of the things you can find out about in this part of the book.

Spacecraft

Rockets have been going into space since 1957. They have taken people as far as the Moon. Spacecraft without people in them have visited distant planets such as Uranus and Neptune.

This American rocket is taking three people to the Moon.

Astronauts

People who travel into space are called astronauts. They have to train for many years before their trip.

This astronaut wears a space suit to "walk" in space. ★

Stars

A star is a blazing ball of very hot gas. The Sun is a star.

Below you can see new stars being made from clouds of dust.

The planet
Neptune

Moons

Most planets have
moons. These are
mini-planets
which travel
around other
planets.

This is Io, one of
Jupiter's moons.

Planets

A planet is an enormous ball of rock or
gas which travels around a star. A group
of planets moving around a star is known
as a solar system.

The planet Saturn

Comets

Comets are balls of dirty
ice, which fly around in
space. Sometimes
they crash into planets.

This is
a comet. ★

Galaxies

Galaxies are huge groups of stars. Our
Sun and its solar system are in a galaxy
called the Milky Way. Scientists think
there are billions of galaxies in space.

This galaxy is called
the Sombrero Galaxy.
It has millions of stars.

Trips into space

People have only been sending rockets into space since 1957. Before then, rockets fell back to the ground before they could reach space. They were not powerful enough to go any farther.

The space shuttle

The first man went into space in 1961. Since then, hundreds of people have followed. From 1981 to 2011, astronauts flew into space in a rocket called a space shuttle. This is how it worked.

Tailfin

When it returned from space, the shuttle's wings helped it to glide back to Earth.

Astronauts had to wear spacesuits to go into the cargo bay or outside the space shuttle.

USA

Endeavour

Booster rocket

Fuel tank

1. The shuttle blasted off from Earth.

2. Two booster rockets fell away when their fuel ran out, and parachuted back to Earth.

3. The main engine took the shuttle into space. The big fuel tank fell away when it was empty.

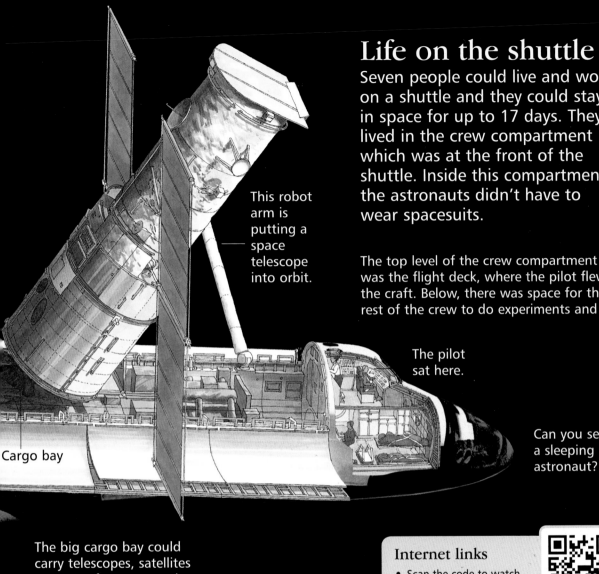

Life on the shuttle

Seven people could live and work on a shuttle and they could stay in space for up to 17 days. They lived in the crew compartment which was at the front of the shuttle. Inside this compartment the astronauts didn't have to wear spacesuits.

The top level of the crew compartment was the flight deck, where the pilot flew the craft. Below, there was space for the rest of the crew to do experiments and rest.

This robot arm is putting a space telescope into orbit.

The pilot sat here.

Cargo bay

Can you see a sleeping astronaut?

The big cargo bay could carry telescopes, satellites or parts of a space station.

Internet links

- Scan the code to watch astronauts board a shuttle and launch into space.
- For more links, go to **www.usborne.com/quicklinks**

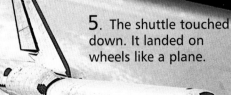

4. On its return, the shuttle glided back though the Earth's atmosphere. Its underside got very hot.

5. The shuttle touched down. It landed on wheels like a plane.

United States

A walk in space

Space is deadly. There is no air to breathe, so outside a spacecraft, an astronaut must wear an outfit called a spacesuit to stay alive. Spacesuits are like body-size spaceships, with their own air and water supplies.

A spacesuit has several very thin but strong layers. These protect the astronaut from tiny meteoroids, and the heat and cold of space.

A camera on the helmet films what the astronaut is doing.

Because his face is hidden by his helmet, this stripe shows other astronauts who is in this spacesuit.

Lights on the helmet help the astronaut to see in the dark.

The suit is flexible enough to allow easy movement.

The astronaut can control the equipment in a spacesuit from this unit.

Walk to work

Astronauts make space walks to repair satellites, build space stations or check the outside of their spaceships. On these pages you can see two American astronauts making a space walk from their space shuttle.

Internet links
- Scan the code to see how an astronaut puts on a spacesuit.
- For more links, go to **www.usborne.com/quicklinks**

Survival equipment

Here is some of the equipment astronauts need to stay alive and comfortable outside their spaceships. Sometimes space walks can last for five hours or more.

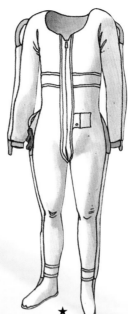

The shiny visor of the helmet protects against blinding, bright sunlight.

This cap holds a radio microphone and ear piece in place.

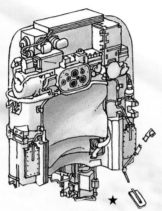

A drink bag has a tube which goes straight to the astronaut's mouth.

This is the "Primary Life Support System". It contains air for the astronaut to breathe.

This outfit is worn next to the body. It has tubes of water which the astronaut can make hot or cold, to warm up or cool down.

Padded gloves have rubber fingertips so the astronaut can feel things more easily.

Boiling and freezing

When astronauts on a space walk face the Sun, its rays are hotter than boiling water. But when their spaceships travel around the dark side of the Earth, temperatures drop way below freezing.

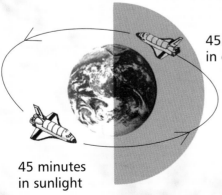

A space shuttle takes 90 minutes to go around the Earth.

45 minutes in darkness

45 minutes in sunlight

Living in space

Space stations are homes in space where astronauts can look at the Earth and do experiments. People can live in them for many months at a time. The first space station was set up over 30 years ago.

The ISS

This is the International Space Station (ISS). It floats around 230 miles above the Earth with six people on board. The first crew arrived in 2000. A space shuttle takes them up and back to Earth. The first part of the station was launched in 1998. More parts were added until it was completed in 2011.

This is the inside of a laboratory where scientists can do tests to see how things behave in space.

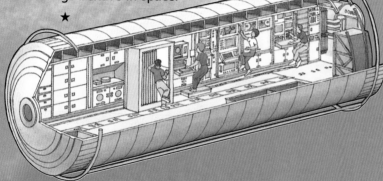

Internet links

- Scan the code to watch a video tour of the International Space Station.

- For more links, go to **www.usborne.com/quicklinks**

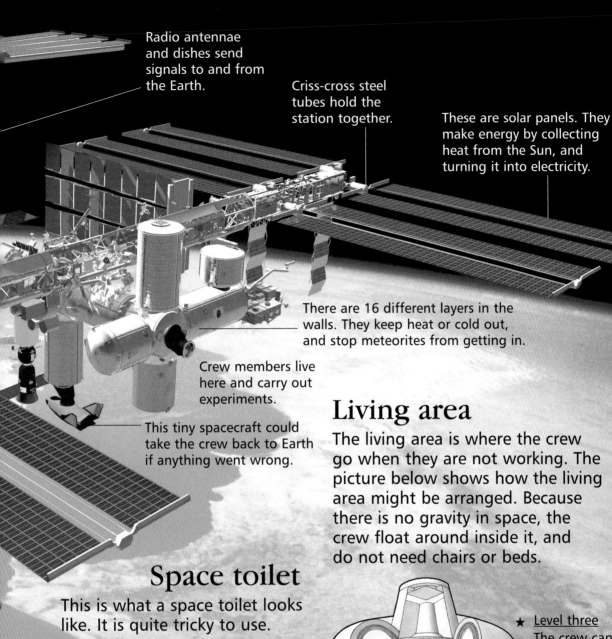

Radio antennae and dishes send signals to and from the Earth.

Criss-cross steel tubes hold the station together.

These are solar panels. They make energy by collecting heat from the Sun, and turning it into electricity.

There are 16 different layers in the walls. They keep heat or cold out, and stop meteorites from getting in.

Crew members live here and carry out experiments.

This tiny spacecraft could take the crew back to Earth if anything went wrong.

Living area

The living area is where the crew go when they are not working. The picture below shows how the living area might be arranged. Because there is no gravity in space, the crew float around inside it, and do not need chairs or beds.

Space toilet

This is what a space toilet looks like. It is quite tricky to use.

★ Handles for the astronaut to hold onto

Seat

Air sucks waste through this tube.

Urine is cleaned and turned back into water. Solid waste is frozen and returned to Earth.

★ Level three
The crew can exercise here.

Level two
Sleeping area. Each person has a small, private space.

Level one
The crew can eat together around this big table.

Satellites and space probes

Satellites and space probes are spaceships with no people in them. Instead, scientists control them from Earth. Most satellites and probes have cameras or other kinds of viewing equipment.

This is the Hubble Space Telescope. It looks deep into space and beams detailed photos back to Earth.

Satellites

Some satellites look down on Earth and others look out into space. Other types of satellites are used to carry television pictures or phone messages around the world. ★

Solar panels

This is the SOHO satellite, which looks at the atmosphere of the Sun. It is also used to find out about the solar wind (see page 262).

254

Space probes

Space probes do similar jobs to satellites, but instead of orbiting the Earth, they visit other planets. All the planets in our solar system have been visited by probes.

The painting on the right shows the Voyager space probe heading toward Neptune in 1989.

Internet links

- Scan the code to watch a video about the space probe, Voyager.
- For more links, go to **www.usborne.com/quicklinks**

Space views

Here are two pictures taken by satellites. Special cameras are used to show particular details, which can also be made clearer with computers.

This ERS picture shows a hole in Antarctica's atmosphere.

This SOHO picture shows the outer edge of the Sun's surface.

A big picture

A satellite named COBE took the picture below. It is a temperature map of the entire universe.

Some parts of space are hotter than others. The red and blue areas show different temperatures.

COBE satellite

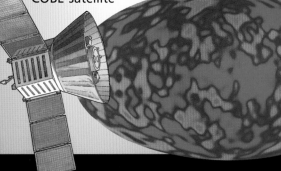

Is anyone out there?

Ever since people first began to study the stars, they have wondered whether there is life in space. At the moment we don't know. Some astronomers think we will find evidence of alien life before the end of the century.

Reaching out

Two kinds of space probes are heading out of our Solar System. Pioneer probes carry a picture of people and a map that shows where Earth is. Voyagers carry a disc with sounds and pictures of Earth. These are to show any alien who may find them what we look like.

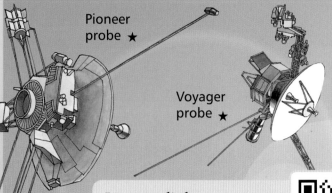

Pioneer probe ★

Voyager probe ★

Internet links

- Scan the code for a video about the search for life on other planets.
- For more links, go to www.usborne.com/quicklinks

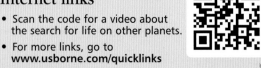

The Voyager disc

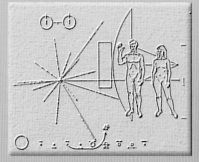

The Pioneer map and picture

New planets

Astronomers have discovered new planets in orbit around stars. Perhaps there is life there. Radio telescopes, such as the one in Puerto Rico shown below, search the skies near these planets, looking for alien signals.

Arecibo radio telescope is the largest in the world.

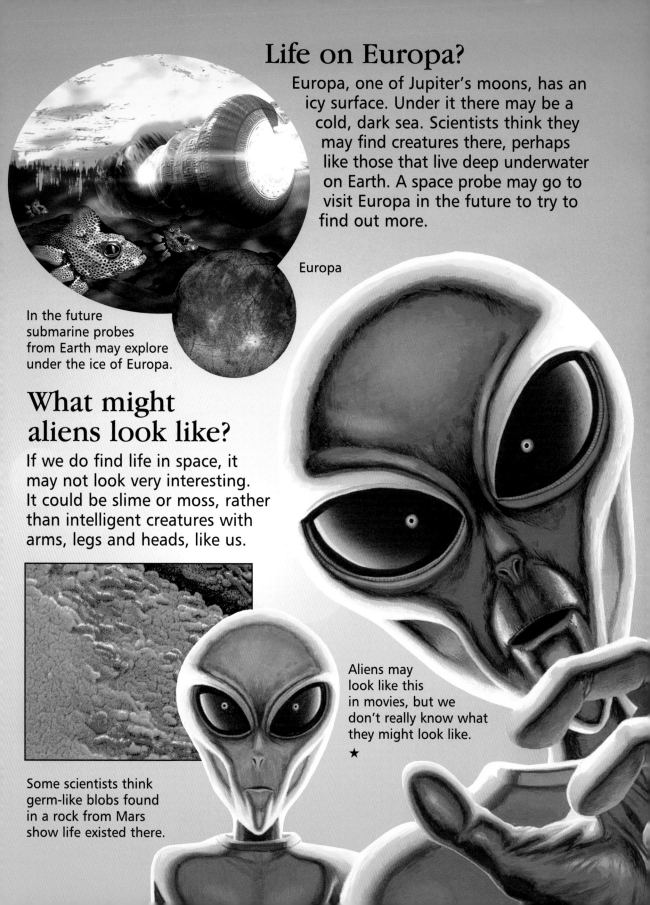

Life on Europa?

Europa, one of Jupiter's moons, has an icy surface. Under it there may be a cold, dark sea. Scientists think they may find creatures there, perhaps like those that live deep underwater on Earth. A space probe may go to visit Europa in the future to try to find out more.

Europa

In the future submarine probes from Earth may explore under the ice of Europa.

What might aliens look like?

If we do find life in space, it may not look very interesting. It could be slime or moss, rather than intelligent creatures with arms, legs and heads, like us.

Some scientists think germ-like blobs found in a rock from Mars show life existed there.

Aliens may look like this in movies, but we don't really know what they might look like.

★

What's in our Solar System?

Our Solar System is the Sun and everything that revolves around it. It includes all the planets and their moons, and space objects such as comets. There are also two vast bands of drifting rocks called the Asteroid Belt and the Kuiper Belt.

In this picture of the Solar System the planets are not shown to scale.

Comets fly around the Solar System.

Days and years

A day is the time it takes for a planet to spin around once. Earth's day lasts 24 hours. A year is the time it takes for a planet to go all the way around the Sun. Earth's year lasts for 365 days.

Earth

A day

Sun

A year

Asteroid Belt

Saturn is the second biggest planet.

Neptune is a gas planet, like Jupiter, Saturn, and Uranus. The gas planets are all much bigger than the rocky planets in our Solar System.

Internet links

- Scan the code to find out how the Solar System formed.
- For more links, go to www.usborne.com/quicklinks

Jupiter is the biggest planet.

Venus

Mercury

The Sun

Mars

Earth

Uranus spins on its side. It has rings like Saturn.

This is Pluto, a dwarf planet (see page 272).

Beyond Pluto lies a band of icy rocks named the Kuiper Belt.

Atmosphere

Most planets have an atmosphere – a layer of gas that covers the surface. Earth's atmosphere is made of air. It stretches up to about 373 miles above us. It provides air to breathe, and helps protect us from the Sun's heat.

Earth's atmosphere

The Moon

The Moon travels around the Earth, just like the Earth travels around the Sun. So far, the Moon is the only part of the Solar System that people have been able to visit.

Sea of Crises

The Moon's "seas" are actually dark patches of melted rock.

Sea of Tranquility

Craters were made by rocks from space, crashing into the Moon.

Sea of Serenity

Apollo 15 landed here in 1971.

Sea of Rain

Earth

If you were orbiting the Moon in a spaceship, this is how far away Earth would look.

When people went to the Moon between 1969 and 1972, it took their spaceships three days to get there.

What is the Moon like?

The Moon is very different from Earth. There is no air, no weather, and no life. It is a dreary, dusty place that is boiling hot by day and freezing at night. The surface is covered with saucer-shaped holes called craters. You can see some if you look at the Moon on a clear night. Some are so huge, a city the size of London could fit inside them.

Where did the Moon come from?

The Moon is about the same age as the Earth. Here is one idea about where it came from.

1. Soon after the Earth formed, a planet hit it. ★

2. Rocks broke off and shot into space. ★

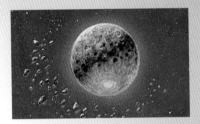

3. The rocks were held in ★ orbit by Earth's gravity.

4. These rocks slowly formed into the Moon. ★

Moon landings

People have visited the Moon six times, but not since 1972. Each spaceship that landed there carried two astronauts. They stayed up to three days before returning.

Internet links

• Scan the code for a video clip about Moon craters.

• For more links, go to www.usborne.com/quicklinks

This is the Apollo 15 Moon landing. See where they are on the Moon, on the facing page.

This spaceship is called a lunar module.

The astronaut is saluting the American flag.

Car powered by electricity

The Sun

The Sun is a star. It is a huge ball of blazing gas that makes vast amounts of light and heat which we call sunshine. It is so big it could hold a million planets the size of Earth. It looks like it's burning, but it's actually exploding like a massive bomb.

The Sun's surface is called the photosphere. The temperature there is 10,000°F. The dark areas are sunspots. The temperature is lower there.

Internet links

- Scan the code for a quiz about the Sun, Earth and Moon.
- For more links, go to
  www.usborne.com/quicklinks

The size of the Earth, compared to the Sun

The solar wind

As well as light and heat, the Sun also sends out a stream of invisible specks, called particles, into space. This is called the solar wind. When the particles pass by the North and South Poles of Earth they can make the air glow beautiful reds, blues, greens and purples.

This is the solar wind lighting up the sky near the North Pole.

This is a solar prominence. It is a massive arch of hot gas, which reaches out into space like a huge, flaming tongue.

Solar surface

The Sun makes sunlight by burning four million tons of fuel every second. You can see in this picture that the Sun's surface is a churning mass of explosions. Solar flares and fiery loops of gas leap out into space.

The photo on the right shows a close-up of the Sun's surface. You can see jets of gas called plasma loops.

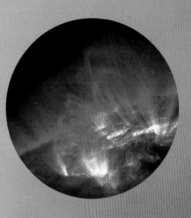

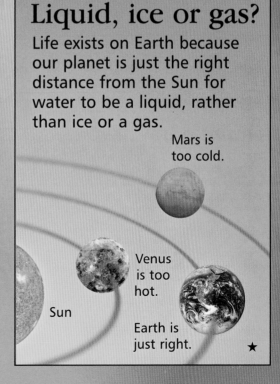

Liquid, ice or gas?

Life exists on Earth because our planet is just the right distance from the Sun for water to be a liquid, rather than ice or a gas.

Mars is too cold.

Venus is too hot.

Sun

Earth is just right.

★

Sometimes, white areas appear on the surface of the Sun. These are called faculae. The temperature here is even higher than that of the rest of the Sun.

Mercury and Venus

Mercury and Venus are the two planets closest to the Sun. Both are small and very hot. Mercury has almost no atmosphere, but Venus is covered with a thick layer of gas.

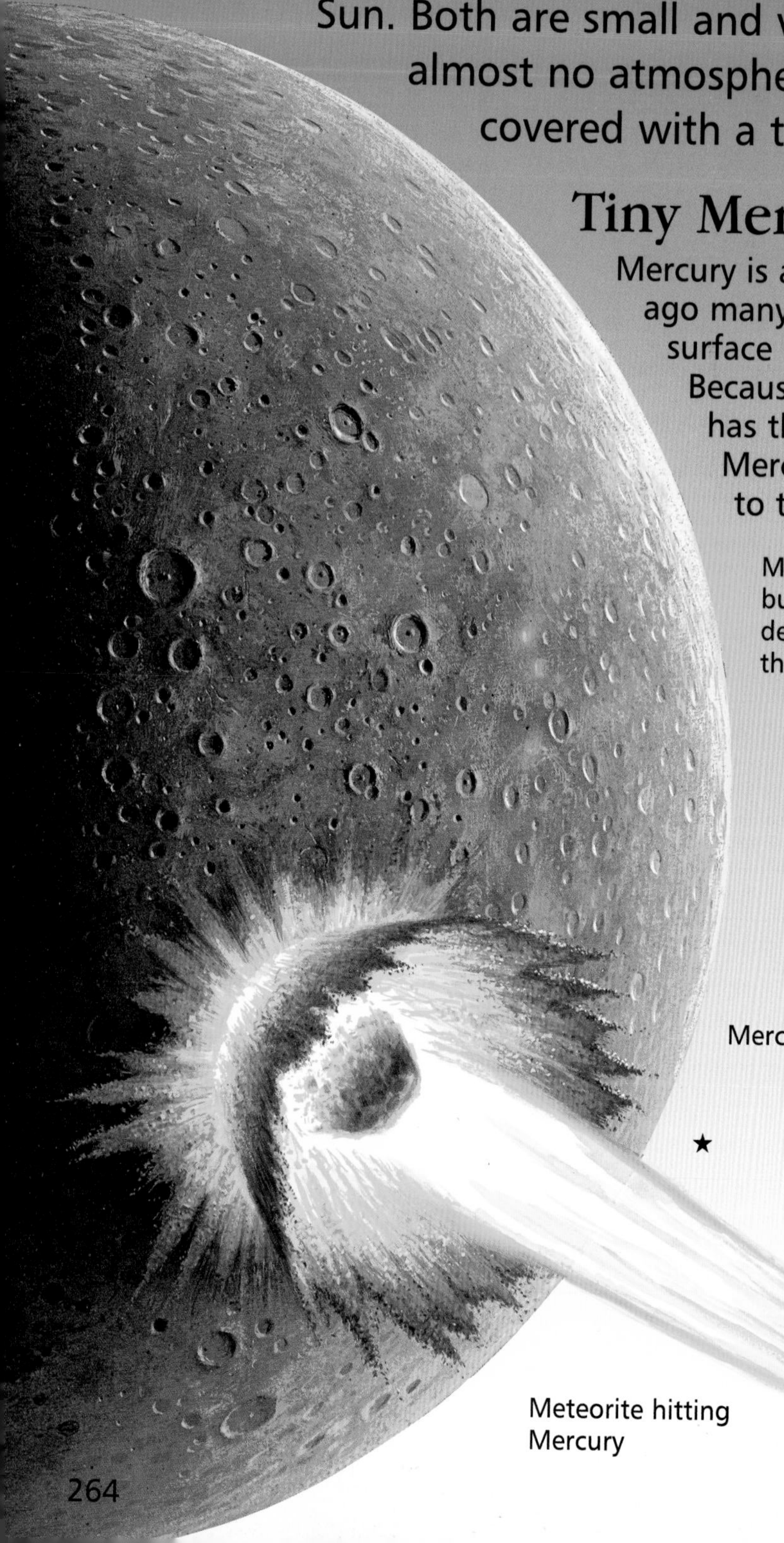

Tiny Mercury

Mercury is a tiny planet. Billions of years ago many rocks crashed into it, so its surface is covered with lots of craters. Because it is so close to the Sun, it has the shortest year of any planet. Mercury takes just 88 Earth days to travel around the Sun.

Mercury is a third the size of Earth, but is almost as heavy. It has a core of dense metal. This makes up nearly three-quarters of its inside.

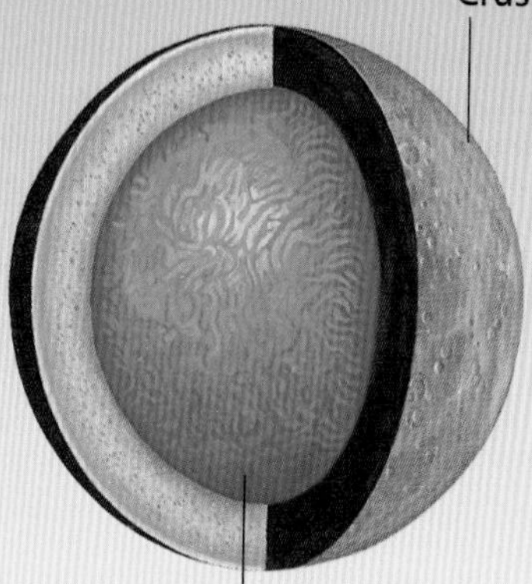

Crust

Mercury

Metal core

Four billion years ago an enormous meteorite crashed into Mercury. It made a massive crater called the Caloris Basin. This is more than 800 miles across.

Meteorite hitting Mercury

Internet links

- Scan the code to see an animation of Venus close up.
- For more links, go to www.usborne.com/quicklinks

Beneath its clouds, Venus is a world of volcanoes, mountains and canyons. The pink and white areas on this computer picture show high, rough areas. Low, flat ground is shown in green.

Sweltering Venus

Venus is the nearest planet to us. Although it is farther away from the Sun than Mercury, its surface is actually hotter. This is because it has a thick atmosphere of the gas carbon dioxide. This atmosphere traps the Sun's heat and stops it from escaping back into space.

Magellan probe

The picture below shows the surface of Venus. It was taken by the Magellan probe which visited Venus between 1990 and 1994.

Mars

If you were standing on Mars, being there would be a little like being on Earth. There is a bright sky during the day, and you could see thin clouds, morning mists and light frosts. But Mars is a lot colder than our planet.

Mars in detail

Mars is half the size of Earth. It is mainly covered with rocks and dust. Most of it looks like a great big desert. It has a thin atmosphere of poisonous gas.

Internet links

- Scan the code to watch an animation of how a robot rover explores Mars.
- For more links, go to www.usborne.com/quicklinks

This is a polar ice cap where water has frozen into a huge field of ice.

These marks are great fields of dark dust. They are blown around by fierce storms.

This is a volcano called Olympus Mons.

This is a volcano called Ascraeus Mons.

This is a huge canyon called The Valles Marineris.

The Viking 1 space probe visited Mars in 1976. It sent down the first craft to land on the surface.

Volcanoes and canyons

Mars has some very interesting features. There are several volcanoes. The biggest one is called Olympus Mons. It is the largest in the Solar System. It rises 15 miles above the surface of Mars. There are also huge canyons and dried-up water channels.

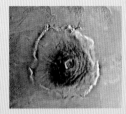

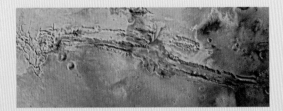

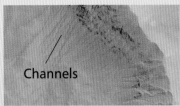

The Olympus Mons volcano seen by a visiting space probe.

The Valles Marineris canyon is a huge crack along one side of the planet. It is so long it would stretch across the entire USA.

Astronomers think that channels like this were made by running water, which has now frozen or leaked away.

Visitors to Mars

Many probes have landed on Mars. Some have carried mobile robots on board that can be moved around by scientists on Earth. The robots conduct experiments and send TV images back to Earth, giving the scientists a better view of the surface.

This photograph was taken by the Pathfinder space probe. Scientists think that these rocks were left here by a big flood, billions of years ago.

The robot on board Pathfinder, Sojourner, was the size of a microwave oven. This picture shows some of its more important features:
Ⓐ Solar panels made power from sunlight.
Ⓑ Small wheels with studded rims gripped the surface.
Ⓒ Radio antenna kept the robot in contact with Earth.
Ⓓ A camera and laser were used to help steer the robot.

Jupiter and Saturn

Beyond the Asteroid Belt lie four huge planets that are mainly made up of gas. The largest of these four are the bright, stormy planets Jupiter and Saturn.

Swirly world

Jupiter is the biggest planet in the Solar System and has at least 63 moons. It also has the shortest day. It takes only 9 hours and 50 minutes to spin around once. Jupiter is a stormy planet. Swirling clouds of gas race around it, in dark and light bands.

The Great Red Spot is a storm three times the size of Earth.

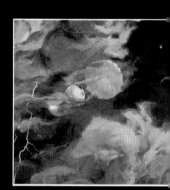

A pod from the Galileo space probe parachuted into Jupiter's gassy atmosphere in 1995.

This space probe photo shows thick, hot gas erupting from volcanoes on the surface of Io, one of Jupiter's many moons.

Internet links

• Scan the code to discover why Saturn has rings.

• For more links, go to **www.usborne.com/quicklinks**

Ring world

Saturn is the second biggest planet in the Solar System. Many broad rings of rock and ice orbit around it. Saturn is very light. If you could put it in a huge swimming pool, it would float there.

All shapes and sizes

The rocks in Saturn's rings may have come from one of its moons. You can see what might have happened below. Some rocks in the rings are as big as a house, others are smaller than a pebble.

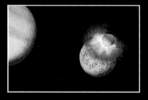

A moon collided with a planet.

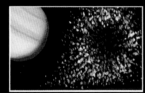

It broke into billions of pieces.

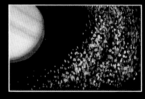

The pieces stayed in Saturn's orbit.

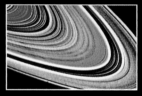

Eventually, they formed Saturn's rings.

Saturn's moons

Saturn has 62 moons, and there may be more. Titan is the largest. It has a thick atmosphere.

Here you can see how big Titan is compared to the planet Mercury and our Moon.

This picture shows what Titan's atmosphere may look like, close up.

Earth's Moon

The planet Mercury

Titan

Uranus and Neptune

Uranus and Neptune are huge gas planets. Both are around four times bigger than Earth. They are hard to spot in the night sky, but you can see them with a telescope.

Uranus   Neptune   Earth

This is how big Uranus and Neptune are compared to the Earth.

Uranus

This world spins on its side. Its outer surface is cloaked by a thin mist, which wraps around a thick gassy surface. Further inside, Uranus has a core of solid rock.

Uranus

Here are some of Uranus's moons.

Umbriel

Ariel

Titania

Puzzle Moon

Uranus has 27 moons. One of them, Miranda, looks like a huge jigsaw puzzle. Perhaps, millions of years ago, it broke into pieces. Gradually time and gravity put it back together.

Oberon

Miranda

★

A comet may have crashed into Miranda.

★

Miranda's pieces drifted together.

★

Miranda slowly put itself back in one piece.

This is what Miranda's surface looks like now.

Neptune

Neptune has the worst storms in the Solar System. Winds of 1,250mph whip clouds of methane around the planet.

Neptune has 13 moons. One, named Triton, is a frozen world. Ice on its surface acts like a greenhouse, magnifying the Sun's feeble rays, and heating gas that lies beneath. This causes hot jets of gas and slush to spout out through the ice and into space.

Internet links

- Scan the code to find out about extreme weather on other planets.
- For more links, go to **www.usborne.com/quicklinks**

Triton orbits in the opposite direction from all of Neptune's other moons.

Visitor from Earth

The Voyager 2 space probe visited Uranus and Neptune in 1986 and 1989. The probe took 12 years to get to Neptune from Earth.

This picture shows what the surface of Triton might look like. A jet of gas and slush is spouting out.

Voyager 2

Pluto and beyond

Pluto lies near the edge of the Solar System. This dwarf planet is so far away it was only discovered in 1930. Unlike the huge, gassy planets Uranus and Neptune, Pluto is a small, solid ball of rock and ice.

Moon-sized

Until 2006 scientists thought of Pluto as a planet. Then they decided it was really too small to be called a planet, so they renamed it a dwarf planet. It's only two thirds the size of our Moon.

★

Pluto's moon, Charon

Pluto

A space probe would take 12 years to get to Pluto. No probe has visited yet, but one may in the future.

Pluto may have a thin atmosphere of nitrogen gas.

Odd orbit

Pluto takes 248 Earth years to go around the Sun. For 20 of these years it is closer to the Sun than Neptune. While all the other planets orbit on roughly the same level, Pluto spins around on a different path. ★

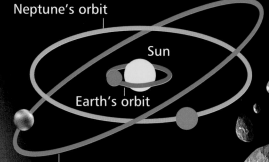

Neptune's orbit

Sun

Earth's orbit

Pluto's orbit

Kuiper Belt

The Kuiper Belt

Beyond Pluto lies a huge ring of frozen rocks known as the Kuiper Belt. These drifting rocks did not merge into one of the planets when the Solar System was formed. Some astronomers think a few of them are bigger than Pluto.

Internet links

- Scan the code to learn more about why Pluto is called a dwarf planet.
- For more links, go to www.usborne.com/quicklinks

Oort Cloud

Even farther away sits a huge, misty cloud, which may be made up of trillions of comets. This is called the Oort Cloud.

The Oort Cloud surrounds the outer edge of the Solar System like a vast, dusty ball.

Solar System

Bits and pieces

Our Solar System isn't just the Sun, the eight planets, and their moons. There are countless asteroids, meteoroids and comets flying around in it too.

This is the Asteroid Belt. Some of its rocks are as big as small moons.

Asteroids

Asteroids are lumps of rocks and metal. Between Mars and Jupiter lies a large band of them, called the Asteroid Belt. One of the biggest, named Vesta, is about 330 miles across. Some asteroids even have their own little moons.

Meteoroids

Meteoroids are smaller pieces of rock from space. Many are no bigger than a grain of instant coffee, but lots are larger. Most burn up in the atmosphere as they fall to Earth, but some are too big to burn, and cause damage when they reach Earth.

Meteoroids that burn up in the sky are called meteors or shooting stars.

Meteoroids that hit a planet are called meteorites. This crater in Arizona, USA, was caused by a meteorite.

Comets

Comets are large balls of ice and dust. They come in from the outer edge of the Solar System to circle the Sun. Once past Jupiter, the heat from the Sun begins to melt the outer layer of the comet, and the solar wind blows a trail of gas and dust behind it.

Deep Impact

Scientists have developed a special probe to find out more about comets. Deep Impact visited a comet called Tempel 1. The probe blasted a hole in the comet, took photographs and collected some of the dust and ice from the blast.

Part of the Bayeux Tapestry shows people looking at a comet in 1066. ★

A comet far away ★ from the Sun has no tail. It is just a solid block of dirty ice.

Closer to the Sun, ★ the outside begins to melt, and forms a trail of gas and dust.

This picture shows the comet Hale-Bopp when it passed by the Earth in 1997.

By the time it flies ★ by Earth the comet's tail is glowing. This makes it easy to spot.

Internet links

• Scan the code to watch an animation about comets.

• For more links, go to www.usborne.com/quicklinks

Galaxies are collections of billions of stars, held together by gravity in one vast group. Most galaxies have a spiral shape, but some have a more scattered pattern. There are billions of galaxies in the Universe.

The Milky Way

The Sun is part of a galaxy called the Milky Way. It has over 100 billion stars, and is about 100,000 light years across. The Milky Way is not the biggest galaxy in the Universe, but it is much larger than many others. Like most galaxies it is spinning around a central hub. ★

Astronomers think the Sun and our Solar System are here.

A long trip

It takes 225 million years for the Milky Way to go all the way around. The last time our Solar System was in the same place in space that it is now, dinosaurs roamed the Earth

If you could see the Milky Way from the side, it would look like a flat plate with a bulge in the middle

The middle of the Milky Way is hidden by great clouds of dust

Galaxy shapes

Not all galaxies look like the Milky Way. There are several other galaxy shapes. You can see three of them on the right.

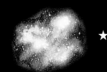

★ This type is known as an irregular galaxy. It doesn't have any real shape at all.

This round type is called an elliptical galaxy. ★

This type is a barred spiral ★ galaxy.

Radio view

A kind of telescope called a radio telescope can "see" the Milky Way much more clearly than other kinds. The picture below shows the big bulge in the middle of our galaxy.

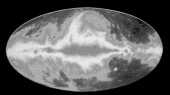

The red patch in this picture shows where most of the stars are in the Milky Way.

How many galaxies?

A hundred years ago astronomers thought the Milky Way was the only galaxy in the Universe. But over the last century, telescopes and radio telescopes have detected many millions of other galaxies.

This photograph shows some newly discovered galaxies. Before this picture was taken, astronomers thought there was nothing in this part of space.

Spiral galaxy

Looking at the night sky

Although many of the pictures in this part of the book were taken using very powerful telescopes, you can still see many amazing things in the night sky just with your eyes.

Milky Way

The Moon

Star cluster. This one is called the Hyades.

Old star. This one is called Betelgeuse.

This group of stars is called Orion.

This star is called Sirius. It is the brightest star in the sky.

These are some of the things you may be able to see without a telescope.

The Moon

The clearest sight in the night sky is the Moon. You can see it glowing brightly in the darkness because it is lit up by light from the Sun. As the Moon orbits the Earth it seems to change shape.

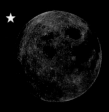

New Moon
When no light shines on the Moon, it is impossible to see it.

Waxing Moon
Gradually a sliver of light returns. The Moon appears to grow.

Full Moon
Once every 28 days all of one side of the Moon is lit by the Sun's light.

Waning Moon
As the Moon moves in its orbit less light falls on it. It seems to shrink.

What you can see

There is a lot to see in the night sky, if you know what to look for. Using just your eyes, you can see the Moon, stars, planets, shooting stars, comets and sometimes even spacecraft.

Stars

A clear night sky is full of stars. There are certain patterns you can look for. These patterns are called constellations, and there are 88 altogether.

This is a star pattern called Orion, which you can also see on the left-hand page. Ancient people thought this shape looked like a hunter.

This is a photograph of the constellation of Orion.

The Milky Way

This is what the Milky Way looks like on a very clear night. You can see it at certain times of the year if you are away from city lights.

Space words

alien a living thing from another world.

asteroid a rock orbiting the Sun. There are thousands of them in a part of the Solar System called the Asteroid Belt.

astronaut someone who goes into space.

atmosphere layers of gas that surround a planet or a star.

cluster a group of space objects gathered together, such as stars or galaxies.

comet a chunk of dirty ice orbiting the Sun which can form a long tail as it melts.

core the middle of a planet, moon, star or other space object.

crater a hollow on the surface of a planet, moon or asteroid, caused by something hitting it, such as a meteorite.

day the time it takes a planet or moon to spin all the way around.

galaxy a group of hundreds of millions of stars all held together by gravity.

gravity a force that pulls objects toward other objects. (Usually smaller objects to larger objects.)

meteor a meteoroid that burns up in a planet's atmosphere. Also called a shooting star.

meteorite a piece of rock or metal from space that is found on the Earth.

meteoroid dust, or small chunks of rock, in orbit around the Sun.

moon a mini-planet in orbit around another planet.

orbit the path of an object in space, as it travels around another object.

planet a huge ball of rock or gas, which travels around a star.

rocket a type of engine in a spacecraft which uses exploding fuel to make it move.

satellite 1) something in space which orbits something else. **2)** an unmanned spacecraft which orbits the Earth.

solar system a group of planets, and other objects, all in orbit around a sun.

spacecraft (also called spaceship) a vehicle that is used for space travel. If it has no people in it, it is unmanned.

space probe an unmanned spacecraft which collects information about objects in space.

space station a large spacecraft orbiting the Earth, where astronauts learn about living and working in space.

spacewalk when an astronaut in a spacesuit leaves a spacecraft and floats in space.

star a huge ball of exploding gas.

Universe everything that exists in space.

year the length of time it takes a planet to travel around the Sun. Earth's year lasts 365 days.

Internet links

- Scan the code to hear how to say lots of space words.
- For more links, go to **www.usborne.com/quicklinks**

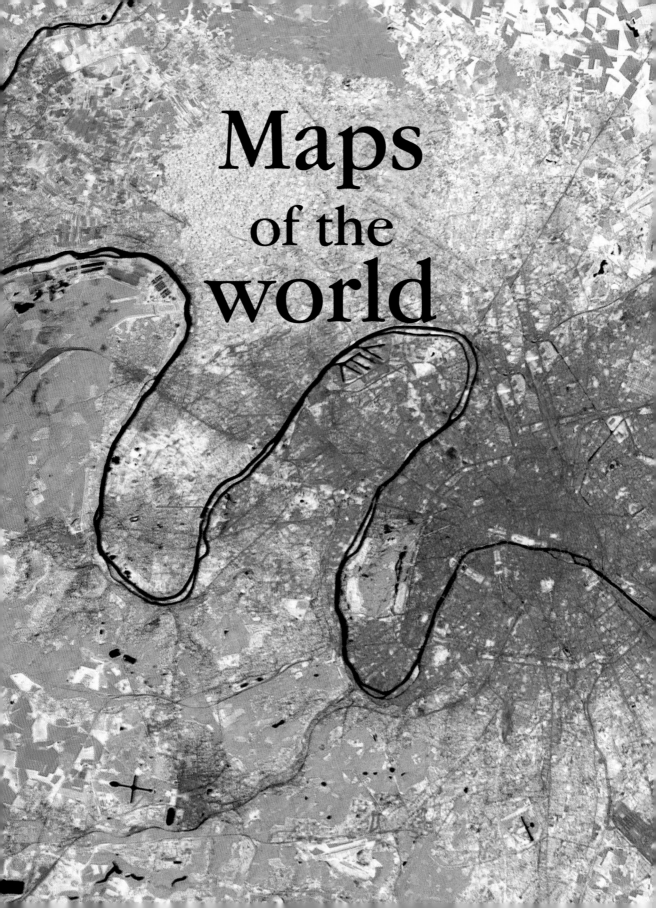

Maps
of the
world

About maps

A map is a picture that shows a particular area of the world. Places are usually shown as you would see them from above and much smaller than in real life. A map can show the whole world or just one street.

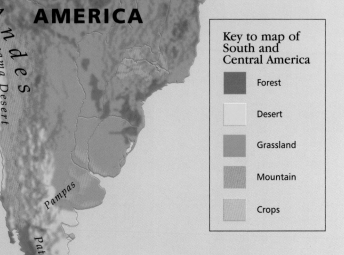

This map shows what the land in South and Central America is covered with.

What will you see on a map?

Maps are designed to be easy to understand. Colors and symbols on a map all mean different things. A key tells you what they all stand for.

The size of a map compared with the area it shows is called its scale. Some maps show this with a scale bar. This is a line that tells you how many kilometers or miles are represented by a certain distance on the map.

Key to map of South and Central America

- Forest
- Desert
- Grassland
- Mountain
- Crops

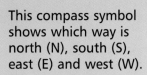

Scale bar — **Approximate scale**

| 0km | 2,000km |
| 0 miles | 1,240 miles |

Which way is up?

The Earth doesn't have a top and a bottom, but north is usually shown at the top of maps. Some maps have a symbol to show which way is north.

This compass symbol shows which way is north (N), south (S), east (E) and west (W).

Kinds of maps

A map can show features of an area in a clear, simple way. There are lots of different kinds of maps. Here are three of them.

Political maps show countries or states. They often show the names of important cities and towns.

Physical maps show natural features such as mountains, rivers and lakes. They usually have a key.

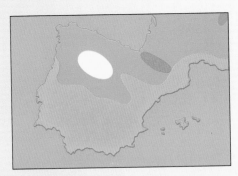

Thematic maps show various types of information, such as which types of plants grow in which regions.

Dividing lines

Map makers divide up the Earth with imaginary lines. These are numbered in degrees (°) and minutes (') to help us measure distances and find places on a map. There are two sets of lines. They are called latitude and longitude.

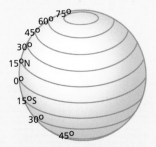

Lines of latitude run around the globe. They are the same distance apart.

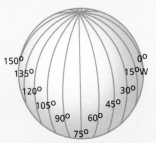

Lines of longitude run from the North Pole to the South Pole.

Here is a drawing of the Earth showing the North Pole and the main lines of latitude and longitude.

North Pole

Arctic Circle (66°30'N)

Prime Meridian Line (0°)

Lines of latitude

Tropic of Cancer (23°27'N)

Equator (0°)

Lines of longitude

Tropic of Capricorn (23°27'S)

The South Pole is at the bottom of the globe, but you can't see it here.

Internet links

- Scan the code to quiz yourself on countries around the world.
- For more links, go to **www.usborne.com/quicklinks**

Countries of the world

This map shows the different countries that make up each continent.

GREENLAND
(Denmark)

ICELAND

Arctic Circle

ALASKA
(U.S.A.)

60°

CANADA

IRELAND **UNITED KINGDOM**

UNITED STATES OF AMERICA

40°

FR.

Azores
(Portugal)

PORTUGAL **SPAIN**

MOROCCO

Canary Islands
(Spain)

WESTERN SAHARA
(Morocco)

THE BAHAMAS

20° N Tropic of Cancer

MEXICO **CUBA** **DOMINICAN REPUBLIC**

HAITI

ALGⁿ

MAURITANIA **MALI**

Hawaiian Islands
(U.S.A.)

BELIZE **JAMAICA**

GUATEMALA **HONDURAS** *Caribbean Sea* **DOMINICA**

EL SALVADOR **NICARAGUA**

CAPE VERDE **SENEGAL**

THE GAMBIA

GUINEA-BISSAU **GUINEA**

BURKINA FASO

COSTA RICA **TRINIDAD AND TOBAGO**

PANAMA **VENEZUELA** **GUYANA**

COLOMBIA **SURINAME**

FRENCH GUIANA
(France)

SIERRA LEONE **IVORY COAST** **GHANA**

LIBERIA

TOGO

PACIFIC

Galapagos Islands
(Ecuador)

ECUADOR

0° Equator

SAO TOME AND PRINCIPE

EQU

KIRIBATI

OCEAN

ATLANTIC

PERU **BRAZIL**

OCEAN

Cook Islands
(New Zealand)

French Polynesia
(France)

BOLIVIA

20° S

Tropic of Capricorn

Pitcairn Islands
(U.K.)

PARAGUAY

CHILE **URUGUAY**

ARGENTINA

40°

Falkland Islands
(U.K.)

South Georgia
(U.K.)

60°

SOUTHEⁿ

Antarctic Circle

Weddell Sea

Approximate scale

0km	3,000km
0 miles	1,860 miles

80°

Key to map of countries of the world

— Boundary, where one country is joined to the next one

Coast

Lake

Some country names had to be shortened to fit on the map. This list has the names written in full:

ARM.	Armenia	B.H.	Bosnia and Herzegovina
AUST.	Austria	CRO.	Croatia
AZER.	Azerbaijan	CZECH REP.	Czech Republic
BELG.	Belgium	K.	Kosovo
		LEB.	Lebanon
		LUX.	Luxembourg
		M.	Montenegro
MAC.	Macedonia		
NETH.	Netherlands		
S.	Serbia		
SLOV.	Slovenia		
SWITZ.	Switzerland		
U.A.E.	United Arab Emirates		

Internet links

Scan the code for a quiz on world capitals.

285

The world's environments

This map shows the different types of land, or environments, such as desert or mountain.

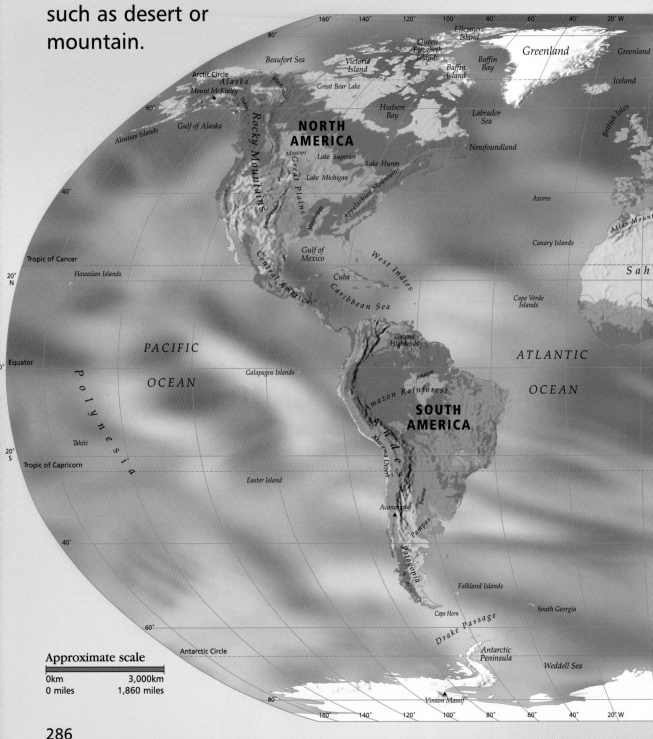

Approximate scale

0km	3,000km
0 miles	1,860 miles

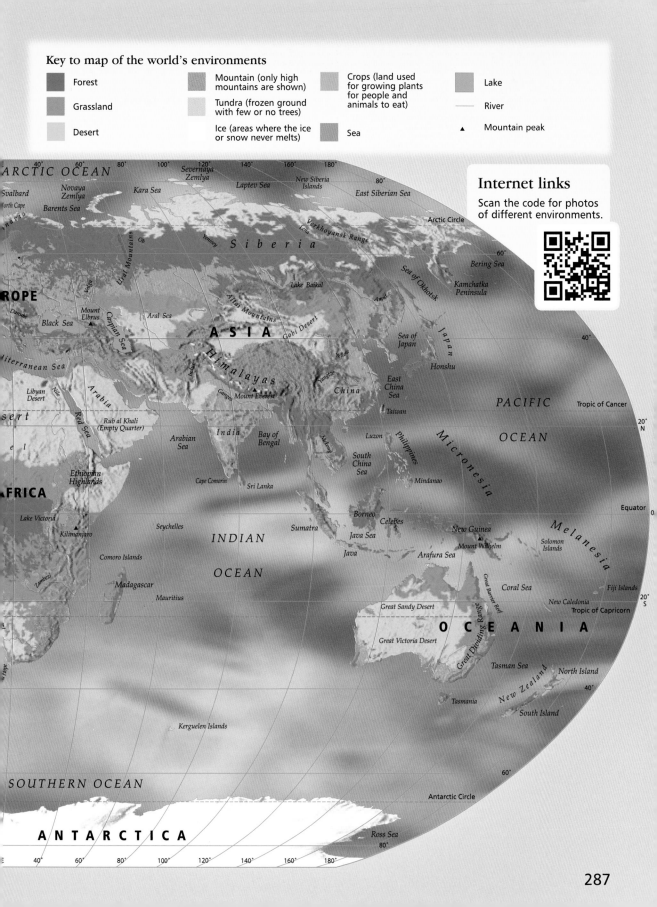

Key to map of the world's environments

- Forest
- Grassland
- Desert
- Mountain (only high mountains are shown)
- Tundra (frozen ground with few or no trees)
- Ice (areas where the ice or snow never melts)
- Crops (land used for growing plants for people and animals to eat)
- Sea
- Lake
- River
- Mountain peak

Internet links

Scan the code for photos of different environments.

ARCTIC OCEAN

40° 60° 80° 100° 120° 140° 160° 180° 80°

Svalbard
North Cape
Novaya Zemlya
Barents Sea
Kara Sea
Severnaya Zemlya
Laptev Sea
New Siberia Islands
East Siberian Sea
Arctic Circle

Siberia
Ob
Yenisey
Lena
Verkhoyansk Range

60°
Bering Sea

EUROPE
Danube
Black Sea
Mount Elbrus
Caspian Sea
Aral Sea
Ural Mountains
Volga

Altai Mountains

Lake Baikal

Sea of Okhotsk
Kamchatka Peninsula

Amur

ASIA
Gobi Desert

Sea of Japan

Japan

40°

Mediterranean Sea

Himalayas
Indus
Ganges
Mount Everest

Yellow
Yangtze

China

Honshu

East China Sea

PACIFIC

OCEAN

Tropic of Cancer

Libyan Desert
Nile
Red Sea
Arabia
Rub al Khali (Empty Quarter)

Arabian Sea

India

Bay of Bengal

Mekong

Luzon

Philippines

Micronesia

20°
N

Desert
el

Ethiopian Highlands

Cape Comorin
Sri Lanka

South China Sea

Mindanao

AFRICA
Lake Victoria
Kilimanjaro

Seychelles

INDIAN

Sumatra

Borneo
Celebes

Java Sea
Java

New Guinea
Mount Wilhelm

Solomon Islands

Melanesia

Equator 0

Comoro Islands
Zambezi
Madagascar
Mauritius

OCEAN

Arafura Sea

Coral Sea

New Caledonia

Fiji Islands

20°
S

Kerguelen Islands

Great Sandy Desert

Great Barrier Reef
Great Dividing Range

Tropic of Capricorn

OCEANIA

Great Victoria Desert

Tasman Sea

North Island

40°

Tasmania

New Zealand

South Island

60°

SOUTHERN OCEAN

Antarctic Circle

ANTARCTICA

Ross Sea
80°

40° 60° 80° 100° 120° 140° 160° 180°

287

North America

This continent includes three very large countries – Canada, the USA and Mexico. It also covers Greenland, the Caribbean, and the countries in the land that joins South America.

ARCTIC OCEAN

Queen Elizabeth Islands

Parry Islands

Point Barrow

Beaufort Sea

Victoria Island

Arctic Circle

Bering Strait

ALASKA (U.S.A.)

Bering Sea

Yukon

Mount McKinley ▲

● Anchorage

Gulf of Alaska

Mackenzie

Great Bear Lake

Great Slave Lake

CANAD

Lake Athabasca

Reindeer Lake

R O C K Y   M O U N T A I N S

Great Plains

Vancouver

Winn

● Calgary

● Seattle

Columbia

PACIFIC OCEAN

Great Salt Lake

U N I T E D   S T A T E

San Francisco

● Denver

Colorado

California

Los Angeles ●

● Phoenix

Lower California

Ciudad Juarez

Te x

Rio

● Hermosillo

Monterrey

Tropic of Cancer

MEXIC

Guadala

Mexico Cit

Acapulco

Key to map of North America
- ■ Capital city
- ○ Major city or town
- ── Boundary (where one country joins another one)
- ── River
- ▨ Coast

Approximate scale

0km	1,000km
0 miles	620 miles

Hawaiian Islands (U.S.A.)

Raccoons are found mainly in North and Central America. They usually sleep in trees during the day and come out at night to feed.

Internet links
- Scan the code to explore America's 50 states.
- For more links, go to **www.usborne.com/quicklinks**

288

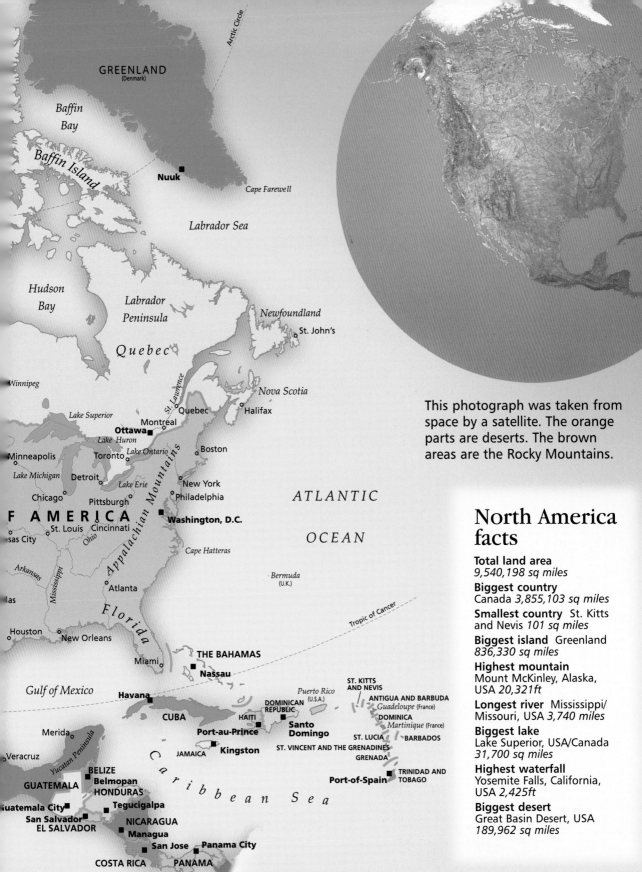

GREENLAND
(Denmark)

Baffin
Bay

Baffin Island

Nuuk

Cape Farewell

Labrador Sea

Hudson
Bay

Labrador
Peninsula

Newfoundland

St. John's

Quebec

Winnipeg

St. Lawrence

Nova Scotia

Quebec

Halifax

Lake Superior

Montreal

Ottawa

Lake Huron

Minneapolis

Toronto

Lake Ontario

Boston

Lake Michigan

Detroit

Lake Erie

New York

Chicago

Pittsburgh

Philadelphia

F AMERICA

St. Louis

Cincinnati

Washington, D.C.

ATLANTIC

sas City

Ohio

Arkansas

Mississippi

Appalachian Mountains

OCEAN

Cape Hatteras

las

Atlanta

Bermuda
(U.K.)

Houston

New Orleans

Florida

Tropic of Cancer

Miami

THE BAHAMAS

Gulf of Mexico

Nassau

Puerto Rico
(U.S.A.)

ST. KITTS
AND NEVIS

Havana

ANTIGUA AND BARBUDA

Guadeloupe (France)

CUBA

DOMINICAN
REPUBLIC

DOMINICA

Merida

HAITI

Port-au-Prince

Santo
Domingo

Martinique (France)

Yucatan Peninsula

ST. LUCIA

BARBADOS

Veracruz

JAMAICA

Kingston

ST. VINCENT AND THE GRENADINES

GRENADA

BELIZE

Caribbean

TRINIDAD AND
TOBAGO

GUATEMALA

Belmopan

Port-of-Spain

HONDURAS

uatemala City

Tegucigalpa

Sea

San Salvador

EL SALVADOR

NICARAGUA

Managua

San Jose

Panama City

COSTA RICA

PANAMA

This photograph was taken from space by a satellite. The orange parts are deserts. The brown areas are the Rocky Mountains.

North America facts

Total land area
9,540,198 sq miles

Biggest country
Canada 3,855,103 sq miles

Smallest country St. Kitts and Nevis 101 sq miles

Biggest island Greenland 836,330 sq miles

Highest mountain
Mount McKinley, Alaska, USA 20,321ft

Longest river Mississippi/ Missouri, USA 3,740 miles

Biggest lake
Lake Superior, USA/Canada 31,700 sq miles

Highest waterfall
Yosemite Falls, California, USA 2,425ft

Biggest desert
Great Basin Desert, USA 189,962 sq miles

South America

South America stretches from just north of the equator almost to Antarctica in the south. Brazil is the biggest of the twelve countries in South America.

Key to map of South America
- ■ Capital city
- ○ Major city or town
- —— Boundary (where one country joins another one)
- —— River
- ▨ Coast

Approximate scale

0km	1,000km
0 miles	620 miles

Caribbean Sea

Maracaibo · ■ Caracas

VENEZUELA

Medellin ○
■ Bogota   Guiana Highl

Cali ○ COLOMBIA   Orinoco

Equator   ■ Quito   Negro

Galapagos   ECUADOR   Amazon
Islands   Guayaquil ○
(Ecuador)

Amazon Rainfores

PERU   M

Ucayali

ANDES

Lima ■

Lake   BOLIVIA
Titicaca
La Paz ■

Sucre ■

Tropic of Capricorn

Atacama Desert

CHILE   San Migu
de Tucum

Cordoba ○

Aconcagua ▲   Rosar

PACIFIC   Santiago ■

OCEAN   ARGENTINA

ANDES

Pampa

Patagonia

Strait of Magellan

Tierra del Fuego

Cape Horn

Drake Passage

Toucans live in the rainforests of South America. They use their long, jagged beaks to pick and eat fruit from the trees.

ATLANTIC

OCEAN

orgetown
Paramaribo
ANA ∎
Cayenne
RINAME FRENCH
GUIANA
(France)

Equator

Reservoir

Amazon

Belem

Fortaleza

Xingu

Tucurui Reservoir

Recife

B R A Z I L

Tocantins

Sobradinho Reservoir

Plateau of Mato Grosso

Sao Francisco

Brazilian Highlands

Salvador

∎ **Brasilia**

Goiania

Belo Horizonte

Parana

Furnas Reservoir

GUAY

Rio de Janeiro

Sao Paulo

Asuncion

Tropic of Capricorn

Curitiba

Porto Alegre

ATLANTIC

OCEAN

UGUAY

∎ **Montevideo**

nos Aires

This is what South America looks like from space. The gray, mottled patch on the left-hand side is the Andes mountain range.

South America facts

Total land area
6,888,063 sq miles

Biggest country
Brazil *3,287,612 sq miles*

Smallest country
Suriname *63,251 sq miles*

Biggest island
Tierra del Fuego *18,302 sq miles*

Highest mountain
Aconcagua, Argentina *22,837ft*

Longest river
Amazon, Brazil *4,000 miles*

Biggest lake
Lake Maracaibo, Venezuela
5,100 sq miles

Highest waterfall
Angel Falls, on the Churun River,
Venezuela *3,212ft*

Biggest desert
Patagonian Desert, Argentina
259,847 sq miles

Internet links

• Scan the code to explore Brazil, South America's largest country.

• For more links, go to **www.usborne.com/quicklinks**

nd Islands
(U.K.)

Asia

Asia is the world's biggest continent, covering thousands of miles. It stretches from the Arctic Circle to the equator, and from the Ural Mountains in western Russia to Japan in the east.

ARCTIC OCEAN

Novaya Zemlya

Barents Sea

Kara Sea

Arctic Circle

St. Petersburg · Arkhangelsk

Ural Mountains · Ob

RUS

Moscow

Nizhniy Novgorod · Kazan

Yekaterinburg

Volga · Samara · Chelyabinsk

Irtysh · Ob

Omsk · Novosibirs

Altai Moun

Rostov

Istanbul · Black Sea · Astrakhan · Aqtobe · Astana

Izmir · Ankara · Caspian Sea · KAZAKHSTAN

TURKEY · GEORGIA · Tbilisi · Aral Sea · Lake Balkhash

Nicosia · ARMENIA · Yerevan

CYPRUS · AZERBAIJAN · Baku · UZBEKISTAN · Almaty · Urume

Beirut · SYRIA · Tabriz · TURKMENISTAN · Ashgabat · Tashkent · Bishkek

LEBANON · Damascus · Ashgabat · Dushanbe · KYRGYZSTAN

ISRAEL · Baghdad · Tehran · TAJIKISTAN

Jerusalem · Amman · Mashhad · Kunlun Moun

JORDAN · IRAQ · IRAN · AFGHANISTAN · Islamabad · Plateau of Tibet

Syrian Desert · Basra · Kabul · HIMALAYAS

KUWAIT · Shiraz · Kandahar

Medina · SAUDI ARABIA · BAHRAIN · Delhi · NEPAL · Mount Eve

Jedda · QATAR · PAKISTAN · New Delhi · Kathmandu · BHU

Mecca · Riyadh · Abu Dhabi · Indus · Ganges · BANGLADESH

UNITED ARAB EMIRATES · Muscat · Karachi · Varanasi

Rub al Khali (Empty Quarter) · Thar Desert · Dhaka

Sana · YEMEN · OMAN · Nagpur · Kolkata (Calcutta)

Red Sea · Arabian Sea · Mumbai (Bombay) · INDIA

Aden · Socotra (Yemen)

Bangalore · Chennai (Madras)

SRI LANKA

Cape Comorin · Sri Jayewardenepura Kotte

Colombo

MALDIVES · Male · Equator

INDIAN OCEAN

Key to map of Asia

- ■ Capital city
- ○ Major city or town
- — Boundary (where one country joins another one)
- River
- Coast

Approximate scale

0km	1,000km
0 miles	620 miles

Giant pandas live in bamboo forests in the high mountains of western China. There are fewer than 2,000 giant pandas left in the wild.

Internet links

Scan the code to discover more about China, or go to www.usborne.com/quicklinks

East
Siberian
Sea

*Laptev
Sea*

Anadyr

Bering Sea

Arctic Circle

Verkhoyansk Range

*Kamchatka
Peninsula*

Lena

Petropavlovsk-
Kamchatskiy

Okhotsk

eria

Yakutsk

*Sea of
Okhotsk*

Lena

Komsomolsk

Amur

Hokkaido

Sapporo

kutsk

Lake Baikal

Qiqihar

JAPAN

Tokyo

Ian Bator

MONGOLIA

Shenyang

**NORTH
KOREA**

Pyongyang

Seoul

Osaka

Honshu

bi Desert

Beijing

Baotou

**SOUTH
KOREA**

Hiroshima

Xian

C H I N A

Shanghai

Hangzhou

*East China
Sea*

Tropic of Cancer

Chongqing

Yangtze

Fuzhou

Taipei

Kunming

Taiwan

Xianggang (Hong Kong)

PACIFIC

MA
MAR)
pyidaw

Hanoi

LAOS

Vientiane

Hainan

Luzon

OCEAN

goon

THAILAND

VIETNAM

*South China
Sea*

PHILIPPINES

Manila

Philippine Sea

ngkok

CAMBODIA

**Phnom
Penh**

Ho Chi Minh City
(Saigon)

Mindanao

Davao

Equator

MALAYSIA

BRUNEI

New Guinea

dan

Kuala Lumpur

Putrajaya

SINGAPORE

Borneo

Celebes

Banda Sea

Palembang

I N D O N E S I A

Java Sea

Ujung Pandang

Arafura Sea

Sumatra

Jakarta

Surabaya

Dili

**EAST TIMOR
(TIMOR-LESTE)**

Java

Timor Sea

The white streaks across
the middle of this satellite
photograph of Asia are
the snowy peaks of
mountain ranges.

Asia facts

Total land area
17,196,187 sq miles

Biggest country Russia
*Total area: 6,592,772 sq
miles Asiatic Russia:
4,934,694 sq miles*

Smallest country
Maldives *116 sq miles*

Biggest island
Borneo *288,869 sq miles*

Highest mountain
Mount Everest,
Nepal/China *29,029ft*

Longest river Yangtze,
China *3,964 miles*

Biggest lake
Caspian Sea, western
Asia *149,190 sq miles*

Highest waterfall
Jog Falls, India *830ft*

Biggest desert Arabian
Desert, the name given to
the deserts of Saudi Arabia
900,000 sq miles

293

ATLANTIC

OCEAN

Mediterranean Sea

Algiers   Tunis
Oran
Casablanca   Rabat   **TUNISIA**
MOROCCO   Tripoli
Marrakech   *Atlas Mountains*   Bengha
                                LIBYA
ALGERIA

S A H A R A   D E S E R

Laayoune   *Ahaggar*
                Mountains
Tropic of Cancer
WESTERN   *Tibesti*
SAHARA   *Mountains*
(Morocco)

MAURITANIA   **MALI**   **NIGER**

Nouakchott   Tombouctou   **CHAD**
                (Timbuktu)   *Lake Chad*
CAPE VERDE   *S*   *a*   *h*   *e*   *l*
Praia   Ndjamena
        Dakar   Niamey
        SENEGAL
THE GAMBIA Banjul   Bamako   *Niger*   °Kano
        Bissau   Ouagadougou   **NIGERIA**
GUINEA-BISSAU   **BURKINA FASO**
        GUINEA   **BENIN**   Abuja
Conakry   *Niger*
                TOGO
SIERRA LEONE Freetown **IVORY** *Lake*   Porto-Novo **CEN**
                COAST *Volta*   **AFRI**
        Monrovia Yamoussoukro **GHANA** Lome Lagos **REPU**
        LIBERIA   Accra   Bangui
                            CAMEROON
                Malabo   Yaounde
                EQUATORIAL
                GUINEA

Equator

                SAO TOME   Libreville **CONGO**
                AND PRINCIPE   **GABON**

                            Brazzaville
                            Kinshasa

Africa

Africa is the second
largest continent, and
the hottest. It stretches
from the Mediterranean
Sea in the north, across
the equator, and far
into the southern
hemisphere.

ATLANTIC

OCEAN

                Luanda

        Benguela   **ANGOLA**

Key to map of Africa

■ Capital city
○ Major city or town
━ Boundary (where one
  country joins another one)
━ River
━ Coast

                        Namib Desert   **NAMIBIA**
Tropic of Capricorn Walvis Bay
                            Wind

Approximate scale

0km   1,000 km
0 miles   620 miles

294

                        Cape Town
                        Cape of Good Hope

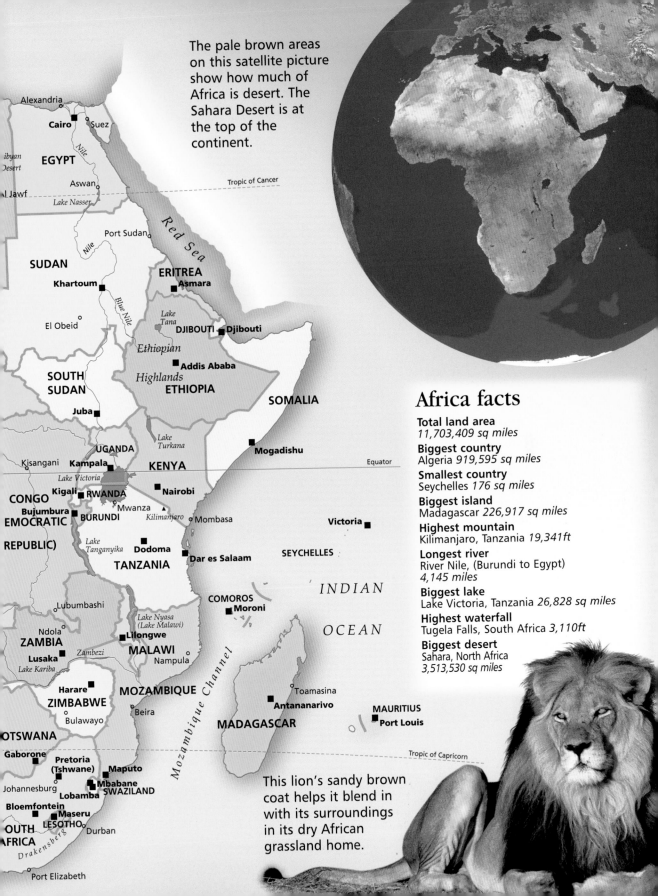

The pale brown areas on this satellite picture show how much of Africa is desert. The Sahara Desert is at the top of the continent.

Alexandria
Cairo
Suez
Libyan Desert
EGYPT
Nile
Al Jawf
Aswan
Tropic of Cancer
Lake Nasser
Port Sudan
Red Sea
SUDAN
Khartoum
ERITREA
Asmara
El Obeid
Blue Nile
Lake Tana
DJIBOUTI
Djibouti
Ethiopian Highlands
Addis Ababa
SOUTH SUDAN
ETHIOPIA
SOMALIA
Juba
Lake Turkana
Mogadishu
Equator
UGANDA
Kisangani
Kampala
KENYA
Lake Victoria
Kigali
RWANDA
Nairobi
CONGO
Mwanza
Bujumbura
BURUNDI
Kilimanjaro
Mombasa
DEMOCRATIC
Victoria
REPUBLIC)
Lake Tanganyika
Dodoma
SEYCHELLES
Dar es Salaam
TANZANIA
INDIAN
Lubumbashi
COMOROS
Moroni
OCEAN
Lake Nyasa (Lake Malawi)
Ndola
ZAMBIA
Lilongwe
Lusaka
Zambezi
MALAWI
Lake Kariba
Nampula
Harare
MOZAMBIQUE
Toamasina
ZIMBABWE
Antananarivo
MAURITIUS
Beira
Port Louis
Bulawayo
MADAGASCAR
OTSWANA
Gaborone
Tropic of Capricorn
Pretoria (Tshwane)
Maputo
Johannesburg
Mbabane
SWAZILAND
Lobamba
Bloemfontein
Maseru
OUTH
LESOTHO
Durban
AFRICA
Drakensberg
Port Elizabeth
Mozambique Channel

Africa facts

Total land area
11,703,409 sq miles

Biggest country
Algeria *919,595 sq miles*

Smallest country
Seychelles *176 sq miles*

Biggest island
Madagascar *226,917 sq miles*

Highest mountain
Kilimanjaro, Tanzania *19,341ft*

Longest river
River Nile, (Burundi to Egypt) *4,145 miles*

Biggest lake
Lake Victoria, Tanzania *26,828 sq miles*

Highest waterfall
Tugela Falls, South Africa *3,110ft*

Biggest desert
Sahara, North Africa *3,513,530 sq miles*

This lion's sandy brown coat helps it blend in with its surroundings in its dry African grassland home.

Europe

Europe stretches
from the Arctic Circle
to the Mediterranean Sea, and from
the Atlantic Ocean in the west to
the Ural Mountains in the east.

Europe is home to
many types of birds,
such as this common
European kingfisher.

Arctic Circle

ARCTIC OCEAN

Reykjavik
ICELAND

Norwegian
Sea

SWEDEN

Bergen

NORWAY

Oslo

Stockholm
Lake Vaner

Gothenburg

British Isles

Edinburgh

North
Sea

DENMARK

Copenhagen

Baltic Sea

Gdansk

Belfast

IRELAND

Dublin

UNITED
KINGDOM

ATLANTIC

Cardiff   London

OCEAN

English Channel

Amsterdam

NETHERLANDS

The
Hague

Brussels

BELGIUM

Hamburg

Berlin

POLAND

Rhine

GERMANY

Elbe

Oder

LUXEMBOURG

Seine

Paris

Luxembourg

Prague

CZECH
REPUBLIC

Nantes

Danube

Munich

Loire

FRANCE

Vienna

Bratislava

Bern

LIECHTENSTEIN

AUSTRIA

Budapest

SWITZERLAND

Vaduz

Bay of
Biscay

Lyon

The Alps

SLOVENIA

Zagreb

Bordeaux

Milan

Ljubljana

CROATIA

Turin

Po

BOSNIA AND
HERZEGOVINA

Bilbao

Adriatic Sea

Oporto

Andorra
la Vella

MONACO

SAN MARINO

Sarajevo

ANDORRA

Marseille

MONTENEGRO

PORTUGAL

ITALY

Podgorica

Lisbon

Madrid

Corsica
(France)

Rome   VATICAN CITY

ALBANIA

Tagus

Barcelona

Tirana

SPAIN

Cordoba

Valencia

Naples

Sardinia
(Italy)

Gibraltar (U.K.)

Mediterranean

Sicily
(Italy)

Key to map of Europe

■ Capital city

○ Major city or town

Boundary (where one
country joins another one)

River

Coast

Approximate scale

0km	500km
0 miles	310 miles

MALTA   Valletta

Sea

North Cape

Barents Sea

Murmansk

Kola
Peninsula

Pechora

Ukhta

Arkhangelsk

U r a l   M o u n t a i n s

Arctic Circle

Oulu

Northern Dvina

FINLAND

...land

Lake Onega

R U S S I A

Perm

Lake Ladoga

St. Petersburg

Cherepovets

Rybinsk
Reservoir

Volga

Nizhniy Novgorod

Kazan

Kama

Tallinn

...STONIA

...nki

...ga **LATVIA**

Moscow

Samara

...HUANIA

Vilnius

Tula

Don

Volga

Minsk

BELARUS

Voronezh

Kiev

Kharkiv

Volgograd

Lviv

UKRAINE

Dnieper

Donetsk

Don

Volga

...KIA

Dnipropetrovsk

Rostov

Astrakhan

Carpathian Mountains

MOLDOVA

Chisinau

Odesa

Sea of
Azov

Crimean
Peninsula

*Caspian
Sea*

...GARY

Cluj-Napoca

ROMANIA

...ade

Bucharest

Caucasus Mountains

Mount Elbrus

Black Sea

...a *Danube*

BULGARIA

Sofia

...kopje

...EDONIA

...CE

*Aegean
Sea*

...thens

Crete
(Greece)

Europe facts

Total land area
3,930,520 sq miles

Biggest country
Russia *Total area:*
6,592,772 sq miles
Area of European Russia:
1,658,077 sq miles

Smallest country
Vatican City *0.17 sq miles*

Biggest island
Great Britain *80,823 sq miles*

Highest mountain
Mount Elbrus, Russia
18,510ft

Longest river
Volga *2,294 miles*

Biggest lake
Lake Ladoga, Russia
6,834 sq miles

Highest waterfall
Vinnufossen, Norway
2,837ft

Biggest desert There are
no true deserts in Europe.

Internet links

- Scan the code to find
  out about different
  European countries.

- For more links, go to
  www.usborne.com/quicklinks

This satellite photograph
of Europe shows how the
continent joins on to Asia
at the right. The white
patch at the top of the
picture is the ice that
covers the Arctic.

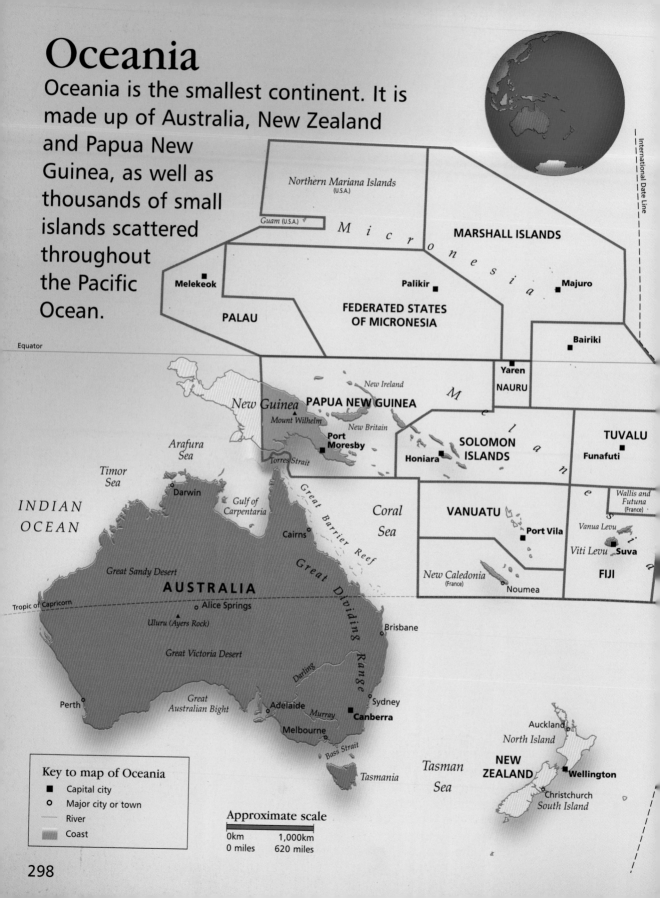

Oceania

Oceania is the smallest continent. It is made up of Australia, New Zealand and Papua New Guinea, as well as thousands of small islands scattered throughout the Pacific Ocean.

International Date Line

Northern Mariana Islands
(U.S.A.)

Guam (U.S.A.)

M i c r o n e s i a

MARSHALL ISLANDS

■ Majuro

■ **Melekeok**

Palikir ■

PALAU

FEDERATED STATES OF MICRONESIA

■ Bairiki

Equator

New Guinea

Mount Wilhelm ▲

PAPUA NEW GUINEA

New Ireland

New Britain

■ Yaren
NAURU

M e l a n e s i a

TUVALU

Arafura Sea

■ **Port Moresby**

Torres Strait

SOLOMON ISLANDS

■ Honiara

■ Funafuti

Timor Sea

Darwin ○

Gulf of Carpentaria

Coral Sea

VANUATU

Wallis and Futuna (France)

INDIAN OCEAN

Cairns ○

■ Port Vila

Vanua Levu

Viti Levu ■ **Suva**

Great Barrier Reef

Great Sandy Desert

AUSTRALIA

New Caledonia (France)

FIJI

Noumea ○

Tropic of Capricorn

○ Alice Springs

Uluru (Ayers Rock) ▲

Great Dividing Range

Great Victoria Desert

Brisbane ○

Darling

Perth ○

Great Australian Bight

Adelaide ○

Murray

Sydney ○

■ **Canberra**

Melbourne ○

Bass Strait

Auckland ○

North Island

NEW ZEALAND

■ **Wellington**

Tasman Sea

Tasmania

○ Christchurch
South Island

Key to map of Oceania

■ Capital city
○ Major city or town
— River
░ Coast

Approximate scale

0km — 1,000km
0 miles — 620 miles

298

Oceania facts

Total land area
3,306,733 sq miles

Biggest country
Australia 2,988,902 sq miles

Smallest country
Nauru 8 sq miles

Biggest island
New Guinea 303,476 sq miles

Highest mountain
Mount Wilhelm, Papua New Guinea 14,793ft

Longest river
Murray/Darling River Australia 2,310 miles

Biggest lake
Lake Eyre, Australia 3,668 sq miles

Highest waterfall
Sutherland Falls on the Arthur River, New Zealand 1,903ft

Biggest desert
Great Victoria Desert, Australia 134,653 sq miles

P o l y n e s i a

Equator

PACIFIC OCEAN

KIRIBATI

Tokelau
(New Zealand)

SAMOA
Apia

American Samoa
(U.S.A.)

Cook Islands
(New Zealand)

ONGA

Niue
(New Zealand)

kualofa

International Date Line

Tahiti   *French Polynesia*
(France)

Tropic of Capricorn

Pitcairn Islands
(U.K.)

Some of the countries in Oceania are made up of hundreds of islands, which are too small to be seen on this map. The red lines show where one country ends and another begins.

This photograph was taken from space. The yellow areas show that much of Australia is desert. The large, white area below Australia is Antarctica.

Internet links

- Scan the code to go sightseeing in Australia.
- For more links, go to **www.usborne.com/quicklinks**

Like this kangaroo, many mammals in Australia are marsupials. This means that they carry their babies in a pouch.

Flags of the world

North America

Antigua and Barbuda

Bahamas

Barbados

Belize

Canada

Costa Rica

Cuba

Dominica

Dominican Republic

El Salvador

Grenada

Guatemala

Haiti

Honduras

Jamaica

Mexico

Nicaragua

Panama

St. Kitts and Nevis

St. Lucia

St. Vincent and the Grenadines

Trinidad and Tobago

United States of America

South America

Argentina

Bolivia

Brazil

Chile

Colombia

... Ecuador

Guyana

Paraguay

Peru

Suriname

Uruguay

Venezuela

Asia

Afghanistan

Armenia

Azerbaijan

Bahrain

Bangladesh

Bhutan

Brunei

Burma (Myanmar)

Cambodia

China

East Timor

Georgia

Asia (continued)

 India

 Indonesia

 Iran

 Iraq

 Israel

 Japan

 Jordan

 Kazakhstan

 Kuwait

 Kyrgyzstan

 Laos

 Lebanon

 Malaysia

 Maldives

 Mongolia

 Nepal

 North Korea

 Oman

 Pakistan

 Philippines

 Qatar

 Russia

 Saudi Arabia

 Singapore

 South Korea

 Sri Lanka

 Syria

 Tajikistan

 Thailand

 Turkey

 Turkmenistan

 United Arab Emirates

 Uzbekistan

 Vietnam

 Yemen

Africa

 Algeria

 Angola

 Benin

 Botswana

 Burkina Faso

 Burundi

 Cameroon

 Cape Verde

 Central African Republic

 Chad

 Comoros

 Congo

 Congo (Democratic Republic)

 Djibouti

Egypt

Equatorial Guinea

Eritrea

Ethiopia

Africa (continued)

 Gabon

 The Gambia

 Ghana

 Guinea

 Guinea-Bissau

 Ivory Coast (Côte d'Ivoire)

 Kenya

 Lesotho

 Liberia

 Libya

 Madagascar

 Malawi

 Mali

 Mauritania

 Mauritius

 Morocco

 Mozambique

 Namibia

 Niger

 Nigeria

 Rwanda

 Sao Tome and Principe

 Senegal

 Seychelles

 Sierra Leone

 Somalia

 South Africa

 South Sudan

 Sudan

 Swaziland

 Tanzania

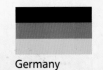 Togo

 Tunisia

 Uganda

 Zambia

 Zimbabwe

Europe

 Albania

 Andorra

 Austria

 Belarus

 Belgium

 Bosnia and Herzegovina

 Bulgaria

 Croatia

 Cyprus

 Czech Republic

 Denmark

 Estonia

 Finland

 France

 Germany

 Greece

 Hungary

 Iceland

Europe (continued)

 Ireland

 Italy

 Kosovo

 Latvia

 Liechtenstein

 Lithuania

 Luxembourg

 Macedonia

 Malta

 Moldova

 Monaco

 Montenegro

 Netherlands

 Norway

 Poland

 Portugal

 Romania

 Russian Federation

 San Marino

 Serbia

 Slovakia

 Slovenia

 Spain

 Sweden

 Switzerland

 Turkey

 Ukraine

 United Kingdom

 Vatican City

Oceania

 Australia

 Federated States of Micronesia

 Fiji

 Kiribati

 Marshall Islands

 Nauru

 New Zealand

 Palau

 Papau New Guinea

 Samoa

 Solomon Islands

 Tonga

 Tuvalu

 Vanuatu

Internet links

Scan the code for facts about every country in the world.

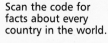

Changing flags

Flags of the world change frequently. New flags are invented as new countries are born, or their situation changes.

For example, in 1991, there were important changes to the way South Africa was run. All adults in the country were allowed to vote in free elections for the first time. To celebrate this, a new flag was designed.

South African flag until 1994

South African flag from 1994

Earth facts and records

The continents

Continent	Area sq miles	Countries
Asia	17,196,187	47
Africa	11,703,409	54
North America	9,540,198	23
South America	6,888,063	12
Antarctica	5,339,573	–
Europe	3,930,520	47
Oceania	3,306,733	14

Internet links

- Scan the code for Earth facts.
- For more links, go to www.usborne.com/quicklinks

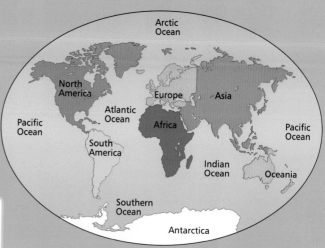

This map shows the Earth's continents and oceans.

Highest mountains in each continent

Continent	Mountain	Other name	Height ft	Location
Asia	Mount Everest	Chomolungma	29,029	Nepal/China
South America	Mount Aconcagua	Cerro Aconcagua	22,837	Argentina
North America	Mount McKinley	Denali	20,321	USA
Africa	Mount Kilimanjaro	Oldoinyo Oibor	19,341	Tanzania
Europe	Mount Elbrus	Gora El-brus	18,510	Russia
Antarctica	Vinson Massif	Mount Vinson	16,046	–
Oceania	Mount Wilhelm	Korel-Khu	14,793	Papua New Guinea

Largest oceans and seas

Body of water	Area sq miles	Deepest point ft
Pacific Ocean	63,803,000	35,827
Atlantic Ocean	31,830,000	27,493
Indian Ocean	28,355,620	24,442
Southern Ocean	7,848,000	23,737
Arctic Ocean	5,440,000	17,881
Philippine Sea	1,931,000	34,577
Coral Sea	1,850,000	25,134
Arabian Sea	1,491,000	19,039
South China Sea	1,423,000	16,457
Weddell Sea	1,081,000	19,685

Climate records

Location	Notes
Death Valley, USA	Hottest recorded temperature on Earth: 136°F (1922)
Vostok, Antarctica	Coldest recorded temperature on Earth: −128.6°F (1983)
Mawsynram, India	Wettest place on Earth: 467.5in of rain in a year
Atacama Desert, Chile	Driest place on Earth: 0.03in of rain in a year

Longest rivers

River	Length miles	Flows from	Flows to
Nile	4,145	Ruvyiranza River, Burundi	Mediterranean Sea (Egypt)
Amazon	4,000	Andes Mountains, Peru	Atlantic Ocean (Brazil)
Chang Jiang (Yangtze)	3,964	Kunlun Mountains, China	East China Sea (China)
Mississippi-Missouri-Red Rock	3,740	Montana, USA	Gulf of Mexico (USA)
Yenisei-Angara	3,442	Tannu-Ola Mountains, Russia	Kara Sea (Russia)
Huang He (Yellow River)	3,395	Kunlun Mountains, China	Gulf of Chihli (China)
Ob-Irtysh	3,362	Altai Mountains, Russia	Gulf of Ob, Kara Sea (Russia)
Parana/River Plate	3,032	Paranaiba River, Brazil	Rio de la Plata (Argentina)
Congo (Zaire)	2,920	Chambeshi River, Zambia	Atlantic Ocean
Amur-Shilka-Onon	2,744	Altai Mountains, Mongolia	Tatar Strait (Russia)

Greatest lakes

Lake	Area sq miles	Depth ft	Location
Caspian Sea	149,190	3,363	Europe/Asia
Lake Superior	31,700	1,332	USA/Canada
Lake Victoria	26,828	270	Tanzania/Uganda
Lake Huron	23,010	750	USA/Canada
Lake Michigan	22,317	925	USA
Lake Tanganyika	12,590	4,823	Tanzania/Congo
Lake Baikal	12,248	5,387	Russia
Great Bear Lake	12,028	1,463	Canada
Lake Nyasa	11,430	2,280	Mozambique/Tanzania
Great Slave Lake	11,030	2,014	Canada

Largest islands

Island	Area sq miles	Location
Greenland	822,706	Atlantic Ocean
New Guinea	303,381	Pacific Ocean
Borneo	288,869	Pacific Ocean
Madagascar	226,917	Indian Ocean
Baffin Island, Canada	195,928	Atlantic Ocean
Sumatra, Indonesia	171,069	Indian Ocean
Honshu, Japan	87,182	Pacific Ocean
Victoria Island, Canada	83,897	Atlantic Ocean
Great Britain	80,823	Atlantic Ocean
Ellesmere Island, Canada	75,767	Atlantic Ocean

Deepest cave

The deepest cave ever explored is Krubera-Voronja Cave in the Caucasus Mountains in Georgia, Russia. It is 1.4 miles deep.

Waterfalls

The widest waterfall is Khone Falls on the Mekong river in Laos. It is 6.7 miles wide. So much water pours over it that it would take only 17 minutes to fill a lake the size of Lake Superior, in North America. The highest waterfall is Angel Falls in Venezuela. It is 3,212ft high.

Angel Falls is over three times as high as the Eiffel Tower in Paris, France.

Space facts

Solar System facts

Name of planet	Distance from the Sun (miles)	Time to travel around the Sun	Time it takes to spin once	Number of moons	Largest moon
Mercury	36 million	88 days	59 days	0	–
Venus	67 million	224.7 days	243 days	0	–
Earth	93 million	365.3 days	23 hours, 56 minutes	1	Moon
Mars	142 million	687 days	24 hours, 37 minutes	2	Phobos
Jupiter	484 million	11.9 years	9 hours, 50 minutes	At least 67	Ganymede
Saturn	885 million	29.5 years	10 hours, 14 minutes	At least 62	Titan
Uranus	1,785 million	84 years	17 hours, 54 minutes	27	Titania
Neptune	2,793 million	165 years	16 hours, 6 minutes	14	Triton

Comparing planet sizes

Distances across planets are given in miles.

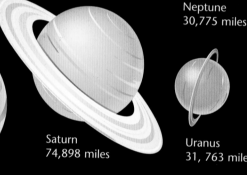
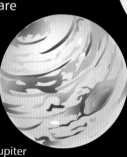

Neptune
30,775 miles

Venus
7,519 miles

Mars
4,222 miles

Mercury
3,032 miles

Earth
7,926 miles

Jupiter
88, 846 miles

Saturn
74,898 miles

Uranus
31, 763 miles

Moon map

This map shows the near side of the Moon, that is, the side which always faces the Earth. The Moon's "seas" are patches of dark rock. The triangles mark places where some important spacecraft landed:

1. Luna 9 (USSR, 1966). The first unmanned spacecraft to land safely on the Moon.

2. Apollo 11 (USA, 1969). The first manned spacecraft to land on the Moon. Two of its crew, Neil Armstrong and Edwin ("Buzz") Aldrin, were the first people to walk on the Moon. They collected rock samples and took photographs of the Moon's surface.

Plato (crater)

Aristarchus (crater)

Sea of Rain

Sea of Serenity

Ocean of Storms

Copernicus (crater)

Sea of Vapours

Sea of Tranquillity

Sea of Crises

Grimaldi (crater)

Kepler (crater)

Sea of Clouds

Sea of Nectar

Sea of Fertility

Sea of Humours

Fracastorius (crater)

Tycho (crater)

Star types

Our Sun is a star – one of billions in the Universe. Stars are huge balls of blazing gas. The Sun looks biggest because it is the closest. Stars vary in size, color, temperature and brightness.

The hottest, brightest stars are blue.

Most stars are the size of the Sun, or smaller. They are called dwarfs. The Sun is a yellow dwarf.

Sun

Compared to other stars, red stars are cooler and dimmer.

The biggest known stars are called supergiants. Rigel is a blue supergiant over 100 times bigger than the Sun.

Stars bigger than the Sun are called giants. Arcturus is an orange giant.

Sailing by the stars

In ancient times, sailors used the stars like a map to find their way at sea. The pictures below show the constellations (star patterns) they used to find the celestial poles – the points in the sky directly above the Earth's north and south poles.

Internet links

• Scan the code to find answers to lots of questions about space.

• For more links, go to **www.usborne.com/quicklinks**

Finding north

The star pattern called the Big Dipper has two stars which, if lined up, point to the Pole Star. This marks the north celestial pole.

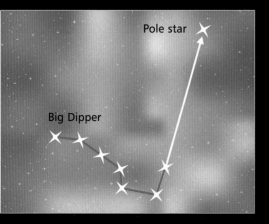

Pole star

Big Dipper

Finding south

To find south, trace one line from the Southern Cross constellation and another at right-angles from two bright stars known as the Pointers. Where the lines cross is the south celestial pole.

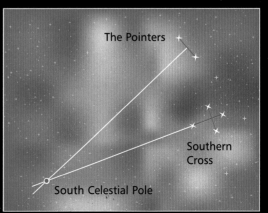

The Pointers

Southern Cross

South Celestial Pole

Animal and plant records

The biggest...

Living thing	"Pando", a grove of aspen trees	Area: 0.17 sq mile	These trees in Utah, USA, are all joined by the same roots.
Animal	Blue whale	Length: 108ft	Longer than a tennis court – the largest animal of all time
Land animal	African elephant	Height: 12ft	Even a newborn African elephant is almost 3ft tall.
Bird (flightless)	Ostrich	Height: 9ft	Lives in Africa
Bird (flying)	Wandering albatross	Wingspan: 12ft	Can fly 600 miles in a day
Reptile	Saltwater crocodile	Length: 23ft	Lives in Australia
Spineless animal	Colossal squid	Length: 46ft	Has the biggest eyes of any animal – the size of basketballs
Insect	Titan beetle	Length: 6.5in	Lives in South America
Tree (tallest)	"Hyperion", a coast redwood	Height: 379.3ft	Grows in California, USA

Comparing animal sizes

Colossal squid

Wandering albatross

Titan beetle

Ostrich   Saltwater crocodile   Blue whale   Human   African elephant

The smallest...

Living thing	*Mycoplasma genitalium*	Length: 0.00001in	A germ living in the human body
Insect	Fairyfly	Length: 0.006in	A tiny wasp from Costa Rica
Fish	Spinyhead seadevil	Length: 0.24in	A minute male anglerfish
Reptile	Dwarf gecko	Length: 0.6in	Lives in the Dominican Republic
Mammal	Bumblebee bat	Length: 1in	Lives in Thailand
Bird	Bee hummingbird	Length: 2.2in	Lives in Cuba

The oldest...

Living thing	Neptune seagrass	Age: 100,000 years (or more)	An ancient meadow of this seagrass grows under the Mediterranean Sea, south of Ibiza
Tree	Bristlecone pine	Age: 5,062 years	Grows in the White Mountains of California, USA
Sea creature	Antarctic sponge	Age: 1,550 years	Grows slowly in the cold Southern Ocean
Land animal	"Jonathan", a giant tortoise	Age: about 182 years	Jonathan was born in the Seychelles in about 1832. He now lives on the island of St. Helena.

The rarest...

Living creature	Rabb's fringe-limbed treefrog	Just one male is known to exist, in captivity, in Georgia, USA.
Land mammal	Long-beaked echidna	These egg-laying mammals are only found on New Guinea.
Sea mammal	Maui's dolphin	Less than 250 are left, around the coastlines of New Zealand.
Reptile	Yangtze giant soft-shell turtle	Only four are left, two of which are in captivity in China.
Plant	Cooke's koki'o	A small Hawaiian tree with red flowers. Just one remains.

The fastest...

Animal (over a short distance)	Cheetah	65mph
Animal (over a long distance)	Pronghorn antelope	55mph
Swimmer	Sailfish	68mph
Bird	Peregrine falcon	112mph

Internet links

- Scan the code for lots of amazing animal facts.
- For more links, go to **www.usborne.com/quicklinks**

Giant tortoises are some of the longest-living animals in the world. This one is from Galapagos Islands, northwest of South America.

Map index

This is an index of the countries named on the maps and their capital cities. The names of countries are written in heavy type **like this**.

Index

Acknowledgements

Every effort has been made to trace and acknowledge ownership of copyright. If any rights have been omitted, the publishers offer to rectify this in any subsequent editions following notification. The publishers are grateful to the following organizations and individuals for their contributions and permission to reproduce copyright material
(t = top, m = middle, b = bottom, l = left, r = right, SPL = Science Photo Library):

Cover: shark, ©Stephen Frink/Science Faction/CORBIS, dinosaur, Harris/SPL, Tutankhamun's mask, Sandro Vannini/CORBIS, all other photos, Digital Vision; p1, monarch butterfly, © Illustration Works/Corbis; p2-3, snowflake variety, © Visuals Unlimited, Inc./Solvin Zankl/Getty Images; p7 Digital Vision; p8b, Digital Vision; p9tr, Digital Vision; p10ml, Digital Vision; p10bl, Digital Vision; p11r, Digital Vision; p11b, Digital Vision; p12, Digital Vision; p12, Richard Hamilton Smith/CORBIS; p14r, Digital Vision; p14m, Douglas Peebles/CORBIS; p14l, Digital Vision; p16ml, Digital Vision; p16m, CORBIS; p16mr, Digital Vision; p16bl, Digital Vision; p16-17, CORBIS; p17mr, Michael S. Yamishita/CORBIS; p20, Joseph Sohm, ChromoSohm/CORBIS; p22t, Digital Vision; p22b, Digital Vision; p22-23b, Digital Vision; p23t, FLPA/Alamy; p25t, Kevin R. Morris/CORBIS; p26-27b, Digital Vision; p27t, Ian Walker, Eye Ubiquitous/CORBIS; p31br, Ron Watts/CORBIS; p35bm, Steve Raymer/CORBIS; p36ml, Gary Braasch/CORBIS; p36-37, Digital Vision; p42-43, Digital Vision; p44-45, Arne Hodalic/CORBIS; p47bm, Chinch Gryniewicz, Ecoscene/CORBIS; p47bl, Digital Vision; p47br, Digital Vision; p48ml, Digital Vision; p48b, Digital Vision; p49b, Digital Vision; p51, National Oceanic and Atmospheric Administration (NOAA)/Dept. of Commerce; p52, Digital Vision; p53, Digital Vision; p54t, Stockbyte; p54b, Digital Vision; p54-55 (background), Digital Vision; p55b, Heinrich van den Berg/Gallo Images/Getty Images; p56t, Prof. P. Motta/Dept. of Anatomy/University, "La Sapienza", Rome/SPL; p57 (main), Dr Linda Stannard, Uct/SPL; p57br, Colin Cuthbert/SPL; p58tr, Digital Vision; p58m, Digital Vision; p58bl, Digital Vision; p59tr, Digital Vision; p59br, Digital Vision; p60l, K & K Ammann/Taxi/Getty; p61tr, Jack Fields/CORBIS; p62, Karl Ammann/CORBIS; p63b, Jean Hosking, Frank Lane Picture Agency/Corbis; p64, George Lepp/CORBIS; p65, Wolfgang Kaehler/CORBIS; p67, Michael Sewell/Still Pictures; p68, Uwe Walz/CORBIS; p69t, Digital Vision; p69b, Jonathan Smith, Cordaiy Photo Library/CORBIS; p70tl, Image Source/JupiterImages; p70br, Heather Angel/Natural Visions; p71, Westend61/SuperStock; p72bl, Jane Burton/Warren Photographic; p72-73, Digital Vision; p73r, Linda Richardson/CORBIS; p74l, Geoff du Feu; p75br, Mick Martin/Planet Earth Pictures; p80t, Bruce Coleman Collection; p80mr, Francois Gohier/ardea.com; p80bl, Georgette Douwma/Photographer's Choice/Getty Images; p80br, David Doubilet/National Geographic/Getty Images; p82tr, Vova Pomortzeff/Alamy; p84bl, Stuart Westmorland/CORBIS; p84-85, Jeffrey L. Rottmann/CORBIS; p85tr, Phillip Cola; p85br, Brandon D. Cole/CORBIS; p86-87t, Francois Gohier/ardea.com; p87br, Johnny Johnson/Bruce Coleman Collection; p88, Digital Vision; p89tl, Digital Vision; p89mr, Digital Vision; p89(main), Horst Schaffer/Peter Arnold/Specialist Stock; p92t, Paul A. Souders/CORBIS; p93b, Gary W. Carter/CORBIS; p95bl, Kim Taylor/Bruce Coleman Collection; p96-97b, Bob Krist/corbisstockmarket.com; p97ml, Digital Vision; p98, Pat O'Hara/CORBIS; p99, Mehau Kulyk/SPL; p101tr, National Cancer Institute/SPL; p101b, Lester V. Bergman/CORBIS; p102bl, Dave Roberts/SPL; p105br, Juergen Berger, Max-Planck Institute/SPL; p106, Mehau Kulyk/SPL; p107br, Stock Connection Distribution/ Alamy; p108tr, Dr G. Moscoso/SPL; p109, Laura Dwight/CORBIS; p111, Rick Gomez/corbisstockmarket.com; p112, Dept. of Clinical Radiology, Salisbury District Hospital/SPL; p113, The Art Archive/ Gianni Dagli Orti; p114b, John Downes/Dorling Kindersley/Getty Images; p115b, Roger Harris/SPL; p117t, Gianni Dagli Orti/CORBIS; p117b, George Roos, Peter Arnold Inc./SPL; p118bl, Johnathan Smith/Cordaiy Photo Library Ltd./CORBIS; p118tr, The Trustees of the British Museum; p120b, Charles & Josette Lenars/CORBIS; p120tr, Archivo Iconografico, S.A./CORBIS; p121tl, The Trustees of the British Museum; p121bl, Gianni Dagli Orti/CORBIS; p121r, Royal Albert Memorial Museum, Exeter, Devon/Bridgeman Art Library; p122b, Fergus O'Brien/Taxi/Getty Images; p123bl, Michael Holford; p124l, National Museums & Galleries of Wales; p125mr, Roger Wood/CORBIS; p126tl, The Vikings, Britain's oldest Dark Age re-enactment society; p127br, Werner Forman Archive/Statens Historiska Museum, Stockholm; p129tr, The Art Archive/University Library Heidelberg/Gianni Dagli Orti; p130l, Alan Levy; p130b, Kevin Schafer/The Image Bank/Getty Images; p131tl, Wolfgang Kaehler/CORBIS; p132tl, L. Clarke/CORBIS; p133tl, The Art Archive/Topkapi Museum Istanbul/Gianni Dagli Orti; p133tr, Asian Art & Archaeology, Inc./CORBIS; p133mr, Asian Art & Archaeology, Inc./CORBIS; p134bl, Photo Scala, Florence; p134tr, Adam Woolfitt/CORBIS; p135t,©Superstock/Superstock; p136tl, Kevin Fleming/CORBIS; p137b, Philadelphia Museum of Art/CORBIS; p138tr, Gala/SuperStock; p139tr, Lebrecht Music and Arts Photo Library/Alamy; p141br, Bettmann/CORBIS; p143br, Mary Evans Picture Library; p144tl, Neil Beer/CORBIS; p145tr, George Hall/CORBIS; p146tl, The Imperial War Museum, London; p146mr, Hulton-Deutsch Collection/CORBIS; p146b, Bettmann/CORBIS; p147tl, Bettmann/CORBIS; p147br, CORBIS; p148, Digital Vision; p149, Galen Rowell/CORBIS; p150t, Bob Krist/CORBIS; p150bl, Digital Visions; p150-151b, Penny Tweedle/CORBIS; p151tr, Laura Dwight/CORBIS; p152, Britstock-IFA/HAGA; p153br, Janet Wishnetsky/CORBIS; p154t, Jeremy Horner/CORBIS; p154-155, Britstock-IFA; p156t, Wally McNamee/CORBIS, p156b, Peter Turnley/CORBIS; p157tr, Lee Snider/CORBIS; p157bl, Peter Turnley/CORBIS; p157br, PoodlesRock/Corbis; p158b, Reed Kaestner/CORBIS; p159b, Julia Waterlow, Eye Ubiquitous/CORBIS; p160tr, Keren Su/CORBIS; p160b, Alan Becker/Stone/Getty Images; p161r, Carl & Ann Purcell/CORBIS; p162t, Yellow Dog Productions/The Image Bank/Getty Images; p164t, Kevin R. Morris/Bohemian Nomad Picturemakers/CORBIS; p165l, Annie Griffiths Belt/CORBIS; p165br, Peter Bowater/Stock Connection Distribution/Alamy; p166t, Stock Connection Distribution/Alamy; p166-167b, John Henley Photography/ CORBIS; p168-169, Wally McNamee/CORBIS; p169tr, Rex Features; p169bl, Wally McNamee/CORBIS; p170b, Joseph Van Os/Stone/Getty Images; p171r, O'Brien Productions/CORBIS; p172r, Rudolph Staechelin Foundation, Chateau de Malmaison, Paris, France/Lauros-Giraudon, Paris/Superstock; p172l, Images-USA/Alamy; p173m, Charles & Josette Lenars/CORBIS; p173b, Steve Vidler/SuperStock; p174tr, Jeffrey L. Rotman/CORBIS; p174b, Elliott Franks/ArenaPAL; p175b, Paul A. Souders/CORBIS; p176b, Lindsay Hebberd/CORBIS; p177l, Robert Harding Picture Library Ltd/Alamy; p177br, Scott Morgan/Taxi/Getty Images; p178, Bushnell/Soifer/Photodisc/Getty Images; p179tr, David Reed/CORBIS;

p179bl, Trip/H. Rogers; p180bl, Adam Woolfitt/CORBIS; p181, Gary Bartholomew/CORBIS; p182tr, Digital Vision; p182m, Samsung Electronics UK: The Samsung SG-A400 is another example of an innovative product from Samsung Electronics UK; p182bl, Michael Melford/National Geographic/Getty Images; p183tr, Mehau Kulyk/SPL; p183br, Sam Ogden/SPL; p184, William Curtsinger/SPL; p185tr, RobertHarding.com; p185br, Roger Ressmeyer/CORBIS; p186b, Digital Vision; p187tr, BSIP, Barthelemy/SPL; p187br, Digital Vision; p188tl, Michael Freeman/CORBIS; p188lm, Adrienne Hart-Davis/SPL; p188bl, Larry Lee Photography/ CORBIS; p189r, Digital Vision; p190tr, foodfolio/Alamy; p190bl, Adrienne Hart-Davis/SPL; p191tl, Reto Guntli/Arcaid,architect Oscar Niemeyer; p191br, Phil Schermeister/CORBIS; p195b, Lowell Georgia/CORBIS; p196tr, Digital Vision; p196b, Alfred Pasieka/SPL; p197t, Dave G. Houser/CORBIS; p198, Courtesy of NASA/JPL/Caltech; p198tr, NASA/JPL/Malin Space Science Systems, USGS; p198br, Courtesy of NASA/JPL/Caltech; p199, Courtesy of NASA/ JPL/Caltech; p199tl, NASA; p199ml, Digital Vision, Courtesy of NASA/JPL/Caltech; p201, Hugh Sitton/Stone/Getty Images; p202m, Brian Bailey/CORBIS; p203tr, Digital Vision; p203br, George D. Lepp/CORBIS; p204tr, TEK IMAGE/SPL; p205tr, Alex Bartel/SPL; p205b, Transrapid International; p206ml, James Jordan Photography/Flickr/Getty Images; p206br, NASA; Digital Vision; p207tl, Digital Vision; p207rm, David Parker/SPL; p207br, Digital Vision; p208tl, Digital Vision; p208mr, D. Robert & Lorri Franz/CORBIS; p209br, Howard Allman; p212 (background), Digital Vision; p213, Digital Vision; p216tr, © Stephen Sweet/Thinkstock; p217br, HP Omnibook 6100; p217bl, Nikon Coolpix digital camera. Image courtesy of Nikon UK Ltd; p217br, Digital Vision; p217 tm, © Kitchner Bain/Thinkstock; p217tr, Digital Vision; p218tr, © Wasanti/123RF Stock Photo; p218ml, © Alexey Dudoladov/Thinkstock; p218-219b, CORBIS; p219tr, DreamWorks Distribution LLC./ Special Anti-Pesto Still/Aardman Bureau L.A. Collection/Corbis; p220tl, Digital Vision; p220tl, © Ryan McVay/Thinkstock; p220 rm, © Paul Wootton/SPL; p220br, Digital Vision; p221b, Digital Vision; p222t, © Paul Fleet/Alamy; p225tr, © Maksym Yemelyanov/Alamy; p227bl, Sankei via Getty Images; p228l, www.TryScience.org TryScience/New York Hall of Science; p228r, Use of screenshot from www.roalddahl (© RDNL) by kind permission of Dahl&Dahl; p228m, Digital Vision; p228-229m, Digital Vision; p229l, BrainPOP 2002 www.BrainPOP.com; p232ml, WildCountry/CORBIS; p232br, London Aerial Photo Library/CORBIS; p235br, Jean-Yves Ruszniewski, TempSport/CORBIS; p241b, www.aviationpictures. com; 244tr Norbert Wu/NHPA/Oceans-Image/Photoshot; p245, Digital Vision; p246-247t, Digital Vision; p247tr, NASA/ NSSDC; p247br, NOAO/SPL; p248bl, Digital Vision; p248-249, Digital Vision; p249br, NASA; p251bl, Digital Vision; p251br, NASA/SPL; p252-253 (background), Digital Vision; p252-253 (foreground), NASA; p254l, Digital Vision; p254tl, © Detlev Van Ravenswaay/SPL; p254-255, NASA/SOHO/ESA; p255tr, Julian Baum/SPL; p255bl, NASA; p255bm, NASA/ SOHO/ESA; p255br, Digital Vision; p256bl, NASA/SPL; p256br, Stephanie Maze/CORBIS; p257tl, Victor Habbick Visions/ SPL; p257ml, NASA/JPL; p257bl, NASA/SPL; p258m, Digital Vision; p258br, Digital Vision; p259l, Digital Vision; p259tl, NASA/SOHO/ESA; p259tl, NASA/NSSDC; p259mt, Digital Vision; p259m, NASA/NSSDC; p259ml, Kenneth Seidelman, U.S. Naval Observatory; p259bl, NASA; p259tr, NASA/NSSDC; p259br, Digital Vision; p260l, NASA/U.S. Geological Survey; p260mr, Digital Vision; p261b, Digital Vision; p262bl, NASA/SPL; p NASA/SOHO/ESA; p263mr, NASA/SPL; p263brl, Digital Vision; p263brm, NASA/NSSDC/Viking; p263brr, Digital Vision; p265t, NASA/U.S. Geological Survey; p265b, NASA/JPL; p266l, NASA/JPL/MSSS; p267, NASA/JPL/Caltech; p267m, NASA/JPL/Caltech; p267r, NASA/JPL/MSSS; p267b, NASA/JPL/ MPF; p268ml, NASA/SPL; p268mr, CORBIS; p268br, NASA; p269tm, SPL; p269mr, NASA; p269bm, Astro-geology Team/ USGS; p269br, Digital Vision; p270mr, NASA; p270m, JPL/CALTECH/NASA/Calvin J. Hamilton; p270ml, JPL/CALTECH/NASA/ Calvin J. Hamilton; p270l, JPL/CALTECH/NASA/Calvin J. Hamilton; p270bl, JPL/CALTECH/NASA/Calvin J. Hamilton; p270bl, JPL/CALTECH/NASA/Calvin J. Hamilton; p270br, NASA; p270-271b, David Hardy/SPL; p271mr, NASA; p274b, John Sanford/SPL; p274l, NASA; p275m, J.Finch/SPL; p277bl, Space Telescope Science Institute/NASA/SPL; p277m, Max Planck Institut für Radioastronomie/SPL; p279bl, Gerry Schad/SPL; p279tr, John Sandford/SPL; p281, Digital Vision; p288bl, Digital Vision; p289tr, Julian Baum & David Angus/SPL; p290bl, Digital Vision; p291tr, Julian Baum & David Angus/SPL; p292bl, Digital Vision; p293tr, Julian Baum & David Angus/SPL; p294tr, Tom Van Sant/Geosphere project, Santa Monica/ SPL; p294br, Digital Vision; p296bl, Digital Vision; p297br, Julian Baum & David Angus/SPL; p299tr, Planetary Visions Ltd/ SPL; p299br, Digital Vision; p300, Craig Lovell/CORBIS; p305br, James Marshall/CORBIS; p309br, Joe McDonald/CORBIS.

With thanks to Louise Baxter and Paul l'Anson at MINI UK (Cars and motorcycles), Vincent Deloménie, Centre audiovisuel SNCF (Trains), CR Frost (Clocks), Kester Sims (Clocks), Christopher Denne (Cameras), Tim Milbourne (Computers, The Internet), Balfour Knox (Toilets and faucets), Albert Milbourne (Cars and motorcycles), Tony Furse (Tractors), Andy Hart, UK SNCF society (Trains), Shipmate Flags, Vlaardingen, The Netherlands, Hawkes Ocean Technologies (H.O.T.) for their permission to feature the Deep Flight submersible in this book. Special thanks to Bob Whiteaker for help with Deep Flight diagram on page 244.

Additional consultancy: Dr. Tom Weston (Science) and Mark Champkins (Technology)
Additional design and editorial: Sam Baer, Verinder Bhachu, Kate Fearn, Georgina Hooper, Vici Leyhane, Laura Parker, Jane Rigby, Leonard Le Rolland, Andrea Slane and Nicky Wainwright
Cover illustrations: Adam Larkum
Additional illustrations: Sophie Allington, John Barber, Verinder Bhachu, Gary Bines, Isabel Bowring, Trevor Boyer, Andy Burton, Michèle Busby, Nicola Butler, Kuo Kang Chen, Adam Constantine, Pam Cornfield, Richard Cox, Gary Cross, David Cuzik, Tony Gibson, Robert Gilmore, Rebecca Hardy, Nicholas Hewetson, Inklink Firenze, Ian Jackson, Colin King, Steven Kirk, Rachel Lockwood, Chris Lyon, Philip Nicholson, Alex Pang, Justine Peek, Maurice Pledger, Leonard Le Rolland, Chris Shields, Guy Smith, Treve Tamblin, Mike Wheatley, Graham White, John Woodcock and David Wright
Answer to question on page 117: The cave painting shows a horse, some deer and a bull.